MARIANNE JEWELL MEMORIAL LIBRARY
BAKER COLLEGE OF MUSKEGON
MUSKEGON, MICHIGAN 49442

The Nazi Holocaust

D0067120

PROPERTY OF
BAKER COLLEGE OF MUSKEGON

Ronnie S. Landau is former education director of
the Spiro Institute for the Study of Jewish
History and Culture. A founding director of the
British Holocaust Educational Project, he writes
widely on modern Jewish history and the Holocaust.
He is currently head of humanities at the City
Literary Institute, London.

The Nazi Holocaust

Ronnie S. Landau

Ivan R. Dee

CHICAGO

PROPERTY OF
BAKER COLLEGE OF MUSKEGON

THE NAZI HOLOCAUST. Copyright © 1992, 1994 by
Ronnie S. Landau. All rights reserved, including the right to
reproduce this book or portions thereof in any form. For information,
address: Ivan R. Dee, Inc., 1332 North Halsted Street, Chicago
60622. First American edition. Manufactured in the United States of
America and printed on acid-free paper.

Library of Congress Cataloging-in-Publication Data:
Landau, Ronnie S., 1948–
The Nazi Holocaust / Ronnie S. Landau. — 1st American ed.
p.   cm.
Includes bibliographical references and index.
ISBN 1-56663-054-1 (cloth). — ISBN 1-56663-052-5 (paper)
1. Holocaust, Jewish (1939–1945)—Moral and ethical aspects.
2. Holocaust, Jewish (1939–1945)—Psychological aspects. I. Title.
D804.3.L355   1994
940.53'18—dc20   93-47275

Contents

Contents

Maps

Source: Martin Gilbert, *Jewish History Atlas*, (second edition, Weidenfeld & Nicolson 1976)

For Michael, Danielle and Rafi
(who's always close, even though he's so far away)
– three exceptional offspring.

Dedicated to the memory of Lola Berstyn,
battling survivor of the Warsaw Ghetto
and wonderful grandmother to Michael
and Danielle.

Author's Preface

The Holocaust of the Nazi era is now increasingly regarded as one of the most momentous events of modern history if not of all human experience. No longer dismissed as a tragic by-product of the Second World War, nor explained away by a whole variety of simplistic, monolithic theses, the Holocaust has become a central reference point for humanity as it stands on the threshold of a new millennium.

The world of scholarship—like virtually every other segment of society—at first received the Holocaust in stunned and awed silence: for almost two decades after the war philosophers, educators, historians, psychologists, and theologians could find precious little to say. Since the 1960s, however, the subject has generated a colossal literature. The awe is still there—well, generally so—but no longer the silence.

The Holocaust as a theme, both in popular contemporary culture and in more academic settings, has proved to be a powerful, highly charged, and malleable subject. At its most inspiring it can be communicated in ways that are spiritually enriching and morally uplifting; but in the hands of the irresponsible, the ideologically motivated, or the malevolent it is easily misrepresented and abused.

One trend that is slowly and thankfully being reversed is the overwhelming preponderance, in the fields of Holocaust scholarship and literature, of those who are themselves Jewish. While it is of course clear why this event should exert such a profound fascination for the Jewish people, unquestionably there has been a viciously circular tendency in the world of academe for the Holocaust to be labeled a 'Jewish' discipline, thus discouraging and *exempting* many of those outside the victim group from trespassing on such 'sacred' territory.

So what sense, if any, have the analytical approaches of philosophy, psychology, history, and political science made of this catastrophe? And—to address that critical yet so often apparently hair-splitting and pointless question: Is the Holocaust an utterly singular historical phenomenon? Or is it in any way comparable to other examples of 'genocide'?

Certainly much of the literature on the Holocaust is dominated—even fixated on—this question of *uniqueness* versus *universality*, at times unhelpfully and frustratingly so. It is almost as though some historians of the Holocaust have felt obliged to adopt a pleading tone—'Please believe us, our "Genocide" was utterly without parallel'—in order to secure recognition for its significance. (So often this approach, notwithstanding its inherent intellectual truth, can prove educationally counterproductive.) It could, I feel, be argued that 'recognition,' to the extent it now exists, has come about precisely because others have been prepared to make a whole series of *connections* (at times, it must be said, superficially) between the Holocaust and other peoples' experiences—between Nazi motives and the intentions of other perpetrators and abusers of power—rather than by isolating the Holocaust from everything else in life...and death.

If this book carries a central message for me, it is this: when assessing the importance of the Holocaust, uniqueness and universality are by no means mutually exclusive or antithetical categories. On the contrary, they are complementary and effective ways of grappling with the Holocaust and its lessons for us all. We must confront our past, not run away from it nor elevate it to a mysterious plane that is utterly beyond our perception and grasp.

The idea for this book grew out of numerous conversations with disgruntled and frustrated teachers who, while wishing to perpetuate the memory of the Holocaust and to transmit its most compelling messages, have suffered both from constraints of time and from a dearth of suitable material both for their students and for themselves. Underresourced and underinformed, they have either chosen not to teach the subject at all or have offered only the most superficial and inadequate treatment—a shortcoming of which they are, in most cases, painfully aware, but to which they have become uncomfortably resigned.

The central problems in communicating the Holocaust involve questions of context, perspective, balance, and emphasis. Very often one or more of the necessary frameworks within which an understanding of the Holocaust may be approached—Jewish history, modern German history, 'genocide' in the modern world, or the fundamental mechanisms of human psychology—is neglected or glossed over in works purporting to treat this subject. Those who tackle the topics of antisemitism and the Holocaust should, I feel strongly, be encouraged to relate these special and apparently baffling phenomena to the larger story of human hatred, prejudice, and bigotry of which they are a part. Persistent antagonism towards the Jewish people has not occurred in a psychological or historical vacuum, any more than has, say, the growth and development of Christianity in European society. They are part of something larger than themselves. But having said that, the Holocaust must also be considered on its own unique terms, properly contextualized, not diluted and potentially lost in a wilderness of empty platitudes. Its strength, power, and integrity must be respected and not subordinated to the political agendas and preferences of countless concerned groups and individuals.

All too often, those who approach so highly charged a theme as the Holocaust have felt obliged to narrow their focus in order to satisfy the demands either of their individual discipline or of the ideological world they inhabit. Most educational systems have a preoccupation with 'subject' boundaries. Academic departments, curriculum builders, boards of education, and even large educational publishing houses function as if the entire human experience were neatly assignable to clearly demarcated areas of study. Though lip service has sometimes been paid (much more successfully in the United States than in older European societies) to the exciting possibilities of a multidisciplinary approach to learning, in practice we have been locked into what often amounts to a series—often competing—of one-dimensional ways of looking at the world. This can pose special difficulties for educators and students who wish seriously to do justice to the Holocaust, a cross-disciplinary subject if ever there was one. For their journey of discovery and inspiration may take them into the very different—sometimes contradictory and mysterious—realms of psychology, theology, moral philosophy, jurisprudence, literature, and art as well as social, political, economic, intellectual, and religious history.

One of the principal aims of this book is therefore to mediate between a vast literature on the Nazi Holocaust (so much of it frankly unapproachable to the average student and the hard-pressed teacher) and those who are grappling with its history and meaning—irrespective of the 'subject' in which they are involved. As such this book is, to some extent, a 'synthesis' of the very best existing scholarship and thinking drawn from many parts of the globe and from a variety of academic fields.

Another important and self-conscious aim of this book is to lift the Holocaust out of the often emotional, ideological, and politically charged realm of 'Jewish education,' and to set its implications before a wider audience. The lessons of the Holocaust are simply too important, too pressing, and of the utmost universal significance to be imprisoned within the world of the 'victim.' To do so is an evasion of responsibility by the rest of humanity. The Holocaust, and its terrifying example, is not, and must not remain, a Jewish possession, an exclusive territory into which few others may intrude. It should of course be studied, remembered, and acted upon by Jews; but its messages and possible meanings should not principally be confined to their world.

The multifaceted nature of this subject has necessitated that I trespass into many areas of specialization. I apologize if this seems to have been an arrogant undertaking. I have enlisted the advice and assistance of many teachers, scholars, librarians, and curators in Britain, Israel, and the United States, and of many of my own students in adult institutes, universities, and schools. It is always somewhat discriminatory to single out individuals for special praise and thanks, but in my preparation of the text I have been particularly grateful to the following remarkable and gifted people: to David March for his outstanding contribution to the chapter on modern German history; to Mark Levene for his inspirational help with all references to 'genocide' in the modern age; to David Bankier of the Hebrew University of Jerusalem, on whose preeminent research I leaned very heavily in my preparation of the chapter on German public opinion during the Nazi era; and to Trudy Gold of the Spiro Institute for her invaluable spadework in helping to conceptualize the final chapter.

I should like to acknowledge my general sense of indebtedness to the Spiro Institute for the Study of Jewish History and Culture, the trailblazing London-based organization with which I worked for most of the 1980s. It was there that I first truly confronted the exhilarating subject of modern Jewish history, and many of the thoughts and conclusions expressed in Chapter 3 were formulated during that period of my life.

I should also like to express my immense gratitude to the following individuals and organizations who, in different ways, provided me with enormous support and encouragement: to Clive Marks, whose initial words of comfort, backing, and loyalty made the project happen; to Nicki Judah for her unfailing faith and love; to Morton Creeger of the Ronson Foundation; to Norman Appleton and Sandra Nagioff; to Christa Wichmann of the Wiener Library; to the B'nai B'rith Anti-Defamation League; to Facing History and Ourselves; to Trevor Chinn; to Mickey Rosen of the Yakar Educational Foundation; to Ian Karten; and to Mel Marcus.

Finally I should like to record my grateful appreciation to the following authors and publishers from whose works excerpts have been included in this book: Yitzhak Arad, Yisrael Gutman, and Abraham Margaliot, eds., *Documents on the Holocaust* (Yad Vashem Publications, 1981); Elie Cohen, *Human Behavior in the Concentration Camp* (W. W. Norton, 1953); Albert Friedlander, ed., *Out of the Whirlwind: A Reader of Holocaust Literature* (Schocken Books, 1976); Gustav Gilbert, *Nuremberg Diary* (Farrar, Straus and Giroux, 1974); Martin Gilbert, *Jewish History Atlas* (Weidenfeld and Nicolson,

1976); Claude Lanzmann, *Shoah: An Oral History of the Holocaust* (Pantheon Books, 1985); Paul Mendes-Flohr and Jehuda Reinharz, *The Jew in the Modern World* (Oxford University Press, 1980); Betty Merti, *Understanding the Holocaust* (J. Weston Walsh Publishers, 1982); Jeremy Noakes and Geoffrey Pridham, eds., *Nazism, 1919–1945*, vols. 2 and 3 (Exeter University Press, 1984, 1988); and Elie Wiesel, *Legends of Our Time* (Holt, Rinehart and Winston, 1968).

R. S. L.

The Nazi Holocaust

Introduction

CHAPTER 1

The Historical, Educational and Moral Significance of the Holocaust

> The Holocaust defies literature. ... We think we are describing an event, we transmit only its reflection. No one has the right to speak for the dead. ... Still, the story had to be told. In spite of all risks, all possible misunderstandings. It needed to be told for the sake of our children.
>
> Elie Wiesel

The Holocaust involved the deliberate, systematic murder of approximately 6 million Jews in Nazi-dominated Europe between 1941 and 1945. It was perhaps the most savage and significant single crime in recorded history; yet it remains, on many levels, an unfathomable mystery. Like all unresolved murders, it continues to haunt those closest to its victims, with the added anguish that most of the dead lie unburied and inadequately mourned. To be punished for a crime that has been committed in violation of laws or a code of behaviour which is known and comprehensible is one thing; but in the case of the Jews of Europe, whose only 'crime' was that they had been born Jewish (in the words of one historian, 'Jewish birth was a sentence of death'), their 'punishment' was – and remains to this day – inexplicable.

The attempt to communicate and transmit this historical event is a task shot through with difficulties. Despite whole libraries devoted to it – at times to the point of 'information overload' – there is still no sure agreement on certain central issues on the part of historians, psychologists, educationists, theologians, dramatists, poets and philosophers. No adequate or simple explanation is possible or indeed desirable. Rather, we should try to identify the right *questions* and then work towards the possible answers and lessons to be inferred.

This is easier said than done – particularly in a scholastic environment, where clear answers are commonly expected from those entrusted with the task of education. At an early stage, the student of the Holocaust must try to rise above the need to stick explanatory labels on everything and to resist the compulsion to reach precise, unequivocal conclusions in answer to the 'big' questions.

Such key questions would include the following (in no particular order of importance):

1. How, why and when did the Nazis determine a policy of total annihilation of the Jews of Europe?
2. How are we to judge the behaviour and responsibility of numerous other groups: ordinary Germans; the citizens of defeated and occupied countries; Germany's allies, such as Italy and Hungary; the various churches throughout Europe; the anti-Nazi Allies, in particular Great Britain, the United States and the Soviet Union; neutral governments, such as those of Sweden, Switzerland, Spain and Eire; and, finally, the Jews themselves?
3. Why did a higher proportion of Jews survive in Fascist Italy and in countries allied to Germany, such as Romania and Hungary than in anti-Nazi Holland with its democratic tradition and long history of toleration towards Jews? Why did so many Jews die in Poland? Does the explanation lie in the religious antisemitism of the indigenous population? Or is the answer much more complex?
4. Why do the Jews *appear* to have offered so little resistance everywhere? (Is that even the right question?)
5. How can we begin to evaluate the degree of moral responsibility of the Jewish leaders and the specially established Jewish police force in the ghettos of Poland?
6. How are we to assess the role of the Reich railway officials who drew up rail schedules and even charged 'package tour' fares to unwitting passengers who were then transported in cattle trucks to extermination camps in the east?

7. How on earth was it possible for such a supposedly civilized society, which had given us Goethe, Beethoven and Brahms, to produce such barbarity, albeit of a largely dispassionate and coolly executed kind?

8. What is the relationship between Nazi anti-Jewish ideology and earlier expressions of anti-Judaism and antisemitism in European history?

9. To what extent was the ferocity of the Nazi onslaught rooted in the peculiar social, economic and psychological circumstances prevailing in Germany in the years following her traumatic defeat in the First World War and the imposition of the humiliating terms of the Treaty of Versailles?

10. Can Germany's descent to barbarism be attributed, to any degree, to a fear of Bolshevism?

11. Is it true that full-blooded Nazi anti-Jewishness had only a very marginal appeal to ordinary Germans, even among those who voted for Hitler?

12. How big a factor is the astonishing human capacity for indifference to the plight of others (present in all societies and arguably on the increase) in explaining the path to Auschwitz and Treblinka?

13. How was it possible for certain individuals, whose role would prove indispensable to the carrying out of the 'Final Solution of the Jewish Question', to be subtly conditioned into believing that to kill Jews was morally no worse than to brush dandruff off their jackets – and, on the contrary, was a morally good thing?

14. What does the methodical slaughter of 1.5 million Jewish children say about the presence or interest of (a) God in human affairs? (This book will not even attempt to wrestle with such theological problems – it is beyond its scope – though other works which address such issues are mentioned in the main Bibliography.)

15. What was the difference between the Jewish experience of Nazism and that of the 5.5 million other civilians – gypsies, Poles, Russians, homosexuals, Jehovah's Witnesses, communists, socialists and others – who were also murdered in cold blood? In other words, why does the term 'Holocaust' strictly refer to the Jewish experience alone?

16. And, finally, a question that dominates Holocaust

literature: is this catastrophe that overwhelmed the Jews
of Europe an incomparably unique historical phenomenon,
or is it a case within the category of genocide?

These questions are mostly of the kind to which we ought to
find no definitive answers. Indeed, if clear solutions are found
to more than a handful of these riddles, then we have probably
gone badly astray. It must be stressed, however, and here we
come to a central, tantalizing, dilemma of Holocaust literature
and education, that the subject can be mystified as easily by
offering no explanation as by offering the wrong one.

The 'Jewishness' of the Holocaust

The struggle to come to terms with the enormity of the
Holocaust, whether through the creative media of literature,
film or art, or through the more analytical prisms of history or
psychology, must strike an often precarious balance between
the need, on the one hand, to hold fast to its Jewish
particularity – to understand its place within Jewish history
and the history of European antisemitism – and, on the other,
to grapple with its universal meaning.

Our emotional and intellectual helplessness in the face of
this tragedy has led some of the 'victim group' – understandably perhaps – to seek to monopolize the event and to be
disinclined to 'share' it with others. What has sometimes
followed – and this is deeply regrettable, and invariably has
the unhelpful effect of alienating those outside the victim
group (a genuinely vicious circle) – is a grotesque competition
in suffering. This may seem inconsequential until it is
appreciated that well over 90 per cent of all the works on the
Holocaust have been written by Jews, who are either
themselves survivor–victims or who culturally, ethnically and,
in terms of their psychological sense of belonging to the Jewish
people, feel part of the victim group.

The author of this book, too, is Jewish and it is a pity, and
perhaps a shame, that it seems, thus far, to have been left
almost entirely to the victim group to carry out the
investigation – at times subjectively and passionately so. After
all, if there is a plane crash, to whom should the responsibility
for conducting the inquiry fall – to the survivors, their family

and friends? Or to those who run the airline? (And the Holocaust was arguably the worst example yet of human civilization 'crashing'.)

> You cannot have loved ones die ... be murdered ... and not have answers.
>
> Parent of one the victims of the Lockerbie air disaster, December 1988.[1]

A human tragedy

The Holocaust has proved so incomprehensible that it has sometimes led to what has been called the demonization of Hitler, Nazism and the crime itself. This is, of course, similar to the medieval Christian view of the Devil as the source of all evil – an entity that remains outside human perception and grasp. Such demonization can lead to an obsession with evil as a purely external force, preventing us from searching for it inside ourselves and, most significantly, within the societies, technological systems and bureaucratic structures we have created.

If there are any lessons to be derived from the Holocaust there is no sense whatever in ascribing its execution to Satanic monsters, for then it becomes unrelated to what is humanly intelligible. What is more, such a reading of Nazism would involve an abstract dehumanization of Nazis – and often indiscriminately of all Germans – which was precisely the Nazi attitude towards Jews.

On the contrary, we must understand that the Holocaust, for all its freakishness, *was* a human event – all too human – which shows that humanity is, on the one hand, eminently capable of doing anything that our technology makes possible, horrifyingly ready to perform unimagined acts of wholesale destruction and self-destruction. To paraphrase Samuel Pisar, a survivor of Auschwitz, the Holocaust was not, as he thought at the time, the end of the world, but possibly the beginning of the end of the world, if we ignore its universal implications.[2]

Humankind is also, the Holocaust shows us, alarmingly prone – especially in the twentieth century – to replace personal ethical standards with collective ones that appear to exempt the individual from accountability. However, the Holocaust also gives evidence that the best is also in us – for some, in their exercise of moral choice, chose good against the polluted stream.

Uniqueness and universality

Without losing sight of the incomparable uniqueness of the Holocaust *as an entire event*, it is educationally essential and, therefore, legitimate to break it down into a range of limited human experiences, motives, crises and responses, with which it might be easier to identify and which can stand comparison with other predicaments.

For example, the pre-Holocaust Nazi anti-Jewish legislation of 1933–8 can be related to attempts by some societies to marginalize certain whole groups by *process of law* – for instance the operation of Apartheid in South Africa (not in itself a genocidal situation but perhaps potentially so). The utter *irrationality* of the annihilation of Jews, inspired by the imagined threat they posed to German civilization, carries echoes of the Armenian genocide at the hands of the Turks during the First World War. The *isolation* of the Jewish victims can, to some degree, be compared with that of the victims of the Kampuchean massacre. The *self-righteousness* of many of the Nazi perpetrators – the prevailing belief in the correctness and holiness of their bloodthirsty undertaking – can be related to almost every massacre in human history, that has been carried out in the name of a religious or imperial mission.[3] These partial analogies are not, of course, exact, but they may be explored; superficial comparisons are as undesirable as the refusal to allow any comparison.

If, on the other hand, the Holocaust is cordoned off from other disciplines, from other peoples' experiences, it will become inaccessible – an impossibly grim and remote area of study or 'remembrance' enacted in an educationally meaning-less vacuum. We should start – and for some this is a painful process – to see the Holocaust as more than a symbol of Jewish fate, Jewish unity and the need for Jewish survival. It is all of these, but it is also a major challenge to assumptions about progress and civilization. The Holocaust shattered Europe-centred, liberal dreams of Western reason and culture as forces that necessarily sensitize and humanize us and which promote genuine tolerance of difference. It also destroyed, once and for all, the tottering belief that science and technology were securely harnessed for the good of humanity, as scientists, politicians, bureaucrats and generals found the means progressively to give destructive expression to their decisions and fantasies. Shortly after the First World War, Albert Einstein, alarmed by mankind's misuse of science, had written:

> In the hands of our generation these hard-won instruments are like a razor wielded by a child of three. The possession of marvellous means of production has brought misery and hunger instead of freedom.[4]

In this regard it is worth reflecting for a moment on the whole history of how human beings have dealt death to one another: the progressive bureaucratization of killing has placed a steadily increasing distance between the perpetrators and the consequences of their decisions and actions.

As the educationist Steve Copeland has pointed out, the Holocaust can also be interpreted as a parable for the darker side of modernity. It was, in part, the outcome of problems of identity – the alienation and isolation of the individual in our modern mass societies, which have become so depersonalized and conformist. Nazism appealed to people's need for a sense of belonging, loyalty and community, a need left dangerously unfulfilled by modern, vast, centralized society. It encouraged a psychological state whereby they could easily be sucked into the entire bureaucratic process. Bureaucracy is a human invention which can subjugate its inventor, undermine human conscience and allow individuals to abdicate personal moral responsibility. 'It's the system's fault, not mine!'

The Holocaust also raises profound and disturbing questions about the ease with which people can fall into a pattern of conformity and obedience to orders, particularly if those orders emanate from a source which is deemed to possess authority.

> When you look at the long and gloomy history of man you will find more hideous crimes have been committed in the name of obedience than have ever been committed in the name of rebellion.
>
> C.P. Snow[5]

The uniqueness and important lessons of the Holocaust should not be sought in the specific and horrific details of its execution – sadly, mass brutality and slaughter are far from new in human history – nor in the behaviour, psychology, religion or ethics of the Jews who were its victims. Its uniqueness, in fact, has remarkably little to do with the harrowing experiences of individual victims. Instead, it lies in the *intentions* of its perpetrators and in the fact that these intentions were, for the most part, translated into reality – for the Jews were the only group marked out for total European annihilation, even in neutral countries and those not yet conquered. And this can – and must – be stated without diminishing in any way the suffering of any other group. The uniqueness of the Holocaust also lies in the unprecedented way that the full might of a twentieth-century, industrially advanced state could be perverted, subordinated to a philosophy of destruction and then directed against a vulnerable, conspicuous, powerless and largely unresisting target.

The Holocaust was a totality – a global event. It was, to be sure, made up of the sum of countless individual stories, attitudes, reactions and dilemmas; but it is also much more than the sum of those parts and cannot be adequately perceived through the prism of any one component. The Holocaust had no precedent and, as an entire event, is a unique phenomenon that resists satisfactory explanation. It was, of course, a Jewish tragedy, but it was not only a Jewish tragedy; it also belongs to world history and to the realm of general humanities and moral studies. Jews, as the special victims of this unique event, are not the only possible victims of such man-made catastrophes, and their wretched experience has implications which go far beyond the Jewish world – implications of concern to the general historian, psychologist, theologian and educationist.

Educational philosophy and scope

If the world could become convinced that Auschwitz never existed, it would be easier to build a second Auschwitz, and there is no assurance it would devour only Jews.

Primo Levi[6]

This book addresses the historical, moral and educational

significance of the Nazi Holocaust. While written primarily for students of history, it is also intended for use by students of psychology, philosophy, sociology, religious and moral studies, humanities and literature. Indeed the Holocaust is perhaps the ultimate cross-disciplinary theme, transcending the rather artificial barriers that so often separate academic subjects, thus narrowing rather than broadening our conceptual range. Many of its themes are highly charged, delicate and controversial, and it is hoped will stimulate discussion, debate and the thrust and parry of differing opinions.

In order that it might answer the needs and frustrations of those engaged in the educational process, many teachers and lecturers have been consulted and interviewed while this book was being prepared.[7] The overall conceptual approach and the resulting part and chapter divisions are, to some extent, therefore, a response to a whole range of different opinions and perspectives on this subject.

What emerged with almost audible insistence from the educators interviewed was the desire for a balanced approach, which avoided, as far as possible, the extreme positions so often adopted by writers on such an emotive topic. For this is a subject that in the hands of an ill-informed, irresponsible or ideologically motivated communicator can very easily be abused, politicized, or misrepresented.[8]

In the hands of a few truly malevolent individuals, the subject of the Holocaust has been drawn into the spotlight purely so that its truthfulness can be manipulated and denied. Far from constituting a serious analysis of the Holocaust, such revisionist history serves more as an example of the kind of twisted thinking that actually contributed to the Nazi horrors in the first place. Of such 'historians', Michael Marrus has written with deserved contempt: 'I see no reason why such people should set the agenda for the subject, any more than flat-earth theorists should set the agenda for astronomers.'[9]

The teachers interviewed were virtually unanimous in their belief that the Jewish experience in general and the Holocaust in particular must be taught in order to combat racial prejudice and the abuse of power. To fulfil this goal it was felt that, ideally, the Holocaust should not be torn from its historical and wider educational contexts (see below p.12) – as so regularly happens – even if time is limited.

This work has consequently been built on the following philosophical and educational premises which it is believed can be adapted to most settings:

1. that the Holocaust was an event which was *both* unique *and* universal, of far-reaching significance for the Jewish people but also with weighty, even mind-boggling, implications for us all;
2. that the story of the Holocaust is potentially the ultimate 'humanities' topic; if taught skilfully and responsibly, it can help socialize and even civilize our students. But, if taught badly, it can titillate, traumatize, mythologize and encourage a purely negative view of all Jewish history, of Jewish people and, indeed, of *all* victim groups;
3. that the Holocaust and its lessons should be approached within the following contexts: (i) that of Jewish history and the history of antisemitism; (ii) that of modern German history; (iii) that of genocide in the nineteenth and twentieth centuries; (iv) that of the misuse of technology and bureaucracy in the twentieth century; and (v) that of the psychology of human prejudice and racism;
4. that the study of the Jewish historical experience, including that of the Holocaust, can serve as a highly effective educational means for sensitizing students to the distinct problem of antisemitism; to the universal issues of minority status and minority identities; to the need most of us have for cultural and national pride; and to the dangers of racial and religious stereotyping and hatred;
5. that the teacher and student of the Holocaust must try to reconcile the intimidating demands of the subject content with their own changing experience, values and awareness and, inescapably, with those of the society and the times in which they live;
6. that no one incident or experience can adequately convey the totality and magnitude of the Holocaust. This catastrophe comprised all kinds of components, each adding a horrifying dimension to the whole. Neither Kovno, nor Treblinka, nor Wannsee, nor Babi Yar can alone represent the others. It is collectively that they express the very worst that human beings can do to each other and to themselves.

Chapter Divisions

The ten chapters have been arranged as follows. The three core chapters (Part 2: Chapters 5, 6 and 7) are devoted to the Nazi period (1933–45), charting the history of the Holocaust, from the beginning of the legal assault on the Jews of Germany up to the liberation of the death camps in 1945. The years 1938 and 1941 represent crucial turning points – hence the chapter divisions in this section. March 1938 saw the Nazi takeover of Austria, an intensification of the onslaught against the Jews culminating in the first major physical assault on the Jews of Germany (*Kristallnacht*), and the British and French climb-down over Czechoslovakia. June 1941 witnessed the Nazi invasion of the Soviet Union and the beginning of the process of mass extermination of the Jewish population.

These three chapters deal 'directly' with the Holocaust and are placed between six other chapters which provide the historical and educational framework. Chapter 2 provides a very brief survey of Jewish history, from Roman times to the threshold of the modern period. Here the emphasis is placed, *not* on suffering, but on *survival*. All too often students of the Holocaust confront no other picture of the Jew except one of unrelieved torment and victimization. This can create an obsessive and utterly unbalanced view of the entire Jewish role in history and, for that matter, of all Jews. This chapter will seek to move away this purely negative image and to explain, in all too few pages, who the Jews are, their historical development, culture, dispersal and contribution to the world. For we must retain some sense of what has been lost – not only the heartbeat of some 6 million Jewish lives but also European, particularly East European, Jewish civilization.

Chapter 3 will explore the modern experience of the Jewish people in Europe, from the period shortly before the French Revolution right up to the years immediately after the First World War. The accent here will be upon four major themes which have dominated modern Jewish history and which are so closely interrelated: emancipation, nationalism, migration and antisemitism.

Chapter 4 examines the history of modern Germany, from its unification in 1871 to the accession to power of Adolf Hitler in January 1933. Here the spotlight will fall on the years following Germany's defeat in the First World War – the period of the Weimar Republic. We shall examine, in particular, the exceptional social, economic and psychological climate that formed the background for the unchecked growth of political extremism.

Chapter 8 examines some of the psychological and motivational forces determining the behaviour and responses of the three central protagonists on the Holocaust stage – the perpetrators, the victims and the bystanders. Many of the book's most challenging, contentious and open-ended moral issues are raised in these pages.

Chapter 9 will probe the vexed subject of the attitudes and reactions of ordinary Germans to the Jewish plight, both in Germany and throughout Nazi-occupied Europe. This is a comparatively under-researched historical area, but one which raises delicate and crucial questions of knowledge, indifference, action and responsibility. It is possible that the reader may conclude from this and other sections that one of the keys to understanding how the Holocaust could have happened lies in grasping the potentially destructive force of human apathy and inaction.

Chapter 10 deals with the immediate aftermath and consequences of the Holocaust (Displaced Persons' Camps, the Nuremberg Trials, etc.). Stress will be placed on the Holocaust's impact on the surviving Jewish world – physically, psychologically and politically – climaxing in the controversial establishment of the State of Israel in 1948. This was itself an epoch-making decision, intimately connected with events in Europe during the preceding 15 years.

Central motifs

There are three further, if often understated, strands that run through much of this book. One is the attempt to lay bare the dangers inherent in our modern forms of technology and bureaucracy – the quintessential products of the twentieth century. For the Holocaust is perhaps the supreme expression to date of what can happen when these weapons fall into the wrong hands.

A second preoccupation, implicit in this work, is to provide insights into the nature of human prejudice. For the Holocaust, despite its singularity, is also the most unspeakable example of what is perhaps only too familiar to us all – the tendency, that appears intrinsic to human nature (and is seemingly ineradicable), to form stereotyped and discriminatory views about groups of 'others' – others who are perceivably different in terms of religion, race, nationality, culture, age, gender or political outlook – and to translate these attitudes into patterns of behaviour.

Thirdly, no study of the Holocaust would be truly serious, or stand a realistic chance of imparting its educational gravity if it were not related, in some way, to other expressions of man's apparently inexhaustible appetite for killing fellow-members of his species. Throughout, the reader should keep in mind that, however unique and incomparable the Holocaust might arguably be, it is also part of something larger than itself and most definitely did not occur in a psychological or historical vacuum. If, on the other hand, the Holocaust were to be isolated from all other historical occurrences and other peoples' experiences, it would become essentially unapproachable – a wholly eccentric phenomenon, devoid of point or meaning.

Without doing damage to the uniqueness of the Holocaust – and indeed to the distinctiveness of other examples of genocide in the modern era – it is increasingly important that the ingredients which the different man-made catastrophes have in common be identified. *For it is the making, not the breaking, of connections that will enable moral and educational lessons truly to be imparted.* Certainly, Hitler appears to have understood the significance of the international community's silence in the face of earlier episodes of genocide:

Genghis Khan had millions of women and men killed by his own will and with a gay heart. History sees in him only a great state builder ... I have sent to the east ... my 'Death's Head Units', with the order to kill without mercy men, women and children of Polish race or language. Only in such a way will we win the 'lebensraum' that we need. Who, after all, talks nowadays of the extermination of the Armenians?

Adolf Hitler, 1939[10]

Genocide in the modern age

Genocide is surely nothing new. The Bible contains apparent examples, as do the chronicles of the ancient and classical worlds. The causes may vary – wave upon wave of human migration, nomadic peoples pitted against settled agricultural societies, 'advanced' civilizations versus loose-knit tribal groupings, the struggle for limited or decreasing natural resources – but the genocidal pattern has been both long-term and unmistakable: the displacement and destruction of one human group by another, and the consequent obliteration of cultures and societies into the sands of time. This is a significant aspect of our recorded history which we ignore at our peril.

Yet the term 'genocide' *is* new. It was the Nazi persecution and eventual extermination of European Jewry in the 1940s which prompted Raphael Lemkin, a prominent international lawyer, to propose it. (*Genos* is the Greek for race or tribe, 'cide' is derived from the Latin *occidere* meaning 'to kill'.)[11] Lemkin's purpose was to bring attention not merely to cases involving the destruction of national or religious groups but also to the potential for such actions. In an international community, he believed, such crimes against humanity ought to be outlawed and punishable.

Significantly, after the Second World War, Lemkin's proposals found an international legal context. In 1946, the newly formed United Nations, still reeling from the horrors perpetrated on civilian communities in Nazi Europe, moved to adopt a Genocide Convention. The General Assembly appointed a committee to study the issue and make proposals on how the convention could best be formulated. At the outset, it sought further to define the problem. Genocide, the committee stated, entailed 'deliberate acts committed with the intent to destroy a national, racial, religious or political group on grounds of the national or racial origin, religious belief or political opinion of its members'.

Although this broad definition was not adopted in the Genocide Convention of 1948, the final text was, theoretically, a breakthrough in that it made genocide, or its intent, a punishable crime. So too were the powers, though somewhat ill-defined, which the United Nations gave to itself to prevent or suppress it. On the other hand, a number of commentators have noted the exclusion both of political and economic groups, and of minorities (national, cultural or religious) from its express protection – an omission which, it has been argued, appeared to come very close to giving member-state signatories a licence to commit the very act which the convention set out to outlaw.[12]

In addition, the convention was weakened by a number of member-states who insisted on emasculating its terms of reference. Prominent in this respect was the Soviet Union, which asserted that genocide, as committed by the Nazis, was bound up with a decaying phase of imperialism, the implication being that the convention would be unlikely to have any future application. Moreover, within the Soviet bloc the specificity of the crime against the Jews came to be subsumed under a general heading of Fascist crimes against the peoples of eastern Europe. Perhaps it was felt that a full definition, enshrined in international law, would in some way encroach upon and threaten the sovereignty of independent states – the very bodies most capable of committing the crime in question. What is quite beyond dispute, however, is that, despite the terrifying precedent of the Holocaust and despite the adoption of this convention by the United Nations, genocide has continued to disfigure human existence on this planet.

Problems of definition

Key questions remain unresolved. In the light of the savagery of human history, in what ways, if any, can genocide be considered a modern phenomenon? To what extent is it, in the final analysis, principally a question of numbers, elevating, say, the crimes of Stalin and Mao above those of Torquemada or Genghis Khan? To be sure, the technology of destruction, the sheer firepower alone, has in our century led to violent death on an unprecedented scale. Sociologists sometimes talk of twentieth-century 'mega-deaths'. But that in itself begs a series of questions. Are all mega-deaths cases of genocide? Alternatively, where the numbers involved are relatively small, can this not also constitute genocide? When exactly do we cross the border? When does inter-communal massacre (e.g.

in the Lebanon or Sri Lanka) become genocide? At what point does violence against individuals or collections of individuals, man-induced hunger, torture and murder, become a cumulative act called genocide? To be more specific, do these acts have features in common? Is it possible or desirable to link (compare?) the main subject of this book – the extermination of the Jews during the Second World War – to other mass killings?[13] There is indeed a danger that by using the term genocide to excess, one might make both the term and the individual instance appear commonplace; conversely, too restrictive a use might limit its preventive and educative effect.

Genocide in action: some common ingredients?

What gives genocide its distinctive characteristics is both the motivation and the ability to carry it out. The potential victims have to be collectively defined, selected, isolated from non-victims, and then obliterated. It is a process which is both deliberate and systematic. If it cannot be carried out all at once, then it is something to which the perpetrators will wish to return. On the other hand, they must be sure that they will be ultimately successful. To do less may be to suffer retribution at the hands of the victims or of some other, more powerful, external agent. Certainly, the Nazi leadership was ultimately concerned to cover their tracks and the pro-Nazi satellite states were anxious to avoid exposure and hence Allied punishment for violations of the Geneva Convention, particularly with respect to crimes against Jewish civilians. Indeed, the true 'state of the art' is the genocide where the act has been so complete, the incriminating evidence so utterly disposed of, that the perpetrators can deny that it ever happened. To this day, the Turkish government continues to challenge allegations that they perpetrated genocide against the Armenian people during the First World War.

Only one body in the modern era has considered such an undertaking with seriousness and equanimity: the state. Only the state is fully equipped with the necessary apparatus for the task: the technology of destruction, the logistical and administrative support systems, the communications facilities with which to coordinate its campaign and, the disinformation agencies with which to lie to its wider population and to the world at large. As we shall see in later chapters, the Nazis went to the most astounding lengths to starve not only their Jewish victims but their own population and the outside world of access to information about the mass slaughter.

And here we come to the heart and essence of the urge to genocide. Why would a state act in such a way against any group either within or outside its political sphere of influence? The answer in short is this: the state would have to be convinced, unshakeably convinced, that the extraordinary crisis it faced could only be resolved by exterminating its selected victim group. Hence the victim group would have to be perceived not simply as a grave but, indeed, as a mortal threat to the state itself. And it is this area – the mentality of the threatened and hence 'vindicated' perpetrator – that the Holocaust arguably bears closest resemblance to some other genocides, most notably the Armenian and Kampuchean catastrophes. The reasoning might go something like this: 'If we do not destroy them, they will destroy us. Our action therefore is no ordinary one and cannot be limited by moral or legal restraints. On the contrary, because "they" are the enemy, a veritable cancer threatening our very existence, our sanction to act, as we propose, is absolute; our mission is "sacred".'

By such a process, therefore, the will to genocide becomes elevated to the 'highest' plane, indeed to a pseudo-religious duty. The corollary is that the victim group must be degraded to the level of *ein Mistvolk*, Adolph Eichmann's term for what he perceived as a garbage nation 'fit only for the dung heap'. This dehumanization, this negation not simply of the victims' human attributes but of their very right to exist, is the necessary prelude to an important aspect of genocide's agenda: not merely the annihilation of the group but its obliteration from the state and wider historical record. (The progressive 'dehumanization' of the Jewish victims of Nazism between 1933 and 1941 as a prerequisite to annihilation during the subsequent four-year period is explored throughout Chapters 5 and 6.)

Even during crises and in exceptional circumstances, one would assume, however, that most states would fall short of this all-embracing response. The record of the twentieth century nevertheless shows us that, where the state machinery is controlled, or has been captured by a highly motivated group or party with its own very definite ideas about the nature and organization of that society, that group has sometimes not shrunk from genocidal intent and action. This is perhaps the final clue and warning signal as to the nature of genocide. Genocide may occur where normal societal restraints have been removed or frozen. More specifically, it happens during or, more often, in the wake of war, revolution or some other massive political dislocation, such as decolonization. In the most complete examples, the Nazi Holocaust being the 'purest' and most tellingly recorded, it is carried out by an ideologically motivated clique, with their own particular sense of destiny who, having consolidated state control, are able to act against the victim group with seeming impunity. For this purpose they will require either the active participation of the wider population, their acquiescence or, failing that, their neutralization. Genocide is the response, almost always, of a totalitarian society – such as Nazi Germany, Stalinist Russia or Saddam Hussein's Iraq – in which dissent or doubt are themselves crimes.

That it is the state or its agents which is the perpetrator of genocide tells us one other revealing fact. Other states will not intervene unless their own state interests are threatened. They may be appalled bystanders but they will remain bystanders nonetheless. One of the hallmarks of genocide has consistently been the international community's inaction until it is too late. In this sense, the United Nations' Genocide Convention has in practice been a dead letter. The failure of the United Nations to invoke the Genocide Convention in the case of Cambodia and, further, the alleged participation of 'representatives' of Pol Pot's Khmer Rouge in the United Nations' efforts to plan the future of Cambodia, has led to widespread popular condemnation. It has consequently even been suggested in certain quarters that the United Nations has somehow forfeited its right to be regarded as a serious bulwark against future genocides.[14]

Constraints and limitations

Although this is an introductory chapter, it has been called Chapter 1 and not the Introduction (which might have preceded the first chapter). This is because readers often skip introductions! And this introduction, in the view of the author at least, is integral and indispensable to what follows. The Holocaust is a vast, almost limitless territory and this book does not, and cannot, stand on its own as an exhaustive treatment of the subject. Its aims are to raise and examine the key issues confronting those who wish to make some sense of a catastrophic event in whose fall-out we all still live. By placing it inside several legitimate contexts, space has inevitably been sacrificed which might otherwise have been devoted, say, to a detailed country-by-country narrative or to a more extensive treatment of the historical background. While no single approach or academic discipline can 'explain' – or, indeed, claim a monopoly on – such a baffling phenomenon as the Holocaust, by removing some of the boundaries between the different perspectives of literature, history, psychology and sociology, it is hoped that this work may help break down the barriers to our understanding of its origins and its import.

The past few years have witnessed enormous upheavals and transformations, especially in Europe. Between 1945 and 1990, Europe remained essentially unchanged, as did the balance of international power. The postwar geopolitical arrangements were largely born out of conditions emerging from the defeat of Nazism. Consequently, there has been, within our culture and society, an organic link to the Nazi period, kept alive by memories and memorabilia (films, books and the like). The new world order and the passing of generations have inevitably dimmed memories. They may also dim the sense of horror and revulsion which, in the industrialized world at least, has served to stem any tendencies for repetition. Should there be any truth in the propositions that forgetting is repeating and that failure to understand is to condone, the purpose of this book is to make a small contribution in helping us both to remember and to understand.

> Like Hiroshima, Auschwitz stands as a boundary stone in history, marking an end and a beginning, a gruesome monument to the mistakes of the past and perhaps a signpost to a better future.
>
> Nicholas de Lange[15]

Part 1

Background and Context

CHAPTER 2

Survey of Jewish History: *c.*300 BC to *c.*1700

What is Jewish history?

It is important to locate the worst tragedy that ever befell the Jews – and, arguably, any other people – within a framework, however superficial, of their own history. This chapter will therefore attempt, in a very brief space, to outline the history of the Jewish people from post-biblical times down to the threshold of the modern period, a history extending over 2,000 years.

The description of a specifically Jewish history presents an immediate difficulty: for who exactly are the Jews? What precisely is 'Jewishness'? And what on earth is Jewish history? After all, there may be a history of Buddhism but there is no such thing as Buddhist history (i.e. a history of Buddhists). There may be a history of Catholicism, but is there a history of Catholics – or, for that matter, of Southern Baptists or Welsh Methodists? The adjective Jewish seems qualitatively different from such descriptive terms as Christian or Scottish. So what does it mean to be Jewish? Is there a difference between Judaism and Jewishness? Is the '*-ish*' suffix significant? After all, we don't call anyone Protestant*ish* or Hindu*ish*. When, in 1960, the British satirical comedian (as he was at the time), Jonathan Miller, said on the stage of a London theatre that he was 'not a Jew, just Jew*ish*!' what did he mean and why did the audience laugh?[1]

Definitions of Jewishness

There are many definitions of the terms 'Jew' and 'Jewish' and, although any attempt at a single, simple explanation that would satisfy everyone is doomed to failure, it would be useful to explore some of the most commonly held beliefs. These include the views that the Jews are a *religious group*, that they are a *racial group*, that they constitute a *nation*, that they are a *cultural group*, and that they are an historical marvel that defies any clear labelling.

The Jews as a religious group?

Many people feel that the religious factor is the single most decisive one in shaping Jewish identity. They believe that it is their ancient religion, rooted in a belief in one God (monotheism) who 'chose' the Jews to receive His law (Torah) and to live in the land of Israel, that has held the Jews together in so many lands of their dispersal, thus ensuring their survival. Seen from this perspective, despite the ravages of modernity and the multiplicity of new identities that have been spawned during the past two centuries, just as it has always been, so it still is, the religious dimension – to the exclusion of all other passing trends and influences – that gives form, purpose and meaning to being Jewish, even in the late twentieth century.

Without denying the centrality of religion to the overall Jewish experience, it is nevertheless quite clear that in our modern, secular societies, at least as many Jews are non-religious as are observant. This would seem, therefore, to be inadequate as a complete definition, since it does not embrace those whose lifestyle and attachment are by no means traditional or orthodox, and who feel no less 'Jewish' for it. The answer, therefore, is plainly more complex.

The Jews as a race?

Many people define Jewishness in racial terms, particularly since the overwhelming majority become Jewish by virtue of being born of a Jewish mother. This, in the eyes of traditional Judaism, is sufficient grounds for conferring membership of the 'club' without the need ever to demonstrate one's Jewishness by any other means – whether through religious observance, becoming a citizen of the State of Israel, eating traditional Jewish food or marrying another Jewish person. The Nazi Party, as we shall see, defined Jews according to strict racial criteria: the Nuremberg Laws of 1935 defined a Jew as having three or more Jewish grandparents and there were later refinements on this law for those with two or even one Jewish grandparent. (For the text of the Nuremberg Laws and the supplementary decree, see Appendix E.) One wit, who clearly has genuine insights into the social and familial values of the Jewish community, would later turn Hitler's definition on its head and defined a 'real Jew' as anyone who has produced three Jewish grandchildren!

In fact, there is no such phenomenon as the Jewish or Semitic race. The concept of a racially pure Jewish group is an historical and biological nonsense. According to anthropologists, there is also no group one could properly describe as belonging to the 'Aryan race'. The terms Semitic and Aryan refer, not to racial categories of people, but to groups of languages, Hebrew and Arabic being Semitic tongues.

According to the latest theories, the Jewish group had its origins in the Mediterranean subdivision of the Caucasian race. Known originally as Hebrews, they migrated and inhabited the coastal plains of Canaan under the name of Israelites. They became known as Jews (Latin *Iudaei*) when the kingdom of Judah was established in 922 BC. After the Romans destroyed the Second Jewish Temple and their state in AD 70, most of the inhabitants were dispersed to various parts of the Roman Empire. They scattered in large numbers to such centres as Egypt, Babylonia, Syria, the Greek islands and Rome itself – all places where Jewish communities had been long established – and they also settled in new communities in Italy, Spain, France (Gaul), Poland, Germany and later in Britain, too. While there are unquestionably dominant physical and racial characteristics within the Jewish group – those of the southern Mediterranean Caucasians – there are many other racial ingredients, including those commonly associated with the majority of the inhabitants of Africa and Asia. This suggests not only dietary and climatic influences but also the incidence of large-scale conversion, intermarriage and sadly, on occasions, forced interbreeding. It is often simply not appreciated that, long before the rise of Christianity and Islam, Judaism itself used to be an actively proselytizing religion. This blending has resulted in a kaleidoscopic racial mix and explains why, in numerous countries throughout all five continents, the local Jews cannot be distinguished by their physical appearance alone from many other inhabitants.

The Jews as a nation?

Long before the establishment of the State of Israel in 1948, Jews were regarded, and often regarded themselves, as members of a nation scattered throughout different lands since the destruction of their state in the first century. For example, in the official documents of the Dutch East India Company during the seventeenth century, Jews are frequently referred to as members of the 'Jewish nation'. Before modern times, if someone was considered a Polish Jew, the noun 'Jew' probably defined him nationally, culturally, religiously and socially; the adjective 'Polish' merely defined his geographical location – and his bags were packed! The term 'Polish' would not in any sense have defined him nationally. The birth of the State of Israel has underscored the belief of many Jews that they have a strong affiliation to their national homeland, even if they choose not to live there. However, this purely national definition is also inadequate, not least because large numbers of Jews, ever since the French and American Revolutions developed the notion of citizenship – of political and cultural loyalties to the nation-states of Europe and America – do not consider themselves as Jewish nationals, but as the nationals of the countries in which they reside. (See Chapter 3 for a fuller exploration of the problem of dual national loyalties, a central feature of the modern period of Jewish history.)

The Jews as a cultural group?

Many people who regard themselves as Jewish – in some cases deeply Jewish – do not measure their Jewishness in terms of religious, racial or national definitions. Indeed, they may be entirely uninterested in spiritual or political expressions of their identity. Yet they feel a strong sense of belonging to an ethnic group and to a cultural tradition. They may display this cultural identity through their preferences in food, the way they dress, the books and newspapers they read, the plays they enjoy seeing performed.

However, because of their continuing dispersal and the collapse of their European languages, Yiddish and Ladino, Jews today no longer speak a common tongue which, until the modern period, was an obvious indicator of the cultural identity of their group (and that of most other groups). They also participate in many different cultures, including radically different 'Jewish' cultures. A Woody Allen film, which is considered so 'Jewish' in the USA would mean little to a Jew from the Yemen. Similarly, Ethiopian Jewish customs would cut little ice with a Jew from north-west London.

If there is now muddle and confusion over what exactly it means to be Jewish, then that is hardly surprising. Jewishness cannot truly be explained in terms of any *one* of these definitions alone; for modern Jewish identity, in all its bewildering diversity, is the product of a very complex historical process. Religious, national, racial and cultural elements are all present within the Jewish group, though not in every Jew. According to Isaiah Berlin, Jewishness is perhaps best defined as having a sense of continuity with the Jewish past – a continuity which may express itself in a great variety of ways.[2]

Outline of Jewish history

Jewish history can loosely be interpreted as the development – social, cultural, political and religious – of the Jewish group over the past 3,500 years. To a greater extent than is the case with the history of most other nations, it is also concerned with the relationship between Jews and other peoples (especially those in a position of power), since for over half of that time Jews lived as minorities in other peoples' lands.

The heart of Jewish 'difference'

The biblical story of the coming out of Egypt and the 'Divine Revelation' on Mount Sinai had signalled the birth of the Jewish nation and the start of its civilizing mission: the Ten

Commandments were destined to be the basis of every civil code in the world. Elsewhere in the Bible, the commandment mentioned more often than any other (36 times in various forms) is 'Love the stranger; for you were strangers in the land of Egypt.'[3] Judaism can be seen, therefore, to contain at its very heart a revulsion at intolerance, prejudice and the dehumanization of others; Jews, it can be inferred, should know from their own historical experience what it means to be persecuted because of cultural, national and religious difference and the powerlessness this engenders. The Exodus from Egypt (c.1250 BC) is the supreme symbol of freedom, not only for Jews but for all peoples. However, in its implicit rejection of the institution of slavery, Judaism would come to be regarded with great suspicion by the powerful empires of the ancient world, by Babylon, Persia, Greece and Rome, who depended for their 'progress' on a massive institutionalized slave-economy.[4]

Not only this rejection of slavery, but its radical monotheism, the belief in a single omnipotent, spiritual God (the principal legacy of biblical Judaism to Western civilization), was in strict opposition to the polytheism of the rest of the world at that time (and later). Some scholars of the Holocaust believe that the origin of antisemitism lies in the strength of this challenge Judaism posed from the start. The God of the Hebrews was not, as was theirs, made in the image of humans and subject to the same appetites for food, sex and power. On the contrary, in Jewish theology humans are made in God's image and are at their most elevated when, in veneration and fear of that Being who created them and the whole world, they display love, moderation, justice and compassion, which are sparks of the Divine.

The start of Hellenism

Fourth and third centuries BC

The latter part of the fourth century BC marks a decisive turning-point in the history of the Jewish state and people. Until then the country had been ruled, or greatly influenced, by the great Oriental powers – Egypt, Assyria, Babylonia and Persia. But from that time until the seventh century AD, the State of Judah (originally the southern territory of the biblical kingdom of Israel, increasingly referred to by scholars as Judea, and later dubbed 'Palestine' by the Romans) came under the sway of empires and cultures whose chief sources of inspiration were Greek (Hellenistic) and, later, Roman. After Alexander the Great's conquest of the Near East, Judea first came under the rule of the Hellenistic Ptolemies of Egypt (301–198 BC) and then passed to the Hellenistic Seleucid kingdom of Syria.[5]

Oppression and rebellion

At first the Seleucid monarchy was tolerant of Jewish culture and religious practices and permitted a fair degree of autonomy. But when Antiochus IV Epiphanes came to the throne in 175 BC, he attempted to suppress Jewish ancestral faith and to impose a pagan Greek way of life, in conformity with the rest of the kingdom (the Jewish upper classes having to some extent already adopted the Greek language and customs). Against the background of a divided Jewish response – the Hellenists in one camp and the Traditionalists in the other – Antiochus ultimately banned all practice of the Jewish religion. For example, the death penalty was imposed on any Jew who observed the Sabbath or circumcised his son. Forbidden food (especially pig's meat) was forced on the population and the Temple was ransacked, defiled and rededicated to Zeus, the father of the Olympian gods of Greece.

Much to Antiochus' indignation and surprise, many Jews, in a climate of fervent messianic expectation and in the prophetic belief of the coming of the End of Days, preferred to suffer martyrdom rather than betray their heritage and faith. This religious belief that the martyr was 'sanctifying God's name' when attacked for no reason other than for being Jewish would recur throughout later Jewish history, including the period of the Holocaust.[6]

This onslaught against Judaism prompted a revolt led by a priestly clan, the Hasmoneans. This rebellion, fuelled by nationalistic and religious resistance to the Greeks, ultimately succeeded. It achieved the liberation and reconsecration of their defiled Temple in 164 BC (commemorated annually by the winter festival of Hannukah – 'the Festival of Lights') and later, in 142 BC, led to the re-establishment of Jewish political independence.

Roman dominion

The Hasmoneans sought to eradicate the political and cultural influences of the Greek world but would prove unable to prevent their state from falling, in 63 BC, into the clutches of the new imperial power – Rome. The Hasmoneans had failed to establish themselves as universally recognized leaders among the Jewish people. Many, including the Pharisees (the party that later became the rabbis), rejected their claim to be legitimate high priests. The Romans, finding division and in-fighting among the Jewish leadership, appointed their own puppet-king, Herod, whose reign was brutal and corrupt. The legacy of Herod's murderous rule was dissension and chaos, with the Romans finally moving into the power vacuum and establishing direct rule of Judea under procurators (governors).

The year 63 BC had effectively marked the end of Jewish political independence; this would not be restored for another two thousand years – until the establishment of the State of Israel in 1948, only three years after the unspeakable horrors of Hitlerite Europe.

The sectarianism that had grown under the Hasmoneans, and developed further under Herod, now blossomed fully under direct Roman rule, and political anarchy swept the countryside and religious disorder the cities. It is against this background that the emergence of new messianic movements, which were both religiously and politically motivated – including that of Jesus of Nazareth[7] – must be understood. So, too, must the rebellion which would culminate in the Great Jewish Revolt against the Romans during the years AD 66–70. Under the new Roman governors, even the pretence of independence had vanished, the Romans introducing severe discriminatory measures to deal with what they regarded as a stubborn people who threatened to undermine the political stability of this far-flung corner of their empire.

The Jewish revolt

The revolt started in AD 66, after the Temple authorities objected to sacrifices being offered to the Roman emperor. Jewish forces destroyed the Roman garrison in Jerusalem and defeated a Roman army sent from Syria. They set up a provisional government but the Jewish population was too divided internally to give it proper support. A huge army was sent by the Emperor Vespasian to put down the rebellion and in AD 70, under the command of Titus (later emperor), Jerusalem was sacked and the Second Temple destroyed.

In both a political and a religious sense, the destruction of the Temple marked the end of an era. Temple sacrifice would give way to prayer, the priests being removed from politics and losing their primary religious function. During the siege of Jerusalem, the rabbinical leader, Yohanan ben Zakkai, escaped from the city and sought refuge in the town of Yavneh. The Romans, in granting this request, allowed him to begin the transformation of Yavneh into a centre of Jewish religious activity. Even though Jerusalem was in ruins, Judaism had been saved.

Sixty years later, the Roman Emperor Hadrian announced the setting up of a Roman colony on the ruins of Jerusalem and another Jewish rebellion (under Bar Kokhba) was sparked off, also inspired by messianic hopes of deliverance. This revolt was put down savagely by the Romans: the Jews of Judea were exterminated, enslaved or forced to flee; only in the northern province of Galilee did a Jewish population remain in the land of Israel. However merciless and decisive these phases of Roman repression may have been, unlike the motiveless and irrational massacres of the Nazi period, they at least had their basis in the brutal governmental logic of Roman imperial power: insubordination had to be crushed.

Diaspora

These events, the destruction of the Temple in AD 70 and the Bar Kokhba catastrophe, represent a major watershed in Jewish history. They accelerated a process already begun centuries earlier – the development of the Jewish Diaspora (dispersal). Jewish slaves, merchants, scholars, exiles and adventurers found their way to virtually every part of the Roman Empire (with the exception of Britain which, it is believed, saw the development of the first Jewish settlement only after the Norman Conquest of 1066). By the third century there was a Jewish presence in lands as diverse (to use their

34

THE JEWS OF THE ROMAN EMPIRE 100-300 AD

Jews filled many occupations, being farmers and cattle raisers (Mesopotamia), street traders (Egypt), slave-traders (Germany), wine and olive-growers (Spain and North Africa), weavers, garment-makers, actors, bakers and shipping-merchants (Italy). They were equally active as agriculturalists and town dwellers

The Jews of the Roman Empire

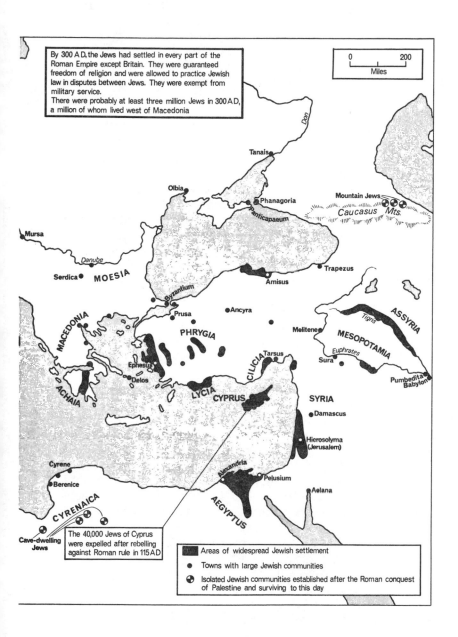

By 300 A.D, the Jews had settled in every part of the Roman Empire except Britain. They were guaranteed freedom of religion and were allowed to practice Jewish law in disputes between Jews. They were exempt from military service.
There were probably at least three million Jews in 300 A.D, a million of whom lived west of Macedonia

0   200
Miles

Tanais
Olbia
Phanagoria
Mountain Jews
Caucasus Mts.
Panticapaeum
Mursa
Danube
Serdica MOESIA
Trapezus
Amisus
Byzantium
Prusa Ancyra
ASSYRIA
Tigris
Melitene MESOPOTAMIA
PHRYGIA
Euphrates
MACEDONIA
Tarsus
CILICIA
Sura
ACHAIA Ephesus
Delos
LYCIA CYPRUS
Pumbedita
Babylon
SYRIA
Damascus
Hierosolyma
(Jerusalem)
Cyrene
Alexandria
Berenice
Pelusium
Aelana
CYRENAICA
AEGYPTUS
Cave-dwelling
Jews
The 40,000 Jews of Cyprus were expelled after rebelling against Roman rule in 115 A.D

■ Areas of widespread Jewish settlement
● Towns with large Jewish communities
⊕ Isolated Jewish communities established after the Roman conquest of Palestine and surviving to this day

modern equivalents) as Spain, Yugoslavia, Germany, Egypt, Greece, the Crimea, Italy, Morocco, Turkey, France, Italy and Iraq – and beyond the Roman Empire in India, Persia and Ethiopia. The simple answer, therefore, to the riddle posed by the spread of Jews into so many different countries – particularly in Europe – is to be found in the extent of an expanding Roman world.[8]

As an inevitable consequence of this scattering over three continents, the major thrust of Jewish history in the Diaspora has been the interaction – and, critically, the changing relationship – between Jew and non-Jew; between an 'alien' social, cultural and religious minority and the 'host' societies at whose mercy they often found themselves. In contrast, the dominant feature of the histories of most other peoples, who were not nomadic and who exerted greater control over their own destiny, has been their *internal* social, cultural and political development. This is not, of course, to assert that Jews in the various countries of their dispersal had no 'power'. Despite being cut off from a political centre, for long periods and in many different lands they enjoyed the sort of autonomy that would allow for the consolidation and creative development of their own religious and cultural traditions.[9]

The importance of study

With the collapse of their independent homeland and Temple-centred religion, the rabbis in Galilee and elsewhere substituted prayer and study in place of sacrifice and pilgrimage to the Temple. The need for a central sanctuary in Jerusalem was thus removed and Judaism became a Diaspora religion (even in the 'Promised Land'), capable of being practised and fulfilled anywhere. In Galilee during the second and third centuries, the corpus of laws known as the *Mishnah* was composed. Just as many modern legal systems comprise written statutes interpreted and developed by the judges, so Judaism is essentially a set of laws interpreted and developed by the rabbis and finally written down.

The major centre of learning and scholarship passed from Galilee to Babylonia, where there had been a large Jewish

settlement since the first exile of the sixth century BC.
Intensive study of the Mishnah ('teaching by repetition') by
later scholars in Palestine (as Judea had now been called by
the Romans) and Babylonia led to the compilation of a vast
array of critical commentaries called *Gemara* ('completion').
The Mishnah and Gemara were then joined together to form
the *Talmud* ('study') – the Palestinian and Babylonian
Talmuds have the same Mishnah but significantly different
Gemara. The Babylonian Talmud, completed in the fifth
century, became the principal religious authority for the whole
Jewish world.

Medieval Europe

In Babylonia the Jewish community and particularly the
rabbinical academies had flourished for several centuries,
exerting a deep influence on the Jewish communities in
Europe. But as the Babylonian centre declined in the tenth and
eleventh centuries, the communities in North Africa and
especially Spain began to thrive. In short, it may be said that
up to the year 1000 the major trends of Jewish history are
principally focused on the East but that, after that date, they
are chiefly concerned with the West. And it was Spain that
succeeded Babylonia as the main centre of Jewish intellectual
creativity.

The impact of Christianity and Islam

The Jewish world had undergone a profound revolution with
the rise of Christianity and Islam in the fourth and seventh
centuries respectively. Jews were now no longer the only
monotheistic people in the world. What is more, they
increasingly found themselves living as a social, cultural and
religious minority among majorities, whose religious systems
were descended, to some extent, from Judaism. Christianity in
particular would adopt a progressively more antagonistic
attitude towards its 'parent' religion. For Judaism had rejected
the messianic, divine claims of Jesus and hence was
irreconcilably at odds with the fundamental tenets of Christian
belief and theology. No matter how successful the Christian
Church was in spreading its message, it still retained an

38   *The Nazi Holocaust*

almost obsessive interest in humiliating and winning over (i.e.
converting) adherents to its religious predecessor – an ancestor
which it regarded as outmoded, discredited and replaced. As a
powerful expression of this hostility, Jews would increasingly
come to be identified in the medieval mind as the 'killers of
Christ' and even as agents of the Devil. The cumulative effects
of so strong a negative stereotype would have implications for
the success, many centuries later, of Nazi anti-Jewish
propaganda.

Before the growth of Christianity as a major force in Europe,
discrimination against Jews in the Diaspora was virtually
unheard of. Jews had previously enjoyed the protection of the
law and lived in comparative peace among the pagan tribes
and peoples. Generally speaking, the Jews under Islamic rule,
too, would enjoy a far greater degree of toleration than did
those living under Christian dominion.[10]

Spain

Medieval Spain is perhaps the best example of the contrast
between the benevolent stance of the contemporary Muslim
world and the hostile position taken up by the Church. Back in
the fifth and sixth centuries, Jews had suffered under the
Visigoth Christians, but under Muslim rule they prospered
and ultimately enjoyed what became known as the Golden Age:
they regularly participated in government and engaged
actively in liberal professions such as medicine. Against the
inspirational background of the flowering of Arabic language
and civilization, the Jews of Spain attained remarkable
heights, particularly in literature and philosophy. Hebrew
poetry in this period included works by Ibn Gabirol, Samuel
Ha-nagid and Judah Halevi, while the philosopher and
religious thinker, Moses Maimonides, produced his monumental works on Jewish law and thought. Jewish mysticism – the
development of the Kabbalah – also blossomed during this
period in Spain.

Upon the Christian reconquest of much of Spain by 1300,
after an initial period of conciliation, conditions slowly
deteriorated, leading to persecution by the Church and
repeated efforts to convert the Jews in order that they might
'bear witness to the truth of Jesus'. Many of the converts,
however were still Jewish at heart and the Church became
determined to take savage steps against heretics.

however, were still Jewish at heart and the Church became determined to take savage steps against heretics. This antagonism culminated in the torture of the Inquisition, which was preoccupied with rooting out 'Judaizing' influences in Christian Spain, and whose climax was the decree of expulsion in 1492. At least 150,000 Jews – a significant element in Spain's commercial and intellectual life – were driven out. Even as early as the fifteenth century, there was a discernible racial ingredient in the manic rooting out of Jewish influence and in the terrifying persecution of Jewish individuals and communities – attitudes which, to some extent, anticipate the later 'biological' criteria of the Nazi genocide.

The Jewish refugees from Spain and, a few years later, from Portugal made their way to many different parts of the world – especially to North Africa, Palestine, Holland, France, Turkey and Italy. The name 'Sephardi', which still refers very loosely to many Jewish communities, particularly in North Africa and Asia, comes from the Hebrew word for Spain. Originally it applied only to the communities which derived their culture and identity from Spain before the great expulsion.

Western and central Europe

As we have seen, Jews had settled in the western part of the Roman Empire long before the rise of Christianity. By the eleventh century they had produced a distinctive Jewish culture in northern France and on the eastern banks of the Rhine. It was in France, for example, that the scholar Rashi produced his famous commentary on the Bible and Talmud.

The First Crusade in 1096 marked a major turning-point in the relationship between Jews and their surrounding societies. On their way to Palestine to win back the Holy Land from the Muslim 'infidel', English and French Christian knights passed through the Rhineland and slaughtered tens of thousands of Jews. The Crusaders left behind plundered homes, broken lives and, more significantly, ushered in a new and depressing era for the Jewish people. Three more crusades in the twelfth century transformed settled Jewish community life into an uncertain existence of forced conversion, mass expulsion and pariah status. The medieval German knight, in his crusader's armour, would later be one of the inspirational visual ingredients in Nazi ritual and pageantry.

In many west European countries, Jews were increasingly channelled into a narrow and demeaning set of economic pursuits, most notoriously moneylending – utterly necessary for the societies themselves but considered an occupation unbecoming to Christians. In 1215 Pope Innocent III defined their degraded status by decreeing that they wear a special badge, to be revived later by the Nazis, and conspicuous clothing. In 1239 Pope Gregory condemned the Talmud as a heresy and a blasphemy against God and Jesus. Worse was to follow: in the mid-fourteenth century the Black Death ravaged western Europe, destroying nearly a quarter of the entire population. The Church, hard pressed to reconcile this unbearable suffering with the existence of a compassionate Jesus, sought to blame the Jews who, it was now alleged, were the emissaries of Satan and had poisoned the wells of Europe!

The Blood Libel

Jews thereafter frequently fell victim to the Blood Libel, whereby Jews were falsely accused of ritual murder of Christian children; this charge had first appeared in Norwich, England, in 1144 and had swiftly spread to the continent. Of all the legends associated with the Jews in medieval Europe, that of using Christian blood for mysterious ritual purposes has perhaps been the most pernicious and enduring. No other example was destined to demonstrate more clearly the extent to which the antisemitism of the modern and Nazi periods would later feed upon the anti-Judaism of the Middle Ages. (For a closer examination of the relationship between modern antisemitism and its medieval predecessor, see Chapter 3.)

The Blood Libel satisfied the dual aim of 'proving' the miraculous powers of Christianity and, simultaneously, the diabolical character of Judaism. Its origins were to be found 'in ancient, almost primordial, concepts concerning the potency and energies of blood'.[11] Christians had themselves been the victims of similar accusations during pagan times.

The fabrication appeared in many versions, but its salient ingredients were essentially the same. A Christian child would vanish – most commonly a male child just short of the age of puberty. A Jewish community – or individuals from that community – would be accused of having kidnapped, tortured and murdered him in order to re-enact, in some symbolic fashion, the crucifixion of Jesus (the episode in their history of which they were presumably most proud!). They were then said to have drained the body entirely of blood for use in the preparation of *Matzot* (unleavened bread) for the festival of Passover. Very often the Christian child, thus martyred, 'miraculously exposed' the crime and was eventually raised to sainthood, while the 'guilty' Jews were slaughtered or banished.

The Nazis would later make unashamed use of the Blood Libel in their anti-Jewish propaganda, both in its original and in an adapted form: the medieval stereotype of the Jew as literal bloodsucker would give way to that of the Jew as bloodsucking capitalist, on the one hand, and as Marxist manipulator of the working class, on the other. The history of the Blood Libel is not without a heavy slice of irony – for the Jewish religion has elevated the sanctity of life to a virtual absolute and strictly forbids the imbibing of the blood of *any* animal.

Expulsions

In the context of a superstitious and suffering medieval society, the Blood Libel and other such primitive and ridiculous accusations became the pretext for persecution, expulsion and occasional massacre. England had already expelled her Jews in 1290. France followed suit in 1306, again in 1332 after several thousand had returned, and finally in 1394. Many of the independent German principalities did likewise, particularly in the wake of the Black Death accusations (the Jews of Spain and Portugal, as we have learned, were expelled at the end of the fifteenth century).

The Jews of Poland

During this era of religious intolerance and expulsion the chief direction of movements by the Jewish population was eastwards. For, in contrast to the ferocious repression that characterized Christendom in the west, Jews were generally welcomed by the kingdom of Poland from the fourteenth

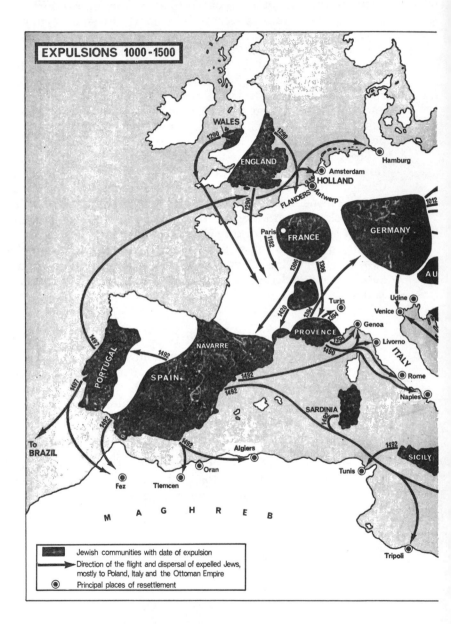

Expulsions, 1000–1500

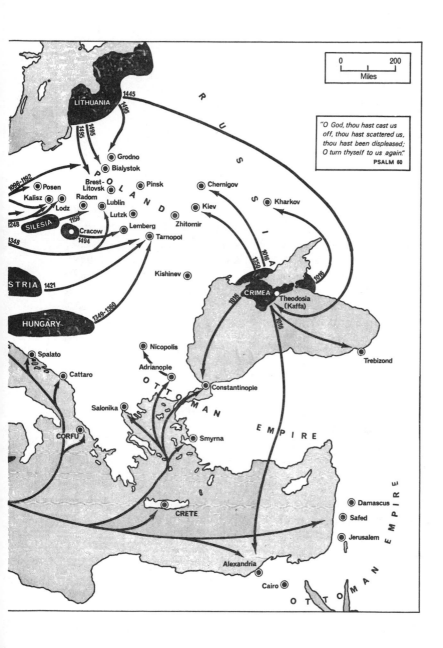

0   200
Miles

"O God, thou hast cast us
off, thou hast scattered us,
thou hast been displeased;
O turn thyself to us again."
PSALM 60

LITHUANIA
1445
1495
1495
1495

Grodno
Bialystok

R U S S I A

1096-1192
Posen
Kalisz
Lodz
Brest-
Litovsk
Radom
Lublin
Lutzk
Pinsk
Chernigov
Kharkov
Kiev
Zhitomir

P O L A N D

1248
SILESIA
1159
1494
Cracow
Lemberg
Tarnopol

1348

STRIA
1421

HUNGARY
1349-1360

Kishinev

1016
1350
1016
1016
1016
CRIMEA
Theodosia
(Kaffa)

Trebizond

Spalato
Cattaro
CORFU

Nicopolis
Adrianople
Salonika
Smyrna

O T T O M A N

Constantinople

E M P I R E

CRETE

Damascus
Safed
Jerusalem

E M P I R E

Alexandria
Cairo

O T T O M A N

MARIANNE JEWELL MEMORIAL LIBRARY
BAKER COLLEGE OF MUSKEGON
MUSKEGON, MICHIGAN 49442

century onwards.[12]

Poland had been devastated by Mongol invasions in the 1240s and needed help to rebuild her shattered economy. For this reason Jews, whose reputation for literacy and financial acumen made them a highly useful immigrant group, were afforded the protection of a charter of liberties issued by successive Polish monarchs. They were employed by the nobility as the managers of estates and tax collectors, frequently acting as middlemen between the landowning classes and the serfs who worked the land. Jews also became traders, craftsmen and, where it was permitted, farmers.

In sharp contrast to our post-Holocaust view of Poland as the most tragic and blood-stained soil on which Jews have trodden, for almost three hundred years – from the mid-fourteenth to the mid-seventeenth century – Jews enjoyed a period of comparative peace, tranquillity and the flowering of Jewish religious life. Eastern Europe – the Kingdom of Poland and Lithuania – was to become the new centre of Jewish spiritual and scholarly activity. There they enjoyed an existence that was, to all intents and purposes, separate from their gentile neighbours – an autonomy that enabled them to perpetuate their culture and sustain their distinctive identity.

The Chmelnicki massacres

This period of peace came to a violent end in 1648, when a lethal cocktail of national, religious and economic tensions erupted in the form of a Ukrainian uprising. Led by Bogdan Chmelnicki, the Russian Orthodox Ukrainian peasants revolted against the Polish nobility and the Roman Catholic Church. The Jews were caught in the middle, a target of Ukrainian hatred not only because they were the 'killers of Christ' but because they had collected taxes on behalf of the despised Polish landlords. Amid scenes of unprecedented brutality, it is estimated that between one quarter and one third of the Jewish population of southern Poland and the Ukraine were slaughtered. The ferocity of the onslaught is captured in the following harrowing description written by a contemporary chronicler:

Many (Jewish) communities ... who were unable to escape,

perished for the sanctification of (God's) Name. These persons died cruel and bitter deaths. Some were skinned alive and their flesh was thrown to the dogs; some had their hands and limbs chopped off, and their bodies thrown on the highway only to be trampled by wagons and crushed by horses; some had wounds inflicted on them, and were thrown on the street to die a slow death; ... others were buried alive. The enemy slaughtered infants in the laps of their mothers. They were sliced into pieces like fish. They slashed the bellies of pregnant women, removed their infants and tossed them in their faces. ... Some children were pierced on spears, roasted on the fire, and then brought to their mothers to be eaten. Many times they used the bodies of Jewish children as improvised bridges upon which they later crossed. ... Many were taken ... into captivity. Women and virgins were ravished, ... Similar atrocities were perpetrated in all the settlements through which they passed. Also against the Polish people these cruelties were perpetrated, against the priests and bishops, ... Scrolls of the (Jewish) Law were torn to pieces, and turned into boots and shoes for their feet ... Some were used for kindling purposes, and others to stuff the barrels of their guns. The ears ring at the hearing of this.[13]

After such a traumatic experience, many Polish Jews fled westwards, moving back into German territory for the first time in centuries; others would turn, in their desperate search for spiritual comfort, to messianic and mystical movements. For a further three centuries, right up until Adolf Hitler's murderous invasion of Poland, Bogdan Chmelnicki would remain the worst bogey-man in Polish-Jewish consciousness.

Pre-modern separation

By the end of the seventeenth century, over half the Jews in the world lived in the joint kingdom of Poland and Lithuania. There were pockets of toleration in Holland and England (Jews were unofficially readmitted into England by Oliver Cromwell in 1655), but everywhere in the pre-modern world Jews lived on the margins of society. Generally speaking, they lived a life of social and cultural isolation, a state of affairs desired both by the Christian host society *and*, for the most part, by the Jewish minority which desperately wished to preserve its separate identity. In some parts of western and central Europe they actually lived in walled-off parts of cities, known as ghettos – a confinement that would be revived by the Nazis in twentieth-century eastern Europe, as a prelude to extermination. (The word 'ghetto', it is now thought, is derived from the name of the district in Venice to which Jews had migrated in large numbers by the beginning of the sixteenth century.)

The legacy of Lutheranism

Hopes that the theological rebellion against 'orthodox' Christianity, the Reformation, would necessarily lead to more tolerant attitudes towards the Jews generally proved unfounded. Indeed, many of the more virulent views associated with medieval anti-Judaism can be found in the later writings of Martin Luther, the deeply influential sixteenth-century German Protestant thinker. In one instance, his advice went to even greater extremes than earlier Christian thinkers on the Jewish question:

What then shall we Christians do with this damned, rejected race of Jews? Since they live among us and we know about their lying and blasphemy and cursing, we cannot tolerate them if we do not wish to share in their lies, curses, and blasphemy. In this way we cannot quench the inextinguishable fire of divine rage (as the prophets say) nor convert the Jews. We must prayerfully and reverentially practise a merciful severity. Perhaps we may save a few from the fire and the flames. ... Let me give you my honest advice.

First, their synagogues or churches should be set on fire, and whatever does not burn should be covered or spread over with dirt so that no one may ever be able to see a cinder or stone of it ...

Secondly, their homes should likewise be broken down and destroyed. For they perpetrate the same things there that they do in their synagogues.

Thirdly, they should be deprived of their prayer-books and Talmuds in which their idolatry, lies, cursing, and blasphemy are taught.

Fourthly, their rabbis must be forbidden under threat of death to teach any more ...

Fifthly, passport and travelling privileges should be absolutely forbidden to the Jews ...

Sixthly, ... all their cash and valuables ought to be taken from them and put aside for safe keeping ... everything that they possess they stole and robbed from us through their usury, for they have no other means of support ...

To sum up, dear princes and nobles who have Jews in your domains, if this advice of mine does not suit you, then find a better one so that you and we may all be free of this insufferable devilish burden – the Jews.'[14]

In the opinion of many scholars, Luther's anti-Jewish stance would remain a critical source of authority for many Germans during the Nazi era – including, naturally enough, many sections of the Lutheran clergy. As we shall see in Chapter 3, it would be the revolutionary modern conditions of the nineteenth century that would give rise to so many new lines of attack on the Jewish people: the modern movement of antisemitism from which the twentieth-century Nazis (and Adolf Hitler in particular) would derive most of their weird and pernicious ideas about Jews. Nevertheless, the preceding era of medieval anti-Judaism should not be underestimated as an essential precondition for the development of these new versions of an old hatred.

CHAPTER 3

The European Jew
and the Modern World

Entry into the modern period

All peoples are marked, to a greater or lesser extent, by their past history and shared folk memories. This is particularly true of pre-modern Jewry, whose beliefs, mores and whole way of life were almost entirely rooted in, and derived from, their past. Yet the modern era has offered an unprecedented challenge to this sense of historical continuity with their religious and cultural traditions: as Jews were allowed to enter the mainstream of society in one western European country after another, there has occurred perhaps the deepest revolution of all in the long history of the Jewish Diaspora.

To understand the paradoxes and hazards of the modern period of Jewish history – including the climate within which the Holocaust would take place – we must begin by briefly considering the effects of two historical processes which would profoundly affect the whole course of European history. The first is the *Enlightenment* of the seventeenth and especially the eighteenth centuries, which engendered deep intellectual and cultural shifts in European ways of thinking. The second is the *French Revolution* of 1789, which to a degree achieved the political realization of the ideas of the French *philosophes*.

The Enlightenment vision

The fundamental tenets of the eighteenth-century thinkers of the Enlightenment were that human nature was essentially the same in all countries and among all races and creeds; that the artificial barriers between particular groups should be broken down; and that the political and economic power of the Christian Church – which, it was claimed, was responsible for so much divisiveness, ignorance, bigotry and misery – should be swept away. In general, the Enlightenment encouraged an altered view of the world – from a religious to a secular perspective. Thus reason and scientific thought were held to replace irrational thinking loosely based on religion and superstition.

In pre-modern Christian Europe, virtually everyone – Jew and gentile – lived in groups, whether religious, economic or regional. Their lives were governed by certain unquestioned assumptions: that it was perfectly natural to be preoccupied with one's own clan or class to the exclusion of outsiders; that it was normal and reasonable to live separately from 'others'; and that to be suspicious of, and even antagonistic towards, those of a different persuasion or background was quite legitimate. Notions of universal brotherhood, toleration, integration and equality were distant, utopian visions for members of all communities.[1] In questioning the very underpinnings of traditional European society, the European Enlightenment was championing the creation of a world in which people would no longer place such destructive emphasis on the differences between them, but instead construct shared and unified lives based on their common humanity.

The French Revolution

The French Revolution is considered by most historians to have heralded the entry of the Jewish people into the modern world. The French Revolution aimed at the establishment of a social and political reality which would make it impossible for individuals or groups to live on the periphery of society, in conditions either of immense privilege or of immense deprivation. Allegiances and loyalties would no longer be owed to the regional, class, religious, or ethnic group to which an individual belonged, but to the centralized nation-state. This was the meaning of the new concept of modern citizenship, an idea which would promote a uniformity of lifestyle, embracing education, language, dress, cultural practices and even beliefs. When Count de Clermont-Tonnerre spoke in the French

Revolutionary National Assembly in support of Jewish equality, he included these words:

> The Jews should be denied everything as a nation, but granted
> everything as individuals ... if they do not want this ... we shall
> then be compelled to expel them.

The Jew, in other words, was expected to conform and no longer give reason to be thought of as a member of 'a state within a state'. It was in this spirit that the Jews of France and, during the course of the nineteenth century, the Jews of every other country in western and central Europe, received emancipation.[2] This would, inevitably, have immense implications for a group such as the Jews, whose very survival – and, arguably, *raison d'être* – depended on its capacity to hold on to its cultural distinctiveness.

Dangers and opportunities

The Enlightenment and the French Revolution were destined to have a contradictory impact on Jewish life. On the one hand, in seeking to curtail continuing Jewish existence as a separate group, they would endanger the very survival of Judaism and a coherent Jewish identity, opening up the possibility of cultural assimilation, Jewish self-denial and the transformation of Jewish life. On the other hand, the Enlightenment and French Revolution brought the legal and political status of the Jews closer to that of their gentile neighbours. They would also help to create an intellectual and political climate which would provide unprecedented opportunities for Jews to participate in the heart of modern society. In time, Jews would function socially, occupationally, culturally and legally on equal terms with their neighbours, enjoying opportunities that had been denied to all but a few in medieval Europe.

The Jews, like all minority groups faced with an overwhelming and suddenly available majority culture, would tread a precarious path between remaining faithful to their ancestral traditions and participating wholeheartedly in modern society. What is more, even those who hurled themselves into their new life were often not considered to have a 'natural' sense of belonging to the majority national culture and were viewed as interlopers, no matter how vigorously they protested and demonstrated their patriotism.

Ironically, it would be during the 150th anniversary of the French Revolution that Nazi Germany would invade Poland, triggering the outbreak of the Second World War with all its wanton carnage.

Transition to modern antisemitism

Once the religious basis of attitudes towards the world and towards fellow-inhabitants began seriously to be questioned, and once traditional society itself was in the throes of transition into the modern secular nation-states with which we are now so familiar, the stage was set for the transformation of virtually everything – including the time-honoured hostility towards Judaism. For, during the course of the nineteenth century, the religiously inspired anti-Judaism of the Christian medieval world was to undergo a change, sometimes subtle and imperceptible, sometimes sudden and more obvious. Against the background of the secularization of western Europe, modern antisemitism (see below, pp.58–63) was to be born – an offspring both of its medieval past and of its modern context.

At first, as the newly liberated Jews struggled for emancipation, acceptance and advancement, the newfangled hostility towards them (and the motivations behind it) appeared in social, economic and psychological forms; later on it became racist and, ultimately, in the twentieth century, as we shall see, it assumed genocidal dimensions. In part it represented something very new, growing as a reaction to the gradually altered status of the Jews and to the increasingly grim social and economic conditions of modern industrialized society. But it was also a development of a very ancient rivalry and hatred, feeding upon what was already there in earlier periods of European history – the demonizing anti-Judaic stereotypes, invented by the Church.

The impact of emancipation

The nineteenth century was a period of exhilarating change for the Jews of western and central Europe. Napoleon may have

been defeated and in many parts of conquered Europe the
emancipating thrust of the French Revolution reversed in
favour of a political and Christian conservatism; but the clock
could not be turned back. The Jews, who had briefly
experienced the thrill of equality, were now generally
committed to political liberalism, social integration and to
participation in the national life of the countries in which they
lived – Holland, France, England, Prussia, Italy and
Austro-Hungary.

As the Jews were emancipated in one country after another,
they responded to the challenge of integration with a whole
range of new religious, intellectual and cultural movements;
the watchwords were *adaptation* and *compromise* as many
strove to strike a healthy balance between the Jewish world, to
which they had been confined for so long – partly by choice,
partly by compulsion – and the realities, demands and
opportunities of the modern, secular world which now
beckoned. Jewish creative and occupational energies, which
had been locked away in the ghetto for centuries, were released
in a flood. Jews entered professions previously barred to them
– law, medicine, journalism and commerce – and achieved
what appeared to some of their gentile neighbours as a
disproportionate and unacceptable measure of success and
prominence.

The astonishingly swift metamorphosis of Jewish life during
the latter half of the nineteenth century catapulted the modern
Jew into what was often a deep state of personal bewilderment.
Emotional crises of identity within such a dynamic context of
change were not uncommon. The speed and visibility of the
alteration in their status also had their effects on the
surrounding society. In Germany, in particular, their
professional and economic progress was highly conspicuous –
especially when compared with their previous obscurity. At
times of depression and unemployment this proved galling and
humiliating for some of their German 'hosts'.

It must be remembered that the Jews had not entered
modern society with a clean slate. Nor did the modern period of
European history emerge unscathed from, and unimpressed
by, its medieval past. For the Jews were accompanied into the
nineteenth century by many images that depicted them in a
negative light. Moreover, in most countries they were not

simply one minority group out of many that were struggling for recognition. They were, in effect, at that time, the only 'alien' group which had been living for century upon century as religious, cultural and national outsiders in so many different parts of Europe (a far cry from our own postwar multicultural societies). Hence they had often borne the brunt of the racial, religious and national prejudices which continue to plague most human societies but which today are diffused more widely.

The role of modern nationalism

The rampant growth of nationalism during the nineteenth century had an ambiguous effect on the Jews. To some extent the national movements tended to look back to and idealize their countries' glorious past – a Christian past – from which the Jews were excluded. Indeed, the image of the Jews as Christ-killers persisted well into the 'secular' age, particularly in rural parts of Europe where a backwash of medieval superstition continued to hold out against the forces of modernity. As the theologian, Norman Solomon, has written:

> The attitudes which enabled the Nazis to 'demonize' the Jews and thus carry out their programme were deeply embedded in the popular cultures of the nations among whom they operated. For so long had Christians taught that Jews were a despised people, the rejectors and killers of Christ, obdurate in their adherence to a superseded faith, that European culture was saturated with this image of the Jew.[3]

On the other hand, the progressive face of the new nationalism was preoccupied with the construction of a single, dominant culture, where differences would be eradicated. The Jew who was prepared to surrender part or all of his Jewish identity – to transcend and accommodate to the needs of the state his attachment to his religious, national and cultural heritage – was apparently to be welcomed as a bona fide member of the new nation. However, in this nationalist climate there remained suspicions about the loyalties of Jews; after all, the Jew was the cosmopolitan *par excellence* – surely, it was argued in some quarters, he was incapable, by virtue both of his religion and of his internationalism (and later of his 'race'), of being a truly dependable fellow-national.

The era of emancipation

Such antagonistic voices must, nevertheless, have seemed of relatively little consequence for the Jews of western and central Europe who, during the second half of the nineteenth century, enjoyed a virtual golden age. Their final emancipation in Italy and Germany, coinciding with the national unification of these countries in 1870 and 1871 respectively, appeared to carry a clear signal that a new era had dawned; 50 years before the accession of Adolf Hitler, far from spelling doom for the Jews, this emancipatory trend would surely place past tensions behind them. Even in the comparatively backward and repressive Habsburg Empire (Austria–Hungary), the Jews had gained their legal and political freedom in 1867. These gains and the prevailing mood emphatically suggested that the classical nineteenth-century liberal view was surely right: that the sheer passage of time and the benefits of a universal, humanistic education, would bring to an end the mindless bigotry, discrimination and violent sectarianism of less enlightened periods of human history; education and scientific advance meant progress; progress meant 'civilization'; and European civilization was a model for all the world, including those parts of the European continent – especially tsarist Russia – which had so far kept at bay the forces of social and political change.

Eastern Europe

During the nineteenth century, the majority of Jews in the world lived in the tsarist Russian Empire. At the end of the eighteenth century Russia had expanded westwards and swallowed the greater part of the former territories of Poland and Lithuania, where, as we have seen, most Jews had previously congregated and developed a flourishing civilization. Unlike countries of western and central Europe, which were actively encouraging the modernization of their political and economic systems, tsarist Russia could be broadly described as an anti-modern society. The tsars were generally determined to retain a stranglehold on their hereditary rule and to resist demands for the introduction of democratic reforms and for the liberalization of their attitudes towards human rights.

Most significantly, there had been no separation of Church and state – one of the hallmarks of a modern nation-state. The Russian Orthodox Church, which was deeply antagonistic both to Judaism and to all movements which supported change, continued to exercise very real power and influence on government attitudes. Tsarist policy towards their largely unwanted but enormous Jewish population was, for the first half of the nineteenth century, a confused blend of repressive, segregationist measures, on the one hand, and crude attempts to integrate them by forcing their conversion to Christianity. The cruellest measure of this kind was that introduced by Tsar Nicholas I in 1827, which made it possible for Jewish boys aged 12 to be conscripted into the Russian army for a period of 31 years. Such a process would almost inevitably have severed links between the conscript and his family (and hence his entire Jewish world). In savagely ironic fashion, it was left to the Jewish communities themselves to fill the quotas of young recruits demanded of them – a vicious foretaste of later Nazi methods. This statute promoted such fear, divisiveness and corruption within the Jewish community that there are even stories of parents maiming their own children to prevent their being press-ganged into service by kidnappers hired by other Jews desperate to protect their offspring.

The Pale of Settlement

Jews were still considered in many sections of Russian society to be a 'contaminating' influence. Consequently, they were obliged to reside almost exclusively in the westernmost provinces of the huge Russian Empire – an area combining what had formerly been parts of Poland, Lithuania and the Ukraine, with additional territories to the south which Russia had recently acquired from the Ottoman Turks. This area became known as the Jewish 'Pale of Settlement'. There, during the course of the nineteenth century, the Jewish population would quadruple, reaching more than 5 million by 1880 and representing almost 12 per cent of the total population of the territory in which they lived (about 3 per cent of the entire population of the tsarist empire).

The Jews of Russia, however, proved very resilient. If the intention was to break their spirit and their attachment to ancestral traditions, it can be said to have failed utterly. The harsher and more discriminatory the measures applied by the tsars to their Jewish subjects, the more committed the Jews became to their religion and way of life. It must be stressed that tsarist Russia was still, in many vital respects, a medieval feudal society; the source of the antipathy towards Jews was, therefore, primarily religious, although economic factors also clearly intervened.

Pogroms and revolution

A turning-point came in 1881, which would have momentous repercussions for the remaining course of Jewish history. In March of that year, a revolutionary group assassinated Tsar Alexander II (the comparatively liberal successor to Nicholas I). The perpetrators belonged to a revolutionary group which included a young Jewish woman named Hessia Helfmann; thereupon, the tsarist government, anxious to divert popular resentment away from its own unpopular and repressive regime, seized the opportunity to pin the blame on *all* the Jews. Not only, it was claimed, had the Jews killed Christ, but they had now murdered the tsar!

Those who had most to gain from the disappearance of the Jews – peasants who owed them money, and small business rivals – leapt into the fray. Throughout the southern districts of the Russian Pale of Settlement, Jews were subjected to violent attack, pogroms breaking out with the apparent connivance of the police and the army. ('Pogrom' is a Russian word denoting violent rioting, involving murder, maiming, rape, vandalism and looting; though originally a general Russian word, it became so closely associated with physical assaults on Jewish communities that its use is now restricted almost exclusively to Jewish victims – in any country.)

Those Jews who had once entertained hopes of liberalization in Russia may have expected support from educated Russians, but they were doomed to disappointment. Some proponents of revolution initially even went so far as to welcome the pogroms: while they regretted the victimization of the Jews, at least it demonstrated what could be achieved when popular anger was aroused – soon it would be the tsarist government's turn to feel the Russian people's wrath. Many Jewish revolutionaries, in despair at this betrayal by their comrades, felt they had little option but to flee the country.

Jewish responses to tsarist oppression

With the traditional Jewish leadership reduced to paralysis and inaction, it was left to the young and the intelligentsia to seize the initiative: in answer to the violence and to antagonistic new legislation, defiant Jewish responses emerged that were destined to have tremendous consequences for the future course of Jewish history. The principal reactions were, firstly, mass emigration to the west, which would bring about the establishment of many new Jewish communities; secondly, increased involvement in national and international socialist movements; and, thirdly, the development of Jewish nationalism, which laid the foundations for the growth of Zionism, an ideological and political movement dedicated to the resurrection of Jewish political independence in the biblical land of Israel (at that time known loosely as 'Palestine' and languishing as an outpost of the Ottoman Turkish Empire).

The tsarist government now intensified its repressive anti-Jewish legislation, compelling hundreds of thousands to move out of the countryside and into the slum districts of the cities. The results could scarcely have been more dramatic: between 1881 and the outbreak of the First World War, nearly 2.5 million Jews left tsarist Russia – one of the largest group migrations in recorded history. The psychological distress caused by the pogroms, combined with the economic collapse of their world, had impelled Jews to uproot their homes and their lives. Of this number, some 2 million went to the United States, while further sizeable groups, each of over 100,000 went to Canada, Argentina and England. Jewish migrants to South Africa numbered 43,000; to Palestine, 70,000.

It was thus against the exhilarating, yet tortured, background of the reign of the last two tsars, before the communist revolution of 1917 removed the autocratic

monarchy and introduced nominal emancipation for all, that
the desire for dynamic political and social change welled up
among the still largely traditional Jews of eastern Europe.
After 1881, the economic and psychological conditions in
Russia were especially ripe for the explosion of socialism and
nationalism. These ideologies had been spawned in western
Europe but had seldom been adopted by the Jews of those
countries, committed as they were to taking full advantage of
the opportunities afforded by emancipation and assimilation.
The need in Russia, however, was simply more urgent.

The tsarist government, in its desperation to outlaw the
'new' ideas merely succeeded in driving them underground and
in strengthening them in other unintended ways. For example,
hundreds of Russian Jews, now barred by restrictive quotas
from attending Russian universities, were obliged to study in
the university towns and cities of western and central Europe.
There, they first encountered and devoured the socialist and
nationalist theories. They then returned to the Pale of
Settlement, bringing their revolutionary knowledge and
fervour back to their own people (whose knowledge of Yiddish
gave them access to much of the German literature), and
making a considerable impact on the general Russian
revolutionary movement too.

The growth of racial and political antisemitism

In Europe, towards the end of the nineteenth century, we have
an apparent contradiction. On the one hand, tsarist ruling
circles, in resisting the momentum for change, which might
have led to the granting of freedom to Jews and other
minorities within Russia's borders, probably ensured that no
sophisticated, western-style antisemitic movement would
develop. Yet Jewish blood flowed in the streets and, as
merciless regulations drove the Jews out of the rural districts
and into the increasingly overcrowded towns and cities, they
were being progressively reduced to the level of paupers.

In western and central Europe, on the other hand, where
nations were eagerly embracing the latest political and
economic developments, it appeared that Jews had never
enjoyed greater protection. Nevertheless, while these advances
enabled the emancipated Jews to take colossal strides within

their societies, a highly intellectual and, in certain respects, 'respectable' new movement was simultaneously ripening: modern 'antisemitism' (the word was first coined by the German, Wilhelm Marr, in 1879)[4] – a volcano that would erupt unbelievably into the horror of the Nazi death camps. At first, the growth of antisemitism had merely a psychological effect on the Jews. To the overwhelming majority, their social breakthrough seemed irreversible, their progress assured; the new bigots were surely a relatively harmless variation on an ancient and outmoded hatred.

Modern antisemitism in Germany

In a climate of fervent nationalism and jingoism, there were increasing allegations of Jewish 'cosmopolitanism' and 'clannish separatism'. Books and pamphlets appeared in France and Germany alleging that the 'Semites' were responsible for everything that was dark, unhealthy, menacing and destructive, whereas all that was pure, creative, heroic and good was the product of 'Aryan' influence. This biological view of human potential and moral worth was, in effect, a pseudo-scientific hotchpotch of the new racial, linguistic and anthropological theories, blended with the vestige of old religious hatreds and fears. The Jews, it was argued, were racially incapable of improvement. No matter how hard they tried to be German – to speak German, to dress German, to convert to Christianity – no matter how great the *impression* of integration, the Jews were depicted as parasitic, scheming, manipulative and venomous, constantly plotting to 'take over' economic control of the state.

The convenient division of humanity into forces of light (Aryans) and forces of darkness (Semites) appealed to crude needs for a black-and-white explanation of the world, and was clearly derived from similar pagan and Christian belief systems ('moral dualism') – especially the medieval fixation with the Devil as the source of all evil and depravity. That the earlier theological image of the Jew as 'anti-Christ' or Satan continued to survive made the task of the modern antisemites much less difficult. The actual categories of Semite and Aryan were borrowed very loosely from the field of linguistics, in which these terms related to families of languages (and not to 'racial' groups). Social Darwinism, with its theory of natural selection – so fashionable in intellectual circles in the late nineteenth century – also provided a rationale for the new antisemitism. Its clichéd slogans on 'the survival of the fittest', when fused with racial stereotypes about supposedly unchanging physiological and mental characteristics of different human 'breeds', produced a concoction that, in the hands of the Nazis, would later prove deadly.

The international 'Jewish conspiracy'

A favourite image from the turn of the century was that of the power-crazed Jews engaged in an international conspiracy to undermine the safe and peaceful world of the gentiles, fomenting wars, revolutions and the collapse of organized religion. The 'Protocols of the Elders of Zion' is the single most notorious antisemitic publication of this type. Hatched in all probability at the court of Tsar Nicholas II, it painted a startling picture of an international Jewish leadership (the sinister 'elders') bent on world domination and using all the forces of the modern world to achieve it. Though it had little impact in Russia itself, it was brought to the west by White Russians fleeing the Bolshevik revolution. It was subsequently translated into several languages and enjoyed wide circulation between the wars, particularly at the instigation of the rising Nazi movement (it is still available in many countries today!).

The birth of antisemitic political parties

In Germany in the 1880s (and later in Austria), political parties sprang up which espoused antisemitism, in its various forms, as a central theme in their electoral campaigns. Indeed, it was the very emergence of mass political movements at this time of rapid democratization and the development of technically advanced communications media that provided the ideal context for the growth of irresponsible extremism and rabble-rousing. The first such group was the Christian Socialist Workers' Party. Since Jews were, for the most part, identified with the Liberal and Progressive opposition, the antisemitic groupings, who might otherwise have remained on the lunatic fringe of respectable politics, were given active encouragement by the ruling Conservatives under Bismarck; his motives were cynical and opportunist, rather than inspired by any genuine sympathy for antisemitic objectives.

Although the nineteenth-century antisemitic parties gained only a handful of seats in the German parliament and could easily be dismissed as an insignificant force in German political life, precedents were established at this time which would have terrifying meaning for the twentieth century and for the Nazi era. Firstly, an avowedly religious Protestant figure, Adolf Stöcker, leader of the Christian Socialists, had preached undisguised hatred for the Jewish people without being restrained or censured by his own Church; and, secondly, a political party spouting barefaced antisemitic sentiments had received the official stamp of approval of the governmental authorities.

In a chilling statement, Eugene Richter, the leader of the Progressive Party, made the following accusation against the Conservative government:

> The government torments the Social Democrats who oppose only the monied classes, but offers protection to the Christian Socialists who advocate hatred against a race ... beware of inflaming savage passions in the undisciplined masses ... do not arouse the beast in Man, for then it will stop at nothing.

The credibility of German antisemitism was also given a boost during the last decades of the nineteenth century by receiving the open support of several highly respected personalities in German cultural and academic life, the most famous being the composer Richard Wagner. Wagner had accused the Jews of being innately incapable of making any truly constructive or original contribution to the arts and wrote:

> I must certainly regard the Jewish race as the born enemy of pure man and of all nobility in them and am convinced that we Germans in particular will be destroyed by them.[5]

Pan-Germanism

A growing force which made blatant use of antisemitic slogans and theorizing was the pan-German movement. Laying claim to all cultural and linguistic German communities scattered

throughout the continent of Europe – later to be a dominant
and obsessive theme in Hitler's foreign policy – the
pan-Germans took their inspiration from the racism underly-
ing much of Western imperialism in Africa, Asia and the
Americas.

Just as the dark-skinned, unchristian natives of far-flung
parts of the world could and 'should' be subordinated to the
'superior' culture of the white European (especially the British
and French) – indeed the mission to 'civilize' them constituted
the 'white man's burden' – so the pan-Germans wished to have
dominance over 'inferior' races in central and eastern Europe.
The Jew and the Slav were targeted as their special enemies,
the wretchedness and natural subservience of these 'species'
being contrasted with the glorious superiority of the Germanic
race. Some historians have gone so far as to suggest that much
of the racial antisemitism in Germany was a kind of substitute,
or compensation, for her frustrated world-wide imperial
ambitions. In other words, Germany was jealous of the British
and French empires.

France – similarities on a different stage

In late nineteeenth-century France, popular and intellectual
antisemitism was arguably even more widespread than in
Germany, perhaps reflecting the resentment that had
snowballed over the decades of Jewish equality (as we have
seen, France had been the very first country to emancipate her
Jews). Here was to be found a similar mixture of religious and
racial antagonism and, in the writer, Edouard Drumont,
France could claim to have one of the foremost proponents of
the new antisemitic creed. As in Germany, there were
occasional financial scandals involving a small number of
Jewish financiers; this fact was enough to stoke the flames of
popular hatred, especially among an emerging middle class
which felt particularly vulnerable to sudden changes in the
domestic and international economies and to the collapse of
banking and commercial institutions.

Conditions in France, however, were in certain critical
respects different from those prevailing in Germany. In
Germany, political parties which sought to disenfranchise or in
some other way to victimize Jews described themselves from

the first as 'socialist'. Hitler's party, in step with this tradition, would later call itself National Socialist. In contrast, French antisemitism was invariably associated with the forces of the political right: chauvinist nationalists, the Catholic Church, those wishing to restore the monarchy and deeply conservative elements within the army.

Most significantly, in France – unlike Germany – whatever the strength of antisemitic feeling on the streets, in the bars and in the universities, political power always remained in the hands of the liberal republicans, a government which never endorsed political antisemitism. When Alfred Dreyfus, an innocent Jewish officer in the French army, was convicted of espionage in 1894, the resulting Dreyfus Affair threatened to split France. Despite his passionate commitment to France and to a Gallic way of life, the very fact of his Jewish origins in Alsace had been enough to convince the court martial of his disloyalty. The ensuing brouhaha indicated that there were as many French citizens prepared to defend Jews as attack them. When the government decided belatedly to intervene, it led to a just conclusion and to the eventual exoneration of the wronged individual.

In Germany, however, the contrast could not have been greater. There, a 'Jewish issue' would hardly have aroused such a furore, and antisemitism was allowed to creep slowly, almost imperceptibly – and virtually unchallenged – into the body politic. It was, as we shall see in the chapters dealing directly with the Holocaust, the supreme indifference, rather than the most active hatred, of most Germans that would permit the fanaticism of a relative few to wreak such havoc.

Indifference is, in most societies, a neutral force which can be harnessed either for good or ill by those who hold the reins of power. By virtue of the very passivity of its nature, the indifference of the many does not allow for direct intervention or active interference in the exercise of power by the few. However, the *indirect* impact of the majority who, through their silence may condone or rubber-stamp the decisions and policies of others, should not be underestimated. Nor should it be overlooked that silence or indifference is a *choice* that individuals make. This, surely, is one of the central lessons of the Nazi era.

The birth of Zionism

Ever since the dispersal of Jewish communities throughout the Roman world, following their loss of independence and the destruction of their Temple in the year 70, pious Jews had prayed for a return to their ancestral homeland. Medieval religious literature is suffused with references to messianic liberation and to mystical yearning for 'Zion' (Zion is a concept, both spiritual and geographical, referring to the Land of Israel in general and to the sacred city of Jerusalem in particular). Religious tradition, however, demanded that Jews wait until God despatched the Messiah to lead them back to the holy land. Until then, they were obliged to reside and, if need be, suffer in their state of exile. It was only the revolutionary atmosphere of nineteenth-century Europe that transformed this yearning into an active, secular political philosophy – and later political movement – which aimed at the establishment of a modern Jewish state in Palestine.

Jewish nationalism was to some extent a development of trends within Judaism but it was far more a response to external conditions, especially to the growth of modern antisemitism in countries which had supposedly welcomed Jewish integration. In a manner wholly symptomatic of the century in which it was born, territorial Jewish nationalism finally sought the restoration of legal and political sovereignty for an oppressed people. It arose in both western and eastern Europe where, despite the obvious differences in social conditions facing them, certain individual Jewish thinkers, deeply impressed with the success of other national movements, especially in Italy, Germany and the Balkans, reached the following breathtaking conclusions: that anti-Jewish feeling was now so deeply ingrained in European society and so easily adapted to changing circumstances that it was incurable; that there must, as soon as was practicable, be an end to the powerlessness and vulnerability that were the inevitable products of Jewish minority status; and that Western progress, civilization and even the legal emancipation of the Jewish people would not provide the security, dignity, power and self-fulfilment guaranteed by a homeland of their own.

Forerunners of Jewish territorialism

Of the trailblazers who advocated the rehabilitation of the Jews in their own state, two at least deserve a brief mention. Though neither could have envisaged the Holocaust of the succeeding century, they offered an unorthodox and, in certain critical respects, remarkably prophetic analysis of the prevailing Jewish condition. Moses Hess, a German socialist and revolutionary thinker, argued in his *Rome and Jerusalem* (1862) that the Jews of Germany were doomed unless they came to appreciate that the source of German hatred was no longer religious, but racial; changing their names, their ways and their religion would not save them, he uncannily predicted – one of the only and certainly the first to record such premonitions. They should seek national salvation in their own land, as part of the universal salvation of all downtrodden and colonized peoples (especially those of Asia and Africa). There, Jewish religion and culture could be revitalized and prove an inspiration to the other peoples of the region.

In 1882, in response to the pogroms, Leon Pinsker, a Russian Jewish doctor, had written a pioneering work, 'Auto-emancipation', in which he had described antisemitism as a 'psychic aberration' and warned that the Jews were an 'indigestible ingredient' among the nations in which they lived. A Jewish majority determining its own political destiny was, for him, the only answer. His passionate essay ends with these words:

> Let 'now or never!' be our watchword. Woe to our descendants, woe to the memory of our Jewish contemporaries, if we let this moment pass by![6]

At first the majority of Jews were either opposed or indifferent to this idea. The reasons were many: firstly, there was the sheer embarrassment and discomfort of those Jews who had already assimilated into their host countries and who had renounced any commitment to a separate Jewish national identity; they were now English, French, Dutch or German patriots and felt completely at home with the culture of their adoptive homes. Secondly, many devout Jews who were still obedient to their inherited way of life regarded the Zionist idea as little short of heresy: to dispense with the need for the Almighty's permission and to accomplish a physical return to Israel on the initiative of mere fellow-humans was a betrayal of their rabbinic tradition. Thirdly, there were those who, though finding the goal attractive and praiseworthy, considered it simply too ambitious and impractical an undertaking.

Theodor Herzl and the development of political Zionism

Although there were many earlier thinkers whose combined arguments ensured that the Jewish public was reasonably informed about the meaning and purpose of Zionism, it was an Hungarian-born foreign correspondent, working in Paris for a Viennese newspaper, who turned this improbable fantasy into a genuine political movement. Theodor Herzl, reporting in January 1895 on the French army's public degradation of the Jew Dreyfus, was genuinely shaken by the French mob's cries of 'Death to Dreyfus! Death to the Jews!' Herzl was an assimilated Jew, who had gravitated westwards towards the country he regarded as the centre of enlightened values and toleration. Of his reaction to the crowd's antisemitic eruption he wrote:

> Until that time most of us believed that the solution of the Jewish question was to be patiently waited for as part of the general development of mankind. But when a people which in every other respect is so progressive and so highly civilized can take such a turn, what are we to expect from other peoples which have not even attained the level which France attained one hundred years ago?[7]

Though his ideas were by no means original, he wrote a short, inspirational book, *The Jewish State* (published in 1896), which made a huge impact, particularly among the Jews of Russia. Later, when he realized that he would not receive backing from the rich and influential Jews of western Europe, he founded the Zionist movement himself. Its aims were to establish a Jewish state in Palestine with the full authority of international law and with the support and influence of powerful European nations. Although Herzl was really opposed to gradual and piecemeal Jewish settlement on the land, the flow of emigration of Jews from eastern Europe to Palestine, begun in 1881 with the outbreak of pogroms, continued. One of the aims of the Zionist movement was, therefore, to purchase land from the Turkish authorities and to provide aid to the new settlers. Herzl used his considerable professional knowledge of communications techniques and his almost manic energy to establish a credibility for the new movement, both within the Jewish world and, perhaps more significantly, among world leaders and statesmen.

Although he died in 1904 without apparently having fulfilled his ambitions, his contribution to the course of modern Jewish history cannot be overstated. Thirteen years after his death, at the height of the First World War, the government of Great Britain would make an astonishing undertaking – later to prove highly controversial – to assist in the establishment of a Jewish home in Palestine (see the Balfour Declaration, pp.69–71 below). This declaration, which was in effect a statement of intent to the entire Jewish world, took the form of a letter addressed to the Zionist Federation of Great Britain. That the Jews now had a recognized voice and a representative body in international diplomacy was due, in no small measure, to Herzl's achievements.

Jewish attitudes towards Zionism

It would be quite wrong, however, to imagine that most Jews at the dawn of the twentieth century were supporters of Zionism. In eastern Europe, while most had by now abandoned realistic hopes of western-style emancipation, their lives were largely dedicated to economic survival, to the maintenance of their traditional lifestyle and to the wish to emigrate, principally to the United States. Though the romantic solution of Zionism had a growing appeal, those who were politically active were more attracted by the socialist remedy to the problems of being Jewish, poor and Russian.

In western and central Europe, meanwhile, in the first decade of a century that would see an attempt on all their lives, most Jews believed that emancipation was proving highly successful, the antics of antisemitic agitators seeming largely peripheral to their lives. Their educational and economic standards were steadily improving and the majority were prepared to try and make sense of their Jewishness in the context of their recent acceptance as national citizens of their respective countries. Progressive and updated varieties of their religion and of religious scholarship sprouted and flourished; this enabled many to reconcile a continuing involvement with a Jewish dimension to their lives – however diluted – with full-blooded immersion in the cultural, artistic and occupational life of the countries in which they lived.

The First World War and its aftermath

On a superficial and deeply ironic level, the First World War saw the Jews of Europe better integrated into their respective nations than ever before. Hundreds of thousands of Jews, serving in the armies of Great Britain, France, Belgium, tsarist Russia and (after 1917) the United States, fought against tens of thousands of Jews represented in the German and Austro-Hungarian forces.

The reality, however, was rather different. As the tide of battle swept back and forth across densely populated areas of Russian Poland and Lithuania (the Jewish Pale of Settlement), the civilian suffering was immense. At a time of national emergency, deep-seated suspicions and stereotypes surfaced, the retreating Russian army uprooting hundreds of thousands of Jewish civilians who were perceived as likely spies and traitors. Amid absurd stories and rumours – according to one Jews had actually been seen tying gold to the wings of geese which were then despatched westwards to aid the enemy – these civilians were forcibly and cruelly marched into the Russian interior. And this despite the presence of almost half a million Jewish men in the Russian ranks! There was also a total ban throughout tsarist Russia on publications in Hebrew and Yiddish, which it was alleged might be used in the service of the enemy. All of which was in sharp contrast to the gentle and humane treatment accorded Jewish civilians in eastern Europe who passed under German control. The good reputation the German army acquired at this time would later have important and tragic consequences during the Second World War: Russian Jews would then be easily deceived into believing the best rather then the worst of their German captors.

In Germany, at the start of the war the Kaiser had proclaimed that he no longer acknowledged any distinctions among those enlisted in the nation's armies. Jews nevertheless continued to be viewed in certain circles as potentially disloyal. In 1916, thanks to mischievous antisemitic accusations that Jews were shirking their responsibilities in favour of black-marketeering, the government was persuaded to institute a special census of Jewish soldiers engaged in active duty on the front. This census was never published, but later research has shown that a disproportionately high number of Jews died or won Iron Crosses while performing their military duties on Germany's behalf.

Two events occurred during the First World War, both in 1917, that would have momentous implications for both Jewish and world history: the issuing of the Balfour Declaration and the Russian Revolution.

The Balfour Declaration

Zionism depended for its success on Jewish unity – the commitment by Jews, in the different countries of their dispersal, to the idea that they belonged to one nation. The First World War, however (quite unlike the Second in the Nazi era), saw Jewish disunity at its greatest: this was the only time in over 3,500 years of Jewish history that large numbers of Jews had fought against each other in the armies of rival nations. It would therefore seem a highly unlikely arena in which Zionism would realize its single greatest achievement. And yet, on 2 November 1917, as British troops in the Middle East were poised for the capture of Palestine from the Ottoman Turks, the British Foreign Secretary, Lord Balfour, issued the following declaration to the British Zionist organization:

His Majesty's Government view with favour the establishment in Palestine of a national home for the Jewish people and will use their best endeavours to facilitate the achievement of this object, it being clearly understood that nothing shall be done that may prejudice the civil and religious rights of existing non-Jewish communities in Palestine or the rights and political status enjoyed by Jews in other countries.[8]

The background to this extraordinary declaration is complex.

No doubt some members of the British War Cabinet genuinely believed that the Jews – particularly the suffering Jews of eastern Europe – had a strong moral case for a homeland of their own. However, the most dominant British motives at this time of international emergency were those of military, economic and political self-interest. There was in certain sections of the Foreign Office an overriding and apparently sincere conviction that the Jews of the world were powerful and influential (a central motif, as we have seen, of much stereotypical thinking on the Jewish question), and that a declaration which favoured them could harness this power to the British military cause; such a declaration, it was thought, would silence Jewish opposition to the war both in the United States – not yet properly committed to the war – and in Russia which, after the first revolution of 1917, was threatening to withdraw from the conflict.

Carrying even greater weight was the view that once the war was over, a friendly Jewish 'home' could extend British imperial interests in a part of the globe whose strategic and economic importance could not be exaggerated. Britain's time-honoured rivalry with France was a major consideration: a Jewish home in Palestine, forever grateful to Great Britain, would act as a useful buffer between British interests in Egypt – particularly the economically vital Suez Canal – and the French sphere of influence in Syria and Lebanon (as these areas are now called).

British diplomatic manoeuvres at this time were not confined to the Zionist option. Earlier in the war (in 1915), the British had made sweeping, if rather vague, promises to the Arabs of independence over vast areas in the Middle East, in return for military support against the Turks – promises which the Arab leadership later claimed were irreconcilable with undertakings made to the Jews. The British had also concluded a secret treaty with the French (in 1916), according to which they were to be granted shared control of much of Palestine. In the event, the British were awarded mandates by the League of Nations to exercise control over Iraq and Palestine (the latter originally including territory which later, in 1921, became Trans-Jordan), while the French were granted mandatory authority over Lebanon and Syria.

The Balfour Declaration was deliberately couched in such

imprecise diplomatic language that its meaning was open to the most flexible interpretation. What exactly was a 'national home' and how much of Palestine was to be Jewish? In subsequent decades, when the whole Palestine question became one of the most explosive issues on the world's troubled agenda, the inconclusiveness of this declaration would prove highly contentious. Nevertheless, when the League of Nations ratified the British mandate over Palestine (in 1922), the text of the declaration itself was included. Thus the Balfour Declaration can be said to have established a legal basis, though ill-defined, for the international recognition of a Jewish national homeland in Palestine.

The impact of the Russian Revolution

In March 1917, as a result of the debilitating and demoralizing effects of the war on both the army and people of Russia, the tsar was toppled as a prelude to the later and more decisive Bolshevik Revolution of November of that year. Almost immediately, the new Provisional Government scrapped all existing legal disabilities under which the Jews had laboured for so long. The revolution's longer-term effects would be highly ambiguous and contradictory. On the one hand, the Jews were now equal before the law; but, on the other, their capacity to enjoy a separate religious and national identity was either severely curtailed or, in many cases and for long periods, made virtually impossible.

In many parts of eastern Europe, the immediate aftermath of the Russian Revolution and the end of the First World War were to see three years of instability, chaos, local wars and famine. During this period of political uncertainty, the suffering of the Jewish population was disastrous, especially in the Ukraine (which had tried to assert its independence from Germany), in Poland and in Bolshevik Russia. There, rival factions competed for control: the pro-Bolshevik Red Army, the anti-Bolshevik White Army, a nationalist Ukrainian army led by Simon Petlura and, in the later stages, an invading Polish army. During these years, Jews were increasingly identified with the new bogeyman of Europe – namely communist and socialist revolution – and became the victims of countless pogroms (far worse than in the tsarist era), especially at the

hands of Petlura and the White Russians. Between 1918 and
1921, it is estimated that between 100,000 and 150,000 Jews
were slaughtered. Much of the evidence for these atrocities,
particularly those committed by the Ukrainian nationalist
irregulars, emerged several years later during the trial of
Samuel Schwartzbard, accused of assassinating Petlura in
Paris (he was, in fact, acquitted by the French jury).

The after-effects of war

The First World War, a conflict of ruthless territorial and
imperial ambition which claimed approximately 25 million
lives, had proved a major watershed, opening the way for
unprecedented levels of human indifference to the plight of
others. In parts of eastern Europe, which had been so ravaged
by war, it could be argued that the local population was
becoming desensitized to mass Jewish – and, indeed, general –
suffering. World opinion, too, so outraged by the murder of tens
or hundreds of Jews during the earlier phases of pogroms in
the 1880s and 1900s, and so divided even by the hounding of
the one, innocent Dreyfus in France, was largely silent.

   In many European countries, the postwar association of
Jews with the dreaded communist revolution – a legacy of the
conspiracy theory expounded for decades by antisemitic
writers and agitators – was most pronounced. A British
Foreign Office official, remarking on the postwar anti-Jewish
excesses in the Ukraine, commented as follows:

> The Jews deserve all they get. Their whole influence in Eastern
> Europe during the war was against us and our allies: nearly all
> the German and Austrian spies were Jews: and now they are
> busily engaged in undermining the foundations of European
> civilization. It is little wonder that the races which have
> suffered most, first from Jewish espionage and then from
> Jewish Bolshevism, should take a truculent revenge on them.
> (J.D. Gregory, 3 February 1919).[9]

Even Winston Churchill, later to be the principal thorn in
Hitler's flesh and thus indirectly a champion of the Jews, had
written in February 1920:

This movement [Bolshevism] among the Jews is not new. From the days of ... Karl Marx and down to Trotsky (Russia), Bela Kun (Hungary), Rosa Luxemburg (Germany) and Emma Goldman (United States) this world-wide Jewish conspiracy for the overthrow of civilization and for the reconstitution of society on the basis of arrested development, of envious malevolence, and impossible equality has been steadily growing.

(*Illustrated Sunday Herald*, 8 February 1920).[10]

The new states of east-central Europe – nationalism and antisemitism

During the peace talks at the end of the First World War, it was acknowledged that the subjugation of national minorities had been one of the principal causes of the conflict. This led to a redrawing of the map of Europe and to the breaking up of large multinational empires. The Austro-Hungarian Empire, the Ottoman Turkish Empire (which had already ceded autonomy to Greece, Romania and Bulgaria during the decades before the outbreak of hostilities) and the western border territories of the tsarist empire now gave way to the rebirth or enlargement of independent nation-states in east-central Europe, including Poland, Hungary, Czechoslovakia, Yugoslavia and Romania.

These new states had sizeable minority populations and the Jews were among the largest and most conspicuous. In Poland there were over 3 million Jews, in Romania 850,000, in Hungary 445,000, in Czechoslovakia 375,000, in Lithuania 110,000, in Latvia 90,000 and in Yugoslavia 68,000. With the exception of Czechoslovakia (which maintained its parliamentary democracy), these countries were the breeding ground of a ferocious new nationalism, fuelled by centuries of suppression which, combined with age-old prejudices, produced illiberal antisemitic right-wing regimes. During periods of severe economic crisis, culminating in the Wall Street Crash of 1929 and the subsequent Depression of the early 1930s, these governments seemed only too willing to exploit popular resentment of the Jews in their midst. Having suffered from German, Turkish or Russian domination for so long, they were deeply suspicious of yet more 'outsiders', who appeared to be so culturally different and, what is more, to have national loyalties of their own (during these years, Zionism's popularity had been developing rapidly among the Jews in these countries).

In Poland, Romania and Hungary, in particular, various antisemitic policies were introduced, severely restricting the rights of Jewish individuals and the freedom of Jewish business activity. Harsh quotas were applied to Jewish university entrance, Jewish firms were sometimes nationalized and there were many other forms of discrimination besides. All this took place despite the express condition attached to the establishment of these new states and their membership of the League of Nations: that they behave fairly and tolerantly towards their racial, national and religious minorities. The result was the growth of a number of bewildered, impoverished and increasingly vulnerable European Jewish communities.

Thus, by the time Hitler came to power in Germany in January 1933, several of the emerging central European countries which contained significant Jewish populations – Poland, Hungary, Romania, Latvia and Lithuania – had regimes installed which would be favourably disposed towards many of his racial policies. This would have the most alarming consequences for their Jewish populations.

CHAPTER 4

Nazism and Modern Germany: From National Unification to Hitler's Accession to Power

> Never forget that our day of reckoning with the Jews will not come about as a result of some laughable single clash, but only when we have the power of the state in our hands to carry out a thorough annihilation [*Vernichtung*] of this international racial parasite ...
>
> The Party Leadership[1]

Introduction

No purposeful investigation of the Holocaust can be divorced from the social, political and psychological conditions prevalent in modern German society. It should not, however, be forgotten that German history did not itself occur in a vacuum; many of the forces shaping that history were pan-European and intercontinental, particularly on the economic and ideological fronts. Nor, it must be stressed, is the Holocaust explicable – if it is explicable at all – in terms of German history alone.

The Nazi accession to power in 1933 was neither inevitable nor, as is commonly supposed, constitutional. The Nazis' own propaganda would create the myth that the hated Weimar Republic had been swept away by a 'national-socialist revolution' backed by the will of the German people. In reality, the Weimar Republic had ceased to function as a parliamentary democracy in March 1930, three years before Hitler's appointment as Chancellor. The rise of the Nazi Party to power was not the cause of the republic's demise but a product of it, the Nazis proving singularly adept at filling the vacuum that resulted from the failure of the parliamentary system.

There was certainly nothing unpreventable about Hitler's appointment as Chancellor. Even in January 1933, many considered the Nazi Party to have only a short-term future, acting in a limited role as junior partner to established conservative interests. Hitler's appointment was intended as a temporary measure, part of a wider scheme (under way since March 1930) by conservative politicians and elites to re-establish a traditional (non-Nazi) conservative German state. This was to replace the liberal republic, harking back to the 'glorious' German Empire that had existed before the end of the First World War. At the start of 1930, the Nazi Party was, in fact, a waning electoral force and seemed likely to disappear like many other short-lived parties that had sprang up on the German political scene since the 1880s.

This chapter will examine four major areas: Nazism in the context of modern German history since national unification in 1871; the growth of the Nazi Party in the interwar years; the Nazi Party's electoral constituency and reasons for its support; and the high-level political manoeuvres of the years 1930–3.

How did German history produce Nazism?

From the last two decades of the nineteenth century, German society was in a state of almost permanent political and social crisis which persisted right up until Hitler's appointment as Chancellor in January 1933. By then, the chances of survival for the postwar democratic Weimar republic were extremely slim. By the late 1920s, support for the Republic was draining away and, while it was quite probable that some sort of right-wing authoritarian government would come to power, the precise form it would take was not predictable. Chance events and decisions of elites and individuals would have fateful consequences for German and European history.

Throughout this period, Germany was troubled by deep social, economic and religious disunity, arising from her strong regionalism and her peculiar experience of modernization; the specific aim and role of the Nazi Party would be to unify the country and to establish a German state that would remain 'permanent for a thousand years'.

1 The foundation of the German Empire in 1871

Before unification, 'Germany' had comprised a varied collection of central European states, several of them weak and dominated by outside powers. In 1871, German was unified into an empire or federation, the smaller states of southern and central Germany submitting to the leadership of Prussia in matters of foreign policy, defence and the economy. Prussia had bound the country together in a series of blitzkrieg wars: in 1866 she had destroyed Austria's domination of the southern German states, asserting her own claim to be the leading force in southern Germany; and, in 1870, she had inflicted a decisive and humiliating defeat on France, which resulted in Germany's assumption of the position as Europe's foremost power (much as reunification in 1990 is believed by many to have done). With unification, Jewish emancipation was granted, principally so that the Jewish minority could make a proper economic contribution to the new German state as part of the mainstream, rather than remain on the periphery of that society.

The Kaiserreich comprised 25 individual states and cities which formed a voluntary union. At the federal level, power rested with the Kaiser (the Prussian king), his Chancellor, Otto von Bismarck, and cabinet. The government consisted in theory of a council or Bundesrat of ambassadors from the separate constituent states, and there was a parliament or Reichstag elected by universal male suffrage. However, in most imperial matters, the Kaiser ruled with the aid of a cabal of ministers and generals who had no accountability to the Reichstag. Indeed, Germany's first parliamentary government was only appointed in October 1918 just prior to the collapse of the Kaiserreich.

The Kaiserreich was not a centralized democratic state, but a federation designed to preserve the political power of conservative interests, namely the Prussian aristocracy, the monarchy, the army and the bureaucracy. Although the Reichstag was democratically elected, it had little effective power and was reluctant to stand up to the imperial clique. In contrast, the constituent states retained their own elitist constitutions; for example, in Prussia, the 'three-class electoral law' of 1850 remained unrevised until 1918, thus preserving the political dominance of the wealthiest section of the electorate, and thereby excluding up to 90 per cent of the remainder.

The persistence of the political power of Prussian elites had important consequences for German history. Germany, unlike Britain and France, quite simply failed to develop a healthy liberalism, the broad mass of her rising middle class resisting ideas of democracy, constitutional government and equality. Whereas in Britain, the Liberal Party put down deep roots in local organizations, and thus constituted one of the main parties until 1922, liberalism in Germany only lasted as an effective political force during the relatively short period of 1860–80. It was the German upper middle classes – an unrepresentative but highly educated minority – who successfully pressed for change during the period 1862–71, and who brought about legal, economic and constitutional unification. But, in the face of opposition from Bismarck and the Prussian aristocracy, they had failed to break the old order, whose political power was actually preserved by the new constitution.

The National Liberal Party, the largest party during the first decade after unification, and the party most closely associated with Jewish rights and Jewish support, lost its majority in the Reichstag in 1879 and, after a brief revival, went into terminal decline after 1887. From 1871 right up to 1933, Germany generally lacked politicians who could negotiate, concede and compromise; her party political system was deeply committed to satisfying sectional interests, with no party succeeding in acting responsibly in the overall interests of the state or of German society. Indeed, the eventual success of Nazism would, to a large extent, rest on its appeal as a party which could transcend sectional interest and thus claim to represent the whole nation. For the Jews, the ultimate failure of liberalism would have the most tragic consequences.

2 The impact of industrialization on German society 1880–1914

The Kaiserreich was a deeply contradictory society, ruled by a reactionary class of pre-industrial elites. Increasingly, during this conservative political era, German society became a breeding ground for the new politics of class war, a proportion of middle- and working-class Germans becoming imbued either with radical nationalism or with socialism. Ernst Bloch described Germany as the 'classic country of unsimultaneity', i.e. a country where different parts of the nation coexisted uneasily, each living in what amounted to different historical eras.[2] The Germany of 1871 was a predominantly rural country which had experienced a certain degree of industrialization; after 1871, however, she underwent astonishing urban and industrial growth that transformed her into the economic giant of Europe, a world industrial power second only in size to the United States (Germany, for instance, produced more than two thirds of Europe's steel, and she led the world in chemical, electrical and engineering production).

However, the process of industrialization was not complete: by 1914, 60 per cent of her population may have lived in towns, but 40 per cent continued to live in the countryside – a large number compared, say, with Great Britain where only 8 per cent still lived in the countryside. Whereas Great Britain was a country of huge urban concentration, Germany was dominated by small to middle-sized towns and a countryside with comparably few urban centres. Thus two radically different cultures coexisted: the modern but ugly industrial landscape of the Ruhr and the charming, chocolate-box small towns and villages of provincial Germany. This societal dichotomy persisted even into the Weimar period: in 1930, just under a third of the population was still rural, which helps explain the deep political divisions within the country.

3   The rise of mass politics and the new right, 1880–1900

Until 1879, German political life, like that elsewhere in Europe, was dominated by landed aristocrats and the professional upper middle classes. Industrialization, however, caused massive dislocation to ordinary people's lives, and politics became dominated by the social consequences of economic change. As the historian Carl Schorske put it, this was the age of 'politics in a higher key'.[3]

The origins of support for Nazism can be traced back to the anti-modern political orientation of the *Mittelstand* (or middle class) which surfaced in the 1880s. Political antisemitism, in so far as it characterized the new political thinking, was itself principally a reaction against many features of modernity. Industrialization, new commercial practices, the 'unfairness' of the free market and of price competition were seen as undermining the smaller farmer and manufacturer. Farmers and shopkeepers disliked the importing of cheap wheat from America and of beef from Argentina; they were hostile to the innovative concept of the American department store introduced into Berlin by the Tietz brothers in the 1880s; and they deeply resented the cheaper mass production of everyday goods and, above all, the banks with their iniquitous rates of interest. This disenchantment led to the appearance of a variety of political parties and sectional organizations determined to fight these new developments and protect the 'small man' from the market economy, a system sometimes termed Manchesterism and attributed by the new antisemitic demagogues largely to the Jews.

This fear of the market economy manifested itself in the rise during the 1890s of lobbies and pressure groups to defend specific economic interests, for instance the Agrarian League or the General League of German Artisans. Some groups were regional and bizarre such as the Württemberg Brewers' League against Station Vending Machines that sold bottled beer, thereby diverting customers from using the local beer-hall, or the campaign by dairy farmers to ban margarine and have it dyed purple and marketed as 'oilslick'. Dissatisfied with the existing political choice, they set up their own parties to oppose banks, Jewish businesses, cooperatives, department stores, indeed almost any expression of modern commercial practice which competed against the local factory or corner shop. What they feared most was the loss of their livelihood, and proletarianization, i.e. their becoming impoverished, unpropertied workers in the grim industrial cities – a real threat given the mass exodus from the countryside to the urban centres. (During the Weimar period the existence of a large number of disaffected middle class voters would be illustrated by the rapid growth of splinter and regional parties in the years 1924–8.)

At the same time as the old middle class was becoming economically distressed, industrialization also gave birth to a

Reichstag – Table of Election Results, 1919–33

Date of election	19 Jan 1919	6 June 1920	4 May 1924	7 Dec 1924	20 May 1928	14 Sept 1930	31 July 1932	6 Nov 1932	5 Mar 1933	12 Nov 1933
1 *Nazis*	—	—	32 (6.5)	14 (3)	12 (2.6)	107 (18.3)	230 (37.3)	196 (33.1)	288 (43.9)	661 (92.1)
2 *Nationalists*	44 (10.3)	71 (13.9)	95 (19.5)	103 (20.5)	73 (14.2)	41 (7.0)	37 (5.9)	52 (8.8)	52 (8.0)	—
3 *Small and splinter parties*	5 (0.9)	9 (0.8)	29 (6.0)	29 (6.0)	51 (10.0)	72 (12.0)	11 (2.2)	12 (2.2)	7 (2.0)	—
4 *People's Party*	19 (4.4)	65 (13.9)	45 (9.2)	51 (10.1)	45 (8.7)	30 (4.5)	7 (1.2)	11 (1.9)	2 (0.5)	—
5 *Bavarian People's Party*	—	21	16	19	16	19	22	20	18	—
6 *Centre*	91 (4.4)	64 (13.6)	65 (13.4)	69 (13.6)	62 (12.1)	68 (11.8)	75 (12.4)	70 (11.9)	74 (11)	—
7 *Democrats*	75 (18.6)	39 (8.3)	28 (5.7)	32 (6.3)	25 (4.9)	20 (3.8)	4 (1.0)	2 (1.0)	5 (0.9)	—
8 *Social Democrats*	165 (37.9)	132 (21.6)	100 (20.5)	131 (26)	153 (29.8)	143 (24.5)	133 (21.6)	121 (20.4)	120 (18.2)	—
9 *Independent Social Democrats**	22 (7.6)	84 (17.9)	– (0.8)	– (0.3)	– (0.1)	—	—	—	—	—
10 *Communists*	—	4 (2.1)	62 (12.6)	45 (9.0)	54 (10.6)	77 (13.1)	89 (14.3)	100 (16.9)	81 (12.2)	—
Total number of seats in Reichstag	421	459	472	493	491	577	608	584	647	661
Total turnout (%)	83	79.2	77.4	78.8	75.6	81.9	84.0	80.6	88.5	95.3

(Figure in brackets = percentage of votes cast)
* The Independent Social Democratic Party ceased to exist after 1924. Some of its members went back to the Social Democrats and the rest joined the Communists.

new middle class of white-collar workers and professionals who worked in the growing bureaucracies of business and government. This new middle class, by contrast, was a much more forward-looking group, which affirmed the modern unified Germany and its rightful place in the sun. By 1907 there were 2 million white-collar workers in private industry and 1.5 million civil servants in central and local government; by 1913 there were 53 different white-collar organizations. Whereas the old middle class would later form the bedrock of Nazi support, the political complexion of the white-collar vote was varied, right up to the collapse of the Weimar Republic.

The *Mittelstand* was destined never really to find a political home in the Weimar Republic – witness the fluctuating performance of all the middle-class parties throughout the period (see table of election results, p.81), none of which succeeded in retaining a solid and sustained level of allegiance, until a change of strategy by the Nazi Party in 1928–9 finally provided them with a sense of belonging.

4 The radical right and antisemitism

For certain sections of the *Mittelstand*, the Jews became the personification of nearly all the hated manifestations of modern life – horse-trading democracy, liberalism, predatory capitalism and 'slave socialism'. For the *Mittelstand*, 'Manchesterism' was the economic war of all against all, where prices ceased to be stable and certain, but were determined by an unjust market. Swindle and speculation replaced the hard work of German peasants or businessmen (the 'productive' classes). Antisemitic parties came into existence in the late 1870s, the term antisemitism being coined in 1879 by the German journalist, Wilhelm Marr, when he founded the League of Antisemites. Other parties included the Christian Socialist Workers' Party, the German Social Antisemitic Party, and the Antisemitic People's Party. (For a more detailed consideration of the growth of modern antisemitism in western and central Europe during the latter half of the nineteenth century, see Chapter 3.)

Such parties did not fare especially well and, by the outbreak of the First World War, had largely failed. At their peak, in 1898, they attracted 250,000 votes (some 4 per cent of the vote) and they achieved their highest number of deputies in the Reichstag in 1907, with 16 out of a total of 397. The Conservative Party, it is true, adopted an antisemitic programme in 1892 but abandoned it in 1896, preferring to exploit antisemitism only if the local political circumstances warranted its use. Even if both pre-1914 antisemitic groupings are taken together – the Conservative Party and the antisemitic parties – they attained at most only 19 per cent of the vote in 1890 and after 1900 went into permanent decline. In 1912, when the last election before the war was held, they polled 11 per cent (10 per cent to the Conservatives and 1 per cent to the antisemites).

The development of political antisemitism was principally a form of *Mittelstand* revolt against existing social and economic crisis. The core of this disaffection was a detestation of banks to whom they paid interest or lost their farms and businesses; a loathing of the mechanism of the market which was often characterized as a 'Jewish swindle'; and a hatred for communists (in antisemitic sloganizing invariably depicted as Jews), who represented the spectre of proletarianization which, as we have seen, filled the *Mittelstand* with special dread. The Nazi Party would later absorb most of the *völkisch* parties of the political right, such antisemitic parties making an important contribution to the party's ideology and structure. (In right-wing German nationalist, racist and, later, Nazi ideology, the term *Volk* was seen as the national community held together by sacred ties of blood.)

However, in terms of overall electoral success the future of the Nazis lay not with antisemitic parties *per se*, but with parties which expressed the resentment and economic distress of the *Mittelstand*, of which antisemitism was a part.

5 The rise of the mass party of the left: the Social Democratic Party

It is all too easy, with hindsight, to read the Holocaust *back* into an analysis of German history and to exaggerate the significance of the Jewish question in German political life. In fact, from 1879 to 1933, the fundamental divide in German politics was caused not by hatred of the Jew, but by fear and hatred of the socialist – though antisemitic parties regularly equated the two. Germany's middle classes were afraid – sometimes to the point of hysteria – of a communist takeover and the fear of proletarianization among the German middle class became very real in a period of accelerated industrial and urban expansion. What is more, to many 'patriotic' Germans the international component of socialism was unwelcome and, in all probability, incomprehensible. Nevertheless, despite attempts by middle-class liberals and conservatives to isolate the socialists, as the Kaiserreich period progressed the Social Democratic Party (SPD) began to flourish.

At a time of intense industrial growth during the 1880s and 1890s, the Social Democratic Party – the pride and model of the Second International[4] – mobilized and recruited the German worker into a well disciplined Marxist party, the largest in Europe. By 1903, the SPD was gaining more votes in the Reichstag elections than any other party, and by 1912 emerged as the largest parliamentary party, with over one third of the vote (4 million). The SPD was run by its 'orthodox Marxist' centre which believed that capitalism was doomed and would collapse in accordance with the scientific laws of history. Until 1914, the SPD refused to cooperate in the Reichstag with any of the 'bourgeois' parties. Its leader, Bebel had said in 1903: 'I want to remain the deadly enemy of this bourgeois society and this political order, so that I will eliminate it if I can.'[5] The party also had a proto-communist left wing, which later broke away to form the Communist Party in 1922, and a reformist right under Eduard Bernstein, who believed that the capitalist system should be reformed by a parliamentary working class. However, keeping in mind the importance of the 4 million members of the free trades union movement, the party generally remained cautious and conservative. On the Jewish question, however, in contrast to the ambivalence of the Communist Party, it was consistently and courageously opposed to all manifestations of political and economic antisemitism.

6 The First World War, 1914–18

Germany fought a two-front war, in western and eastern Europe, as well as a submarine war against the British blockade. In alliance with Austria-Hungary and Turkey, the

Central Powers exercised control over land from Belgium to Baghdad until 1918. Only very rarely did Germany actually fight on her own soil, and, because of the paucity of accurate information, the general population remained largely ignorant of the reality of Germany's position right up to the end of the war in 1918.

Germany is believed by many commentators to have been the prime mover in the outbreak of the war, attempting to satisfy her ambitions for political and economic expansion in central and eastern Europe. The need to fight the war on many levels, both political and economic, meant that she was increasingly ruled by the military. From 1916 she was effectively led, not by the Chancellor, but by her two leading generals, Hindenburg and Ludendorff. Germany's war aim was expansion: to win colonies abroad; to annexe land in Poland and the Baltic in the east, and Belgium and France in the west; to dismantle the tsarist empire; and to create a pro-German Ukraine. Before 1914, imperialist ideas may only have been held by a minority, but the war created a wave of patriotism and imperialism which spread virtually throughout the German middle class – and beyond. Not only did such expansionist notions pervade the general population, but the experience of fighting also strengthened important strands of right-wing political ideology: the idea of fighting for a national cause of salvation, the sense of comradeship in the face of death, and the commitment to the virtuous struggle of nations.

During four and a half years of war Germany fought on enemy soil, yet the impact on the home front was considerable. In order to wage a war of attrition that was costly in both men and resources, she developed the first modern centralized economy. This proved problematic and divisive, and had the effect of radicalizing the population. For the farmers and small producers resented the increase in government controls while, at the same time, the trades unions assumed a more central and powerful position in ensuring the smooth running of the war economy. In the meantime, the British had blockaded the North Sea, which forced the German government to exercise even more controls. As for war losses, in 1916 alone Germany lost 281,000 men at Verdun and 450,000 on the Somme. By 1918 over 4.5 million Germans had died.

1917 proved a year of contrasts. The Russian revolutions in

February and October would eventually lead to the end of the war on the eastern front and the imposition, in early 1918, of a disastrous peace for Russia at Brest-Litovsk (an unquestioned triumph for German imperialist designs). Yet the success of Bolshevism in Russia and the fear it engendered in the west would have profound implications for the cause of anti-communism and antisemitism at home.

In March 1918, after the war on the eastern front had ended, Germany mounted her last great offensive in the west, in an effort to take Paris in one big push. By July 1918, however, this had palpably failed, and as the French successfully counter-attacked and the build-up of United States forces was becoming an unanswerable ingredient, the German High Command realized that the war could not be won. Hindenburg and Ludendorff recommended that an armistice be sought on the basis of President Wilson's 'Fourteen Points' (of January 1918), which envisaged a just peace and the establishment of a democratic world order. In October, Prince Max von Baden became the first Chancellor to be appointed with parliamentary support, a manoeuvre intended to signify to the allies that constitutional change within Germany was under way and that their preconditions for an armistice – that Germany should first remove the government that had caused the war – had been fulfilled.

However, what actually brought the war to an end was the outbreak of the 'German Revolution'. This began when the ordinary sailors in the German fleet at Kiel mutinied on 28 October 1918 and refused to put to sea. This disaffection quickly spread to the army and to the cities. Alarmed at the possibility of a Bolshevik-style revolution at home, the Social Democratic Party took matters into its own hands and on 9 November, upon the abdication of the Kaiser, proclaimed a republic. On the 11 November the First World War came to an end.

The circumstances which saw the demise of the Kaiserreich were to plague the Weimar Republic right up to the accession of Hitler. From the documents of the period, it is clear that the army High Command had no stomach to take on the humiliating task of negotiating a defeat. They therefore called upon the socialists and Catholic politicians to do their dirty work. Hence, was born the 'stab in the back' legend, namely that the honourable German army had been betrayed by socialists and Jews. To many patriotic Germans, this accusation seemed to have an element of truth because, until the last moment, the army High Command had not informed the populace of the true state of the war. They were therefore more inclined to believe the allegation that it was an internal collapse, engineered by 'Bolsheviks', socialists and Jews, that had undone Germany.

The First World War and the Jews

During the period 1914–16, Jews could have been forgiven for imagining that the war might have the effect of harmonizing and strengthening Jewish–German relations. After all, never had Jewish devotion to the Fatherland been on such public display; and all Germans were now surely united in the face of a national emergency. The Kaiser, moreover, had announced at the war's outset that he recognized no distinctions among Germans.

The long-term reality, however, was that the war, and the humiliation, economic distress and political extremism it would spawn, spelled unprecedented danger for the Jewish community. But these effects could not have been predicted then, despite the malevolent activities of some antisemitic splinter groups. As the war started to go wrong, accusations that Jews were shirking front-line duty, were engaged in anti-German black-marketeering and were generally craven, exploitative and unpatriotic, even led to an official census ordered by the Prussian War Ministry to investigate Jewish wartime activity. Though its results were never published, the damage had been done: the Nazi Party could later claim, without published evidence to the contrary, that the census revealed damning evidence of Jewish 'treason'. In point of fact, the statistical evidence shows that Jewish losses at the front and, indeed, the number of Iron Crosses won by Jewish soldiers was proportionally much higher than their numbers, a reflection of the zeal with which German Jews sought to prove their loyalty.

7   The German Revolution of 1918–19 and the establishment of the Weimar Republic

The revolution began with the spontaneous establishment of 'councils' of sailors and soldiers within the armed forces, and of civilians in the domestic cities. Germany had been brought to her knees by hunger and exhaustion, and the population had grown resentful of the increasing overregulation by government, which had especially impoverished the small producers. Like the Russian Revolution, the German version was not strictly a 'communist' revolution, but one instigated by ordinary, but radicalized, citizens who took matters into their own hands following the collapse of their government; what they now wanted was to replace the defeated old order with a new, democratic republic.

The supreme irony of the early Weimar years was that the Social Democrats were obsessed by the fear of a Bolshevik revolution that would supplant the old order with a dictatorship of the proletariat, accompanied by nationalization and the sweeping confiscation of property. For this reason Friedrich Ebert, the Chairman of the Council of People's Delegates, sought to steer events towards the establishment of a parliamentary and liberal order. In point of fact, the revolutionary councils themselves overwhelmingly supported a new parliamentary regime. Because of the fear of Bolshevism, however, Ebert succeeded neither in pushing through wide-ranging reforms within the state-run institutions nor in democratizing the army, judiciary, bureaucracy and universities. Instead, the Social Democrats made a pact with the army and used the old Prussian elites to maintain the status quo. In January and April 1919, the army and Freikorps (paramilitary formations of the right) were used to put down the movement of left-wing councils and to quell all political agitation. Consequently, despite the 'revolution', key areas of the state remained wholly unreformed. The Social Democrats had missed the opportunity to put the republic on to a sound democratic footing for fear of what was, in fact, a non-existent threat of communism. As will be explained later, the persistence of Prussian elites and of the threat – real and imagined – to their power base, would play a key role in the collapse of the Weimar Republic and in Hitler's fateful coming to power.

In January 1919, elections to the National Assembly resulted in a victory for the Weimar coalition of Social Democrats, Centre Party and Democrats, who together polled over 75 per cent of the vote. The Democrats, Germany's only equivalent of a genuine liberal party, polled 18 per cent, but this was merely a a temporary success (see above, p.81), indicating that during the years 1918–19 Germany was bound in a brief spell of radicalism and distrust of the old order. The old Prussian conservatives and liberals were, at first, paralyzed by defeat, a factor accounting perhaps for the temporary success of the Weimar coalition. They only began to organize successor parties to the old imperial bourgeois parties – by this time called the National Party and People's Party – in the years after 1918–19. They remained temporarily stunned by the loss of the monarchy and the Prussian constitution, but had not yet developed a coherent anti-republican and 'German' programme.

The Weimar Constitution was adopted in January 1919 and, for the first time, Germany became a centralized democratic state, ruled by a Reichstag whose members were elected by all men and women aged 21 and over. Governments relied upon the support of the Reichstag, although Article 48 of the constitution allowed for the exercise of emergency presidential powers at times of political crisis. Elections were to be held on the basis of proportional representation, which meant that any party gaining at least 60,000 votes would have a deputy elected. The previous constituent states now became *Länder* or state provinces and were subordinated to the central government in Berlin.

8 The Versailles Treaty and its consequences

Germany had asked for an armistice in November 1918 on the basis of Wilson's Fourteen Points. However, in May 1919 the German delegation was presented with a draft peace treaty that showed that American idealism had given way to the French desire to punish her old enemy: Germany, it seemed, was to be permanently emasculated and France restored to her position as Europe's primary power. As a result, Scheidemann's socialist government resigned on the grounds that the treaty was unacceptable, but the socialist Bauer formed another government and signed.

The impact of the Treaty of Versailles on the infant republic was profound and far-reaching, though its precise effects would also later be shrouded in myth and propaganda. Germany lost substantial assets: 13 per cent of her territory and 6 million subjects (she was forced to surrender Posen and Upper Silesia to Poland, and Alsace-Lorraine to France); she lost her colonies, all assets held in enemy countries, and control over two important economic regions – the Saarland and the port of Danzig; she had to accept the permanent demilitarization of the Rhineland and allied occupation of the left bank for 15 years; she also endured the loss of 14 per cent of her arable land, 26 per cent of her coal, 68 per cent of her zinc, 74 per cent of her iron ore. Her navy and army were also severely cut back. Most significantly and painfully, she was required to accept the 'War Guilt' clause, whereby Germany shouldered all the moral responsibility for the war (from which no protagonist can truly be said to have emerged with honour intact), adding shame and humiliation to her wounded national pride. Finally, in order to help France restore her devastated northern *départements*, and to enable the allies to repay their own American loans, an unspecified sum was to be paid as compensation for the cost and damage of the war suffered by Great Britain, France and Italy. In May 1921 the final account for reparations was settled at 132 milliard gold marks (*c.*$33 billion).

In 1922, the Wirth government attempted a policy of 'fulfilment' by payment of the sums due, but by the end of 1922 Germany announced she could make no further payments (her economy was by now in dire straits). In January 1923, French troops occupied the Ruhr, and the German government financed a permanent strike by German workers. Within one year, the German currency had collapsed and a new settlement was reached – the Dawes Plan of 1924 – which sought to limit reparations in the first five years to allow the German economy time to recover; in addition, 800 million gold marks were lent largely by American banks to help restructure the German economy.

The Versailles treaty deprived Germany of important resources, yet it did not cripple Germany and it was not responsible, as propaganda suggested, for her subsequent economic difficulties. Indeed, after the Dawes Plan, Germany received foreign loans and aid equivalent to the reparations she paid. The Young Plan of 1929 virtually halved the real reparations bill and provided generous financing in the form of a loan to be repaid over 50 years. Finally, in the wake of the Great Crash in 1931, a one year moratorium was announced, followed in July 1932 by cancellation of the debt.

However, the political and psychological consequences of Versailles were much more important. Many Germans felt that they would never have negotiated an end to the war had the treaty's terms been known. Moreover, successive German governments of both left and right exaggerated the unfairness of the treaty and its crippling effects, in order to prepare the ground for its complete revision. In reality, this exaggeration only benefited the political right, which campaigned vigorously on an anti-Versailles nationalistic platform. The considerable losses sustained by the Weimar coalition in the first Reichstag elections of June 1920 (their vote slumped to under 50 per cent) are generally attributed to popular outrage at the terms of the treaty. Indeed, so fearful were the Weimar parties of the impact of the treaty that the planned presidential election of Ebert was cancelled, and he was appointed instead by the government. In the long term, the Weimar Republic would be damned with responsibility for such a 'humiliating' treaty, even though it had been faced with no alternative. Much of Hitler's appeal would rest on his revulsion at the treaty, on his promise to make drastic revisions to its terms and on his pledge to reunify the 'dismembered' German territory and people.

9 The Jews of Weimar Germany

As we have seen in Chapter 3, by the time of the establishment of the Weimar Republic, German Jews had enjoyed the fruits of legal and political emancipation for almost half a century. Despite the emergence of a modern antisemitic movement, they would generally occupy a comfortable position – at least in relative terms – within the economic and cultural fabric of German society. However, as Donald Niewyk has pointed out:

> The role of Jews in the economy and, indeed, in the culture of Weimar Germany has been exaggerated by both Nazi and

anti-Nazi writers, the former to disparage alleged Jewish decadence and domination, the latter to praise Jewish achievement and to identify antisemitism as being rooted in part in jealousy and envy.[6]

Nevertheless, the statistical evidence does suggest a disproportionate penetration by Jews into prominent professions that would have fuelled the stereotyping on which antisemitic prejudice and hatred fed. There were approximately 550,000 Jews in Weimar Germany, making up just under 1 per cent of the overall population, but holding, between 1919 and 1933, more than 3.5 per cent of positions in the middle-class professions of law, medicine, trade, banking and commerce. By the time of Hitler's accession in 1933, Jews comprised over 16 per cent of Germany's lawyers and 11 per cent of Germany's doctors. Just as conspicuously, during this period Jews emerged as owners of a number of large American-style department stores in several major German cities, while nearly 60 per cent of all clothing outlets – both wholesale and retail – were in Jewish hands. Jews were also prominent in privately owned banks and in some of the larger publishing houses.

However, a significant section of the German Jewish population (about one-fifth) was made up of refugees from the various postwar revolutions and upheavals in eastern Europe. A much less happily integrated group, they frequently fell victim to unemployment and economic distress, becoming easy targets of antisemitic accusations of cultural outsiderhood and economic parasitism. One consequence was that the wealthier, more sophisticated and more successfully assimilated sections of the Jewish community could more readily believe that antisemitic agitation, even of the later Nazi variety, was aimed not at them but at these *Ostjuden* (eastern Jews).

Taken as a whole, according to all the available evidence, the Jewish community was, quite contrary to right-wing smears and propaganda, destined to be just as hard hit as any other section of German society by inflation and the Depression.

10   The Great Inflation

Between 1919 and 1924 Germany experienced increasing economic difficulties leading to hyper-inflation in 1922–3 and, finally, to monetary collapse. During this period the mark devalued from 14 marks to the dollar in 1919 to the mind-boggling level of 4,200,000,000 marks to the dollar in November 1923. The original reason for the inflation lay in attempts to finance the war of 1914–18, which the government had previously paid for simply by printing money. After 1918, the government refused to reduce the budget and to introduce deflationary measures, principally because it wished to buy time for the republic in a climate of acute political instability; it needed to pay for the transition to a peace-time economy – to provide pensions for orphans, widows and the war-disabled and, of course, to make reparations. Rather surprisingly, Germany actually avoided the postwar slump of 1920–1, experienced in both Britain and the United States.

The Great Inflation had an undoubted impact on the fortunes of the Nazi Party, whose vote in the first election of 1924 was quite pronounced. But by December 1924 the Nazi vote had slumped, indicating that its support was really only crisis-related. More significantly, perhaps, Hitler was in prison and, after his release, was banned from speaking; deprived of his oratory, the party had little if any appeal; without his leadership it split into warring factions. Over the subsequent four years, the Nazi Party virtually collapsed. For the working classes the impact of the inflation was huge in 1923 (when it was hyper-inflation), and stabilization in 1924 made for immediate, 'permanent' mass unemployment. For those members of the middle class who had mortgages or who dealt in real property or goods, the inflation had only a comparatively moderate impact. But those who lived on fixed incomes suffered the most severe difficulties, with countless members of this section of the middle class generally being thought to have lost their life savings. The main effect of the inflation, therefore, was to *divide* the middle class.

The most damaging repercussion of the inflation, however, was on the psychology of successive German governments, which grew obsessed with the spectre of inflation. Consequently, when the slump of 1930–2 occurred, following the Wall Street Crash, the government deepened the recession, causing dramatically high levels of unemployment, so as to avoid any recurrence of the inflation.

The rise of the Nazi Party to power

Adolf Hitler

Adolf Hitler was born in 1889 in a small town on the Austrian-Czech border. He was a citizen of the Austro-Hungarian Empire, at a time when the dominance of the ruling Germans was being undermined by rising Slav nationalism. His father was a customs official who died when Hitler was still a child. At school he appears to have been a moody daydreamer who lacked industry and purpose. He failed to gain entrance to art school and lived in Vienna without employment until 1913. There he would have experienced the drab and depressing existence of modern urban life among the poor working class and unemployed; he would have cast envious eyes on the prosperity of Vienna's highly Germanized and prosperous Jewish middle class and, according to his own writings, been 'repelled' by the poor, culturally 'alien', immigrant Jews from Polish Galicia and tsarist Russia. He would also have witnessed the successful antisemitic strategies of mayor Karl Lueger and his Christian social politics which protected the 'little man' against capitalist (and Jewish) enterprises. In 1913 he fled the city, possibly to avoid conscription, but from 1914 he served as a brave front-line soldier in a Bavarian regiment. This must have had a profound impact upon him, particularly as he had now found a purpose and the exhilaration of comradeship in the struggle for life. He became a corporal and was decorated with the Iron Cross. After being temporarily blinded by a gas attack in 1918, he suddenly found that the war had ended in shameful defeat for Germany.

Returning to Munich, he became an undercover agent for the army, spying on the many small conspiratorial right-wing groups that inhabited the beer-cellars. One of these groups was the German Workers' Party – embryo of the Nazi Party – founded by a railway worker, Anton Drexler. Hitler appears very quickly to have assumed its leadership.

The growth of the Nazi Party

The Nazi Party was founded as the German Workers' Party in

Munich in 1919. Throughout 'the period of struggle', until the accession to power in 1933, the Nazi Party's electoral support remained in a constant state of flux. Between 1919 and 1924, the party was confined to Munich and Bavaria, and attracted extreme right-wing groups of ex-soldiers, anti-communists and tsarist émigrés. This early phase during the turbulent first years of the Weimar Republic culminated in the failed Beer Hall Putsch of November 1923: Hitler had attempted to seize power in Munich and to proclaim a 'national revolution'. Found guilty of treason, he received only the minimum sentence of five years. In the event, he served only nine months in the fortress prison at Landsberg. There he wrote the first volume of *Mein Kampf* (*My Struggle*), in which he spelled out a political philosophy which gave pride of place to anti-communist, antisemitic and pan-German ideas. (For an explanation of the philosophy of pan-Germanism, see Chapter 3.)

The Nazi Party had been antisemitic from its inception, at first repeating all the familiar accusations against 'Jewish capitalism', 'Jewish Bolshevism', and characterizing Germany's defeat in the war as the product of Jewish treachery, cowardice and profiteering. Throughout the 1920s and 1930s, it developed more fully a bizarre conception of the Jew as a parasitic, biological 'germ' which threatened the purity of the Germanic race. According to this theory, the Jews constituted a supreme danger against which the German people must defend themselves. Nevertheless, although Adolf Hitler himself and the Nazi Party clearly attached central significance to the 'Jewish problem' in the formation of their ideology, their success in winning over the German electorate had, as we shall see, comparatively little to do with the active or latent antisemitism of ordinary Germans. The view that their eventual staggering triumph at the ballot box can largely be attributed to their overt antisemitism has, quite simply, been greatly exaggerated.

In 1925, the party was reorganized on more centralized lines, the decision having been taken to fight its battles legally in elections rather than to plot coups in sweaty beer-cellars. In particular, it developed its proletarian wing outside Bavaria, under the leadership of Gregor Strasser, in northern, western and eastern Germany, in order to attract the working class.

The party's title revealed that one of its main goals had been to 'rescue' the working class from the clutches of international socialism.

The Nazi Party first participated in national elections in May 1924. It gained 6.5 per cent of the vote, but in the December 1924 election, in the wake of economic stabilization and calmer political conditions, its share of the vote fell to 3 per cent.

Regional and splinter parties

Of greater long-term importance to the eventual Nazi success was the growing strength of regional and splinter parties, whose share of the vote now rose from 3 per cent in the 1920 elections to 8 per cent in 1924. Such parties as the Economy Party, Business Party, Tenants' Party, Bavarian Peasants' and Middle Class Party gained votes from the established Reichstag middle-class parties which were loyal to the republic (i.e. the German People's Party and the German Democrats). Long before the Depression, sizeable numbers of the German middle classes were deserting the Weimar coalition to set up their own protest parties. This was of consequence because the viability of the Weimar Republic depended on alliances involving the Social Democrats and the Catholic Centre Party, together with both liberal parties (i.e. the German People's Party and the Democrats). However, the Weimar bourgeois parties failed to extend themselves beyond merely representing narrow sectional interests and were thus unable to command the broad support of the German middle classes (i.e. including the 'small men' with small to medium-sized farms or businesses).

The period between 1924 and 1928 was a time of comparative political and economic tranquillity for the Weimar Republic, clearly reflected in the 1928 election results. The Nazi Party received only 2.6 per cent of the vote (800,000 votes) and seemed well on the road to insignificance or even extinction. However, important political changes were taking place beneath the surface, as mirrored in the fortunes of other parties. The Democrats and German People's Party were both continuing to lose support, thus further weakening the middle ground in German politics. More striking still was the decline of the established conservative Nationalists, whose anti-Weimar stance had previously enabled them to make such headway between 1919 and 1924 (and who probably had taken votes from the more liberal and pro-republican middle-class parties). But in 1928 their share of the vote fell from 20 per cent to 14 per cent.

Most significantly, in 1928 independent splinter parties almost doubled their vote. For example, the Economy Party, established in 1924 to represent artisans and shopkeepers, who were dissatisfied with the larger middle-class parties, saw its number of seats rise from 17 to 23. Thus in 1928, at the height of the so-called years of stability, the political centre of the Weimar Republic and the conservative parties of the German establishment were both haemorrhaging. The NSDAP (the Nazi Party) was just one of many such splinter parties that had emerged, jostling (unsuccessfully at this stage) for these 'detached' voters.

The twin path to success

However, in the depths of its failure, the Nazi Party stumbled across the key to its later startling progress. In the election of 1928, much to their own surprise, the Nazis found considerable support in the northern provincial farming communities – in Schleswig-Holstein, Lower Saxony, Thuringia, and in Bavaria. At this point, the party abandoned its emphasis on Strasser's 'urban plan' and adopted two strategies which were to mark a new beginning for the party: (a) the establishment of 'formations' (or organizations); and (b) the decision to agitate among the rural and provincial communities.

(a) Establishment of 'Formations'

'Formations' were created which would appeal to factional interests or infiltrate existing organizations or communities. Such 'informal agitation' involved the establishment of networks, recruiting key local individuals and spreading the party word by hand or mouth. In 1926, youth had already been targeted with the establishment of the Hitler Youth and the National Socialist German Students' Association. In 1929 the

NS Union of School Pupils was set up, mainly attracting upper middle-class children attending grammar schools. The students' association was the most successful of these bodies (the student world had traditionally – since the 1870s – been an important breeding ground of antisemitism in many European countries), and had effectively 'captured' at least nine universities by 1930.

In 1928 the Association of National Socialist Jurists was founded to encourage within the legal profession the 'renewal of a system of law in a patriotic and national socialist sense'.[7] In 1929 came the NS Association of German Physicians and the NS Teachers' Association. The League of Struggle for German Culture was an organization intended to attract 'culturally active persons', 'to rally all defensive forces against the powers of corruption that at present dominate German culture'.[8] Jews, who were conspicuously over-represented in the professions, universities and in cultural life in Weimar Germany, were easy scapegoats and, at a time of high unemployment, middle-class Germans were encouraged to close ranks against their Jewish competitors in the struggle for bourgeois success.

The Nazis projected the image of a party that identified with the needs and anxieties of the 'small man' faced with the dangers posed by the modern practices of big business. Consequently, they infiltrated the militant Combat League of Middle Class Traders, whose chief purpose was to agitate against chain-stores and consumer cooperatives. Important, too, was the Nazis' infiltration in 1929–30 of the German-National League of Commercial Employees (a body which had previously supported the Nationalists) and organizations representing the interests of the war-disabled, war-pensioners, and civil servants.

(b) Rural agitation

The second strategy was agitation in Protestant areas amongst the rural and provincial *Mittelstand* – in particular the farmers – and penetration of existing agricultural communities and peasants' organizations. This was to be a critical turning-point in the fortunes of the Nazis, the party establishing its Office for Agriculture in 1930. After the 1928 election, the Nazi Party developed a network of local advisers to spread propaganda among the farmers and to report back to Munich on the political state of the agricultural community. Later, the main organization representing farmers in Germany, the Landbund, was effectively in Nazi hands. Farmers were ripe targets for Nazi efforts because they had become radicalized by the alarming drop in farm incomes during 1926 and 1927 and by increases in taxes and interest rates. Many had voted for the Democrats in 1919, because of their commitment to deregulate farm prices after years of wartime controls, but in 1920, after the Treaty of Versailles, they switched to the Nationalists. From 1928, however, the Nationalists themselves began to experience mass defections (it is estimated that the rural vote for the Nationalists declined from 39 per cent to 27 per cent across Northern Germany).

The agricultural depression preceded the industrial depression by some three years. Farm income by 1928 had declined to a level 44 per cent below the national average and indebtedness soared by 35 per cent between 1923 and 1929; foreclosures and forced sales doubled in the years 1929–30. On 28 January 1928 a new era in farm politics dawned when 100,000 farmers marched on town squares in Schleswig-Holstein. This led to the foundation of independent peasants' parties such as the Christian National Peasants' and Rural People's Party and the Landvolk Party or the Bavarian Peasants' Party. In the summer this in turn led to a widespread tax revolt, acts of violence against tax collectors and bank officials, and even bomb throwing. These activities exposed the presence of disaffected middle-class groups in German society, from whom the Nazi Party would later draw such strong support. Nazism did not bring such forces into existence but it could offer them a political home.

Though antisemitism was by no means the principal weapon in the proselytizing armoury of the Nazi Party in its appeal to the rural communities, it is nevertheless true that, in the country districts particularly, there survived primitive – even medieval – attitudes towards the Jews which could be aggravated by crude stereotypes and scapegoating tactics.

Electoral roller-coaster

Thus, the infiltration of urban middle class groups and the

development of the farm vote largely accounts for the astonishing growth of Nazi support in the election of September 1930 – from 800,000 to 6.5 million (2.6 per cent to 18.3 per cent, and from 12 to 107 seats), the party now becoming the second largest represented in the Reichstag behind the Social Democrats. In the previous year, Hitler had gained national publicity and a measure of respectability by standing on the same platform as the Nationalists and other right-wing groups during the campaign against the Young Plan on the issue of reparations. More importantly, the collapse of the liberal parties (Democrats and People's Party) had spread to the Nationalists who now declined from 14.2 per cent to 7 per cent. The special interest parties still held on, losing nothing to the Nazis. Given that the electorate grew from 31 million to 35 million between 1928 and 1930, we can conclude that the Nazis took votes from young voters, and from supporters of the Nationalists, Democrats and People's Party, especially the farm vote in Protestant areas (but not yet from the splinter parties).

In the election of July 1932 the Nazis' support reached its apogee with 37.3 per cent of the vote, making them the largest single party in the Reichstag (note that even at their height, they never attracted more than a third of the electorate – the March 1933 election should be discounted, since it was not really a 'free' election). So, where did the votes come from? In addition to continued defections from the bourgeois parties, they now came from the splinter and regional parties which declined from just under 14 per cent to 2 per cent (the farmers' and other middle-class splinter parties had by 1932 joined the Nazi Party). They also came from first-time voters, especially young people, from women, and from a significant part of the working class, especially in areas with weak socialist traditions. Nevertheless, it should be stressed that the Nazi vote of 13 million was much bigger than the number of defections from other parties.

Six months later, however, a shock awaited the Nazis. In the election of November 1932, they lost 2 million votes and 34 seats, their share of the vote falling to 33.1 per cent. The Nationalists and communists, on the other hand, increased their representation. Many ascribe this Nazi decline to Hitler's refusal to join a government unless he was appointed

Chancellor. Part of the attraction of the Nazi Party had been its claim to energy and power that would sweep away the Weimar Republic; they had clearly found it difficult to sustain the momentum which had been such an integral part of that appeal. Many also consider that Brüning's economic policy (see p.108 below), although so disastrous in its initial stages, was now bringing about economic recovery. The economic indices for employment, production and real wages all started to climb from the low point of 1932, *before* the Nazi economic policies could have had any effect. Thus Hitler was appointed Chancellor, not on the triumphant crest of a wave, but just as his electoral fortunes were beginning to wane. (As we shall see, he would ultimately be appointed primarily because of conservative fears of a communist takeover).

Who voted for Hitler?

Until 1929 the Nazi Party had been a failure, and seemed doomed to political extinction. What transformed the fortunes of the party was the dramatic domestic situation which arose in that year and the impressive ability of the party to adapt, organize and appeal to a diverse constituency of anti-Weimar voters.

In 1928, the Nazi Party had been shrinking. Hitherto, as we have seen, it had operated on the basis of the 'urban plan', inviting support from the urban working classes on the basis of a nationalist form of socialism. This electoral strategy was a failure. But, as the established political parties began to collapse, for reasons largely unrelated to the existence of the Nazi Party, and with the onset of the particular economic circumstances of 1929–30, the Nazi Party proved able to gather together these pre-existing discontented groups under a catch-all party banner. Martin Broszat describes the appeal of the Nazis as 'sudden but undramatic', the Nazis setting in motion the sort of political bandwagon that would appeal to a large number of people in search of a political home.[9] The principal political message was that of the *Volksgemeinschaft*, a key political and racial concept in Nazi ideology, that German society could become unified under the banner of the 'national community', irrespective of, and transcending, class, religion and previous political affiliation. The concept of *Volk* and race was essentially a universal and centrifugal political idea that could bind together a deeply divided society. As Goebbels said: 'The class parties of the right and left must be overcome and a new way opened for the creation of a genuine party of the people.'

In considering the election results after 1928, modern research has shown that the Nazi constituency was neither so static nor so narrow as previously thought. The claim to be a broad-based national people's party was, to a certain extent, true.

Those who did not vote for Hitler:

Three particular constituencies stand out:

1. The Catholics (the Centre Party and Bavarian People's Party): generally speaking, politically organized Catholics seem to have remained remarkably immune to Nazi infiltration.
2. The *organized* working class: workers who had previously voted for socialist parties and who worked in heavy and large-scale industry. Although the Social Democratic Party lost many votes to the Communist Party and some to the Nazis, the organized working-class vote remained remarkably coherent and was generally resistant to the Nazis' electoral appeal.
3. The Jews: a very small group who constituted less than 1 per cent of the German population, they remained to the end the principal supporters of liberal democratic politics by retaining their allegiance to the German Democratics (later the German State Party) and the Social Democratics. (There was obviously no question of Jews voting for the Nazi Party, except perhaps in very rare individual cases, for reasons of eccentricity, frivolousness, or total 'blindness' to reality!)

Groups that did vote Nazi:

1. First-time voters, i.e. the young. In all three post-1928 elections, the Nazi Party was more successful in attracting the youth vote than any other party. This is not too

surprising given the intensive efforts by the party to infiltrate student and youth organizations. In contrast, the Weimar parties appeared middle class, unexciting and 'elderly'. Only the Communist Party could appeal to youth on a similar basis.

2. The farm vote (see above, pp.98–9).
3. The disaffected *Mittelstand*: retailers, small businessmen and civil servants.
4. Traditional supporters of the established middle-class parties – the Nationalists, the Democrats and the People's Party. In the September 1930 election, the split in the total Nazi vote was as follows: 14 per cent had voted Nazi in 1928; 23 per cent had not voted at all previously; 31 per cent had voted for parties of the bourgeois centre (i.e. Democrats and German People's Party); 21 per cent had voted for the Nationalists; 9 per cent for the SPD; and 2 per cent for the small splinter parties.
5. The upper and upper middle classes. The view that the Nazi electorate was lower middle class is not entirely true, although no one would deny that such groups formed its bedrock. However, it is now clear that the upper and upper middle classes were much stronger supporters than previously imagined. The Nazis gained better-than-average results in upper middle class districts in Berlin, Hamburg, Essen and Dortmund – areas with a high percentage of Jewish inhabitants. Interestingly enough, the Nazis won relatively large support from voters who were registered as being away on their summer holidays – strongly indicative in the 1930s of those who were better off than average.
6. The unorganized (i.e. non-socialist) working class in small to middle-sized enterprises. Only the committed and organized working class remained immune. The sort of workers who did vote Nazi included farm labourers, home-workers, craftsmen and artisans, those working in small to medium-sized enterprises, and 'uniformed' workers in municipal and service industries, such as the post office and railways.

Contrary to popular belief, the unemployed did not form a particularly noteworthy section of the Nazi vote. About one third of all workers who voted in 1932–3 were unemployed, and most voted for the Communist Party and, to a lesser extent, for the Social Democrats. The Nazis only picked up significant support from the unemployed white-collar voter. The white-collar vote as a whole was much less important an explanation of Nazi success than previously thought, 60 per cent voting either for socialist or liberal parties.

It is now clear that the essential appeal and success of the Nazis lay in their claim to be a national people's party that could bind and heal German society. On the other hand, although Nazi 'integral nationalism' had, for the first time, achieved this end, it was naturally impossible for the party to fulfil its obligations to so many diverse and conflicting sections of the population. Thus the Nazi coalition would be inherently contradictory and unstable in the period after 1933.

Nazi ideology and political mobilization

In looking at what the Nazi Party stood for, it is important to distinguish between Hitler's own thoughts and the official programme of the party, and between the pre-1928 propaganda of the party, when it was a minor *völkisch* party and the period after 1928, when it sought to present itself as a respectable party to which the government of the country could safely be entrusted.

Hitler's own philosophy

Hitler's ideas were based on a *völkisch* and biological racism which explained human history in terms of a primeval romantic fantasy. His ideas and aspirations were not new but were common in the nineteenth century among *Mittelstand* parties and ideologists: the primacy of a German blood-nation free from foreign influences (i.e. Jewish, Bolshevik, liberal and even Christian); a unified organic national community which transcended class conflict by the promotion of national consciousness; the principle of leadership and obedience; a commitment to Darwinian meritocracy and natural selection of the strong; the central role of the German *Mittelstand* – especially the peasant – as the repository of true German virtue; the importance of the concepts of manliness and struggle; the necessity for a national re-awakening by the liberation of the Germanic race from domination by foreign creeds; the need for German 'living space' (*Lebensraum*) in the east; the re-establishment of a German warrior peasantry and re-breeding of the stock; the 'world-historical' conflict of great nations; the existence of the Jews as a mortal enemy both of the German people and of all mankind – a group capable of fomenting the division and dissolution of entire societies and cultures. (For a selection of Hitler's recorded views on the Jews, see Appendix C.)

The party's electoral approach

To what extent, then, was Nazi mass appeal founded on articulating its racial ideology in the years 1930–3? To Hitler the Nazi Party was a vehicle of social transformation. In *Mein Kampf*, he had written:

> The ideology is intolerant and cannot be content with the role of a party among other parties. It imperiously demands its own exclusive and unqualified recognition as well as the complete transformation of the whole public life according to its views ... the national conversion of the mass of the people.[10]

Implicit within this statement are two important concepts: firstly, that such ideas were sacrosanct and unalterable; and, secondly, that Nazi ideology was intended as the means of social engineering, that is to create a *new* society. The ideology explained Germany's current difficulties and the way to re-establish its purity and permanence. In Hitler's view, the German people were too infected with Marxism, liberalism, Christianity and Judaism for the party to appeal to the electorate with an open declaration of its ideological goals. For this reason, Hitler's unadulterated 'philosophy' (in particular his obsession with the Jewish question) was not a constant motif of Nazi electoral propaganda. Propaganda had a different purpose before and after the seizure of power. The purpose of Nazism *after* the seizure of power was to saturate the German population with its ideology and mobilize it in a crusade of conversion to Nazism. Hitler often remarked that it would take perhaps 30 or 40 years before the Germans could be completely Nazified; those who had already been enslaved by Christianity,

Marxism and Judaism were a lost generation.

Before 1933, much of the success of the Nazi Party lay not in appealing to people with overt propaganda, or in wooing them with romantic notions or ideals. Rather, the sole purpose of propaganda was to achieve power by legal means, which entailed emphasizing and exploiting popular discontent and anger, insinuating that the Nazi Party was the sole means of securing a brighter economic future. Ordinary voters saw their own material self-interest and values rooted in what the Nazi Party had to offer; they cared little or nothing for utopian visions of a new Germanic civilization.

After 1928, Hitler's speeches and Nazi electoral propaganda in general toned down the *völkisch* and full-blooded antisemitic elements of Nazi ideology. There were, to be sure, plenty of references to Jews, but not the more outlandish image of the Jews as 'non-humans' which was by now a fundamental axiom of Nazi racial ideology. The appeal to the German people was, instead, largely based on a complete rejection of Weimar democracy, on the German nation's wounded pride and the lure of a vague but brighter economic and political future for an awakened nation. Indeed, Martin Broszat has written that voting for Hitler was not so much a deliberate acceptance of National Socialism as a decided rejection of the Weimar system of democracy and capitalism, and an acknowledgement that the Nazis were the only effective instrument of change.[11] Seen from that perspective, voting for Hitler was 'undramatic' and prosaic rather than an earth-shaking vote for *Lebensraum* or an 'Aryan' future built on wholesale depopulation or mass murder (even assuming that this was remotely on the horizon for committed Nazis).

The significance of antisemitism

In Ian Kershaw's view (a view opposed by many Zionist historians), antisemitism was 'secondary to Nazi electoral success' and was 'taken on board' by a majority of the Nazi supporters rather than being a prime motivating factor.[12] In Merkl's study of long-serving Nazi members, only 12.5 per cent saw antisemitism as their most salient concern, while only 8 per cent of the total sample espoused 'strong ideological antisemitism'.[13]

Antisemitism was an important factor in areas where Jews were important in the cattle or grain trade or in providing credit, for example in Hesse, Westphalia, Middle Franconia, or stretches of the Rhineland. Antisemitism was also important in the 'formations' of teachers and students, principally because of the preponderance of Jews in key areas of upwardly mobile middle-class life. But such antisemitism tended to reflect the distress of middle-class groups, not an unswerving belief in the inherent legitimacy or necessity of racial ideas or hatred of Jews.

High-level politics and the presidential 'camarilla', 1930–3

Given the transitory nature of Nazi support, how did Hitler come to be appointed Chancellor?

In March 1930, the last government to enjoy a majority in the Reichstag fell from power over the issue of increased unemployment benefits. Until the resolution of the crisis in January 1933, power effectively passed from the Reichstag to the President of the Republic, Paul von Hindenburg, who appointed a succession of 'presidential cabinets', none of which was put into office by a parliamentary majority. Instead, these 'presidential' governments ruled by use (or rather abuse) of Article 48 of the Weimar Constitution which allowed for emergency decrees where the parliamentary system had broken down. The collapse of the parliamentary system can be charted as follows: the Reichstag sat for 94 days in 1930, 42 days in 1931 and just 13 days in 1932; 98 laws were passed in 1930, 34 in 1931 and 5 in 1932; conversely, the number of emergency decrees passed under the presidential powers increased from 5 in 1930 to 44 in 1931 and to 66 in 1932. For the Nazis the road to power was far from easy; even though they constituted the largest party in the Reichstag after July 1932, it took six months for Hitler to be appointed.

Return to conservatism

Until 1918, the imperial governments had been appointed by the Kaiser and run by a cabal of Prussian aristocrats, army officers and conservatives. With the failure of parliamentary government in March 1930, this form of rule eventually returned. Around the ageing figure of the neo-kaiser, Field Marshal-cum-president, Paul von Hindenburg, a group of politicians and army figures worked consciously for the destruction of the Weimar system and its replacement by a new conservative order – possibly monarchical – recalling the good old days of the Kaiserreich, safe from democracy, socialism and political challenge. These politicians included General Kurt von Schleicher and other army officers, who were in collusion with conservative politicians drawn both from the Nationalist and Catholic Centre Parties, and from the influential lobbies of heavy industry and landowning. Thus, from 1930, it was the president, his entourage, the army and bureaucracy, in collaboration with various conservative lobbies, who would decide Germany's political fate and who would push executive control over daily government far beyond constitutional propriety.

It is quite clear from the evidence that such politicians were not driven by circumstances or compelled by political crisis to demolish Weimar's democratic structure; rather it was a conscious choice to place Germany back on a conservative footing. Indeed, even before the political crisis that brought Hermann Müller's government down in March 1930 – as far back as Easter 1929 – plans were afoot to replace Müller's socialist-led government with a presidential cabinet.

The election of 1930 – the Nazi breakthrough

In March 1930 Hindenburg appointed Heinrich Brüning as Chancellor. Brüning was a Centre Party politician of the old conservative mould, whose avowed aim was to bury the Weimar Constitution. His solution to the economic crisis was to impose swingeing cuts in government expenditure and a deflationary budget. When the budget was refused by the Reichstag he dissolved it, calling an election for September 1930. This is considered the first major departure from the spirit of the Weimar Constitution because, in effect, he punished the Reichstag for refusing his decree – as they were entitled to do. This election (see above, p.81) led to the permanent weakening of the parliamentary system, with the Nazi Party gaining an astonishing 107 seats, and the Communist Party enjoying similar success with 77 seats. The centre middle class parties collapsed and there was no chance of a viable coalition. Brüning survived, however, for two years, until May 1932, governing not with the support of a positive parliamentary majority, but because the SPD decided to 'tolerate' the government's decrees: they refused to support motions of no confidence, but managed to avoid direct association with the painful economic medicine being administered by Brüning.

Brüning's economic measures

In its attempt to cope with the Depression, Brüning's economic policy was so severe that it led to massive increases in the level of unemployment, the numbers rising between 1932 and 1933 to approximately 6 million. Brüning's principal aim was to force the cancellation of further payment of reparations by demonstrating that Germany could no longer afford it; this he chose to do at the expense of huge unemployment for the foreseeable future. Indeed, there is evidence to suggest that Brüning could, in mid-1931, have accepted foreign credits to help finance a reflation, but this would have hampered his policy of non-payment of reparations. In the longer term, it is believed, he intended to sweep away the Weimar Constitution and re-impose a Hohenzollern monarch. On the other hand, it has been argued in Brüning's defence that he had no other option since, after the experience of 1922–3, there was widespread terror at the prospect of another bout of hyper-inflation. In the event, a one-year moratorium on reparations was later agreed in June 1931, and in July 1932 – two months after Brüning's fall from office – they were totally cancelled.

The most important political consequence of Brüning's economic policy, however, was that it severely polarized the electorate to the left and to the right. Brüning was removed in May 1932, largely at the behest of Prussian army circles which now surrounded the president. One officer who was to have a profound impact on the course of events, culminating in Hitler's appointment in January 1933, was General von Schleicher. Schleicher was Minister of Defence from June 1932, and sought to impose a permanent authoritarian right-wing government, independent of the Reichstag and backed by the army – in effect a version of the pre-1918 constitution. He was the principal mover in Brüning's downfall and was the guiding spirit behind the von Papen cabinet of May–December 1932 (von Papen was Brüning's successor as Chancellor); he it was who was shortly to suggest that Hitler could be 'tamed' and the Nazi Party used on *his* (i.e. Schleicher's) terms, in particular by incorporating the Brownshirts (Hitler's bully boys) into a new expanded state army.

1932: crisis year

Schleicher secured the appointment of von Papen as Chancellor, a conservative Centre Party politician who, failing to get the support of the Reichstag, called an election for July 1932. His government, hoping to use the Nazis for their own purposes, lifted the ban on Hitler's Brownshirts on 15 June. Not content with that, on 20 July von Papen did even more of the Nazis' work for them by removing from power the Social Democratic government of Prussia by way of a *coup d'état*. No resistance was offered by the Prussian socialists – a tame ending to the party once feared by Bismarck. The results of the July election were sensational: the Nazi Party reached its highest level of popular support securing 13.8 million votes and more than a third of the Reichstag seats (230 out of 603). The July 1932 election was a turning-point because, thereafter, both radical ends of the political spectrum, the Nazis and the communists (who gained 89 seats) together held more than half the seats in the Reichstag. Permanent democratic paralysis now set in.

A remarkable feature of the unending crisis of 1932 was that, under the normal rules of democracy, Hitler as leader of the largest party should have been appointed Chancellor. But Hitler adamantly refused to join any government unless he was appointed Chancellor. This was acceptable neither to Hindenburg nor to his conservative aristocratic camarilla. Meanwhile, von Papen was working towards a policy of dismissing the Reichstag and refusing to stage new elections, as required. This would not only have laid the Weimar Constitution to rest, it would also have denied the Nazi Party its claim to substantial political power. Between July and

November 1932 no action was taken because von Papen was immediately voted down in the Reichstag and new elections called.

In November 1932, in the second election of the year, remarkable new trends revealed themselves. The SPD, Centre Party, Democrats *and* the Nazi Party all lost votes. The more respectable Nationalists, the People's Party and the Communist Party all gained ground. As well as losing 2 million votes and 34 seats, Hitler also saw substantial losses for the Nazi Party in Thuringia in December 1932. What seemed to be emerging was that the Nazi bubble had burst: the coalition of pro-Nazi constituencies was beginning to wane now that Hitler had shown himself unwilling to enter the government.

Von Papen proceeded with plans to dismiss the Reichstag without summoning elections; at this stage, he intended to use the army and police to put down any civil war or insurrection, and to disband political parties and all other quasi-political organizations. The possibility of civil war was repugnant both to the army and to Schleicher. Consequently, on 3 December, von Papen was dismissed, and Schleicher appointed in his place as Chancellor. Schleicher lasted less than a month, primarily because he tried to appease the left by courting both the trades unions and Gregor Strasser's proletarian wing of the Nazi Party. This tactic greatly alarmed the right, prompting Schleicher to move in an entirely contrary direction.

Hitler appointed Chancellor

Von Papen initiated retaliatory political manoeuvres to remove Schleicher and replace him with a von Papen–Hitler–Nationalist government. The appointment of this coalition was the only option President Hindenburg was able to accept, given that the alternative was dissolution of the Reichstag and rule by state of emergency. On 30 January 1933, Hitler was appointed Chancellor. Von Papen became Vice-Chancellor and there were eight other conservatives, including the Nationalist leader Alfred Hugenburg, and two other Nazis in the cabinet. *But*, it is important to note that Hitler's cabinet was a presidential cabinet, not a Reichstag government – he could never have formed a government with a majority of the Reichstag, since together they commanded only 42 per cent of the vote.

Conclusion

Three major themes emerge from the process that culminated in the events of 1933. Firstly, the Weimar system had failed prior to, and independently of, the success of the Nazi Party. Secondly, the Weimar system was consciously sabotaged by conservative pre-Weimar elites. Lastly and most astonishingly, even though he led the largest party in the Reichstag, Hitler could never have come to power by conventional means; he could never have formed a proper parliamentary government with the support of the majority of the Reichstag deputies. Hitler assumed the reins of government only with the assistance of the old conservative elites, who naively continued to believe that Hitler would pay them deference. Electorally, the constellation of pro-Nazi voters was already dissolving by late 1932. What gave Hitler his break was the colossal miscalculation that Hitler could, as a junior politician, be tamed and used by the Establishment.

Meanwhile, the Jewish question – so central to Hitler's own world view – was, both to his new political partners and to most other Germans, a largely peripheral concern. What followed, therefore, is all the more puzzling and alarming, a terrifying indictment of the power of human indifference and passivity.

Part 2

The Holocaust: A History

CHAPTER 5

Nazi Germany, 1933–8: Anti-Jewish Policy and Legislation

> The broad mass of a nation will more easily fall victim to a
> big lie than to a small one.
>
> Adolf Hitler, *Mein Kampf*

Introduction

When Hitler came to power in January 1933, no one could
reasonably have anticipated the outcome: that those political
and economic forces which had propelled him into government,
in the belief that he would be little more than a puppet, would
be utterly unable to contain him; that, after rebuilding
Germany's economy and shattered national pride, he would
plunge his country and indeed much of the rest of the world
into a war that would cost over 50 million lives and radically
change the political shape of Europe.

Hitler's obsessive preoccupation with the 'Jewish question'
was, and remained right up to the last moments of his life,
absolutely central to his view of the world. Yet it would be quite
wrong to suppose that he regularly and *explicitly* revealed the
extent of his hatred for the Jews – including his fantasies
about their total elimination – to the German people. Hitler
was even advised that his anti-Jewish philosophy was too
bizarre and too extreme ever to be fully comprehended or
tolerated by ordinary Germans.

It would also be quite incorrect to imagine that, from the
moment Hitler assumed the reins of power, he launched a
genocidal policy against the Jews aimed at their total

annihilation. In fact, the 'war against the Jews', was a multi-dimensional, considered process, embracing different tactics and distinct phases: it involved their gradual exclusion from German – and, later on, from occupied European – society by legislation, social pressure and intimidation; it encompassed the partial and eventually wholesale confiscation of property, forced emigration (providing, that is, that other countries were willing to accept them) and constant public humiliation; and it culminated in internment and, finally, in extermination. These policies were by no means coherent, consistent or without contradiction. And they were certainly neither predictable nor inevitable.

The murder of approximately 6 million European Jews did not happen overnight. Nor were there clear signs of its imminence that might have been visible to Jews, Germans and others at the time. Only those employing the luxurious logic of hindsight can say that 'the writing was on the wall' for all who wished to see it.

Intention versus improvisation

One of the major questions that have exercised the minds of historians of the Holocaust has been whether Hitler always intended to kill the Jews of Germany and later of Europe. If so, did the policy always match the intent? Or, on the contrary, was this policy of industrialized extermination essentially improvised? Was it determined at a much later date in accordance with the logistical and bureaucratic rationale of those operating within the context of a world war, in which Germany had gained, or seemed on the point of gaining, possession of literally millions of unwanted Jews? (For a consideration of the brutalizing context of the Second World War, see Chapter 7.)

It is possible to argue that in Hitler's ideal world no place for Jews could ever have been found and that since the First World War – or even earlier – he had dreamed of a 'purified' planet in which no Jew existed. Yet, when the historical evidence is examined, it becomes apparent that the chief thrust of Nazi governmental policy from 1933 to 1938 was to wage a legal war of attrition against the Jews. The objective was to invade the Jewish economy, to push the Jews out of the German economy and to deprive them of every opportunity and any possibility of participating in German national, civic and cultural life. In short, life was to be made so unendurable that the Jews would 'voluntarily' leave the country. It was arguably only the reluctance of other countries to receive Jewish refugees that would lead to their ultimate imprisonment in Hitler's European fortress in conditions of almost total isolation, powerlessness and choicelessness.

The Holocaust was, in the final analysis, the product of a deliberate genocidal plan drawn up by the legally established government of a country that was considered to be in the vanguard of European civilization and cultural progress. This plan was the logical, if highly improbable, extension of an ideology that was both racist and antisemitic, that had been in the public domain for many decades and which had slowly come to condition many Germans and other peoples in Nazi-dominated Europe – both conquered and allied – to regard the Jews as something less than (or other than) human.

Jews, who in the full-blooded Nazi ideology were considered unimprovably evil – an 'anti-race' – were ultimately to be the sole targets of a policy of *comprehensive* annihilation. Several million others (according to the most reliable estimates, approximately 5.5 million) – Slavs, gypsies, homosexuals, Jehovah's Witnesses, mental defectives, socialists, communists and others – who were described variously as enemies of the German state or as social or racial 'inferiors' would also be murdered, in equally horrible circumstances. But in each of these cases there was no intention – at least no recorded intention – to kill *all* of them. Whether or not Hitler and his entourage would have ended up treating gypsies and other groups in exactly the same vein as Jews, had they enjoyed the time and had they won the war, is an interesting, if depressing, hypothetical question. But there is no evidence on which to base an answer.

State-sponsored ideological slaughter

The production-line murder of 6 million Jews would be painstakingly designed and systematically implemented with all the legal, technological, bureaucratic and propagandist means available to the German state. Ultimately, the destruction of the Jews would be so intrinsically desired by the Nazi state that even when it was clear to all but the most fanatical and self-deluded that Germany was heading, inescapably, for military defeat, her anti-Jewish policy would be carried out with even more rigour and determination. What is even more remarkable and noteworthy is that this policy continued to be enacted with ruthless efficiency even though it often worked directly against the German war interest. It is, therefore, possible to assert with some assurance that Hitler's murderous campaign against the Jews was a *separate* ideological struggle from that which he was conducting against the armies of Great Britain, the Soviet Union and the USA. In other words, the Holocaust cannot be explained merely as a by-product of the Second World War or as a consequence of the brutalization of the German populace at a time of national emergency. The path to the death camps had been prepared many years before the outbreak of that war.

The Holocaust would only be made possible because of the active participation or passive compliance of many groups and individuals, first within Germany, then in Austria and later in other countries under Nazi occupation or sway. Worldwide forces that might have acted to prevent the implementation of this horrific plan were either inadequate, slow to act, under-informed, disbelieving, or downright unwilling to adjust their priorities in order to save Jewish lives.

Taking an overview of 1,600 years of Jewish history in Christian Europe, the historian Raul Hilberg, in his monumental and trailblazing work, *The Destruction of the European Jews*, outlined the development of anti-Jewish measures in the following way:

> Since the fourth century after Christ, there have been three anti-Jewish policies: conversion, expulsion and annihilation. The second appeared as an alternative to the first, and the third emerged as an alternative to the second.[1]

In this chapter we shall see that the Nazis were uninterested in converting Jews to Christianity, because they viewed the Jews in purely racial terms and because Nazism was in most important respects a post-Christian (anti-Christian?) ideology. In order to 'remove' Jews they concentrated initially on a policy of exclusion and emigration. When they were confronted by the reality of a total war which encompassed parts of Europe – especially Eastern Europe (including the Soviet Union after June 1941) – in which millions of Jews would be 'acquired' by their expansionist empire, they decided that emigration was no longer a feasible solution to their 'Jewish problem'. It was then that they produced the third and, in all of human history, quite unprecedented anti-Jewish policy.

Nazi policies towards the Jews, 1933–8

The Holocaust was the end product of a cumulative process of depersonalization (robbing the Jews of a sense of legal personality and individuality) and, later, of dehumanization. They were increasingly cut off from their German non-Jewish neighbours and their feelings of isolation and vulnerability were consequently intensified, hastening the collapse of their morale and inner resources. The growing distance – social, economic, legal and psychological – between Jew and Gentile helps explain how the Nazis could 'remove' a community virtually without protest from the rest of the population – a population which gradually felt, and was gradually persuaded, that it had precious little in common with the unfortunate Jews. The problems 'they' (the Jews) faced could be shrugged off as remote, as happening 'somewhere else', as 'nothing to do with us'.

As soon as they came to power, the Nazis launched a programme of subtle conditioning and indoctrination of their own people. This programme was masterminded by Joseph Goebbels, the Propaganda Minister, who controlled all the communications media – radio, newspapers, film, theatre and books. It also coincided with the beginnings of the Nazification of the educational system. All new teaching appointments to state schools would soon be confined to Nazi Party members; subjects such as history, German literature and biology were revamped in accordance with Nazi ideology, particularly its racial components; and there was a growing emphasis on the glorification of militarism and the strengthening of a regenerated Germany. As the Reich Minister of Science, Education and Popular Culture, Bernhard Rust, put it: 'The whole function of education is to create Nazis.'

Hitler's own educational philosophy was made abundantly clear in *Mein Kampf*:

> The whole organization of education and training which the People's State is to build up must take as its crowning task the work of instilling into the hearts and brains of the youth entrusted to it the racial instinct and understanding of the racial idea. No boy or girl must leave school without having attained a clear insight into the meaning of racial purity and the importance of maintaining the racial blood unadulterated.
>
> *Thus the first indispensable condition for the preservation of our race will have been established and thus the future cultural progress of our people will be assured.*[2]

The construction of a totalitarian state

Hitler's Nazi Party would establish its iron, mesmeric grip on the German people by combining totalitarian elements found in Stalin's Soviet system with the Fascist dictatorial model provided by Mussolini's Italy. When these ingredients were added to the Nazis' racial theory the result was a potent and apparently irresistible brew.

On his appointment as Chancellor Hitler now possessed all the advantages of state power to ensure decisive success in the fresh elections he immediately called for March 1933. The police came under the control of the two Nazi ministers – Göring had been made Minister of the Interior of Prussia, Frick the Reich Minister of the Interior. Göring purged the police of anti-Nazis, while 50,000 SS (*Schutzstaffeln* or Guard Troops) and SA (*Sturmabteiling* or Stormtroopers) men were engaged as auxiliary police and employed as a violent means of repressing left-wing opponents. They were also empowered to take over state governments should these fail to introduce the necessary measures to ensure public order. In this way, over the ensuing weeks, Hitler managed to secure the resignation of many local governments, replacing experienced politicians and personnel with amateur Nazi functionaries.

On 27 February 1933, the Reichstag was set on fire under mysterious circumstances (a Dutch leftist named van der Lubbe was later accused of arson). Amid hysterical and paranoid reactions to Nazi claims of an impending communist-led insurrection, President Hindenburg signed an emergency decree, 'For the Protection of the People and the State'. This decree went a considerable way towards removing all the fundamental rights of a free, democratic state: freedom of speech, freedom of property and the right to privacy. Throughout the country, thousands of political opponents were beaten up, intimidated and arrested. The radio network now presented Hitler in a favourable light.

The March election itself was a disappointment for Hitler, since it failed to give him the overwhelming mandate he sought from the German population. He gained only 43.9 per cent of the vote, but with the Nationalists gaining 8 per cent he now had a slim but overall majority in the Reichstag. This convinced Hitler that he must move even more swiftly away from the democratic process.

The Enabling Act, March 1933

On 23 March 1933 Hitler prevailed on the German parliament to pass the Enabling Act which gave the new government dictatorial powers. The Reichstag had met in an atmosphere of massive intimidation both inside and outside the parliament building, after many of the 81 Communist Party deputies had been arrested. The bill which was to give the Reich government full legislative and executive power for a period of four years – including the right to pass any laws needed to consolidate the 'National Revolution' – needed a two-thirds majority since it entailed constitutional change. With Hitler muttering threats about what would happen if the bill were not passed, the Enabling Act became law with the support of the Centre and liberal Parties. Only the socialists and communists refused to vote. It was a sad reflection on Weimar democracy that only 15 Catholic or middle-class deputies would have deprived Hitler of this key instrument in the introduction of Nazi rule. The Nazis would now be able to pass laws and decrees without the consent of parliament, even though this was strictly in violation of the Reich constitution. Thus, from the outset, the rule of law and standards of moral behaviour normally expected of democratically elected governments were openly discarded. Parliamentary authority had been virtually surrendered to the Nazis; perhaps this was because strong, charismatic and uncompromising leadership was still seen as a favourable alternative to the indecisive liberal and democratic coalitions which in the preceding decade had presided over mass unemployment, economic depression, social unrest and German 'humiliation'. The industrial, landowning and army interests persisted in their belief that the principal threat to law and order was represented by the political left and that Hitler – 'their man' – could be tamed and held in check once this storm had been ridden.

Hitler was thus given *carte blanche* to terrorize and neutralize all effective political opposition. On the same day as the Enabling Act was passed, the first concentration camp was opened at Dachau, near the city of Munich. At first it was intended as an internment and punishment centre for political adversaries of the regime, especially socialists and communists. Very soon Dachau and other camps like it were to become synonymous with systematic brutality, torture and the deprivation of human rights and dignity.

Initial measures against the Jews

The Nazi Party's 25-Point Programme of 1920 had declared:

> Point 4. Only nationals can be citizens of the State. Only persons of German blood can be nationals, regardless of religious affiliation. No Jew can therefore be a German national....
>
> Point 7. ... If it is not possible to maintain the entire population of the State, then foreign nationals (non-citizens) are to be expelled from the Reich.[3]

There were early attempts to popularize this anti-Jewish manifesto by encouraging the general population to become involved in acts of boycott, intimidation and violence. This was not especially successful at first, since non-party members themselves often had to be bullied into participation. Generally speaking, the mass of ordinary Germans were hugely indifferent, rather than actively hostile, to the Jews in their midst. This indifference, however, was to contribute decisively to the eventual fate of the Jews.

Legislation proved a far more effective means of shutting the Jews out of German society. The legal onslaught against the

Jews can be divided roughly into three stages. The first, from April 1933 to the middle of 1935, was characterized by laws aimed at preventing Jews from taking any part in German professional and cultural life, especially in the public sector. The second phase started with the passing of the Nuremberg Laws in September 1935. These laws officially defined the Jews in purely racial terms (according to the number of Jewish grandparents they had) and, at a single stroke, stripped them of their citizenship. The third phase began in 1938 when Jewish communities were placed under the direct authority of the Gestapo (Security Police) and all Jews were obliged to register their property and assets – both at home and abroad – as a prelude to confiscation.

The anti-Jewish measures taken between 1933 and 1935 include the following:

1 April 1933.   The Nazis proclaimed a boycott against Jewish shops, businesses and professional services. Stormtroopers took up positions as pickets in front of Jewish-owned stores, holding placards which read: 'Don't buy from Jews!' They daubed anti-Jewish slogans on the windows of Jewish businesses and attacked their clients verbally and, on occasions, physically. Although this economic and psychological assault on the Jewish community, launched very early in the life of the regime, was effective in frightening and demoralizing its bewildered victims, it was a comparative failure. The conviction that Jews were naturally fit only for subordination and degradation had not yet penetrated the German consciousness. There were, in addition, still enough Germans employed in Jewish-owned stores who insisted on going to work in defiance of the boycott. Moreover, at this stage Jews still had friends – many of them former comrades-in-arms from the First World War who were not yet ready to abandon them. Most significantly, the boycott had not been officially instigated by the government; it had been promoted by the party but lacked the full authority and force of law. Nevertheless, Goebbels was able to place the following entry in his diary that day:

> I drive along the ... street in order to observe the situation. All Jews' businesses are closed. SA men are posted outside the entrances. The public has everywhere proclaimed its solidarity. Discipline is exemplary. An imposing performance![4]

An early Jewish reaction

One remarkable Jewish response to the boycott was a stirring and defiant call for Jewish solidarity from Robert Weltsch, editor of a Zionist periodical. In his article he urged the renewal of Jewish national and cultural pride in the face of Nazi hostility. He did not, of course, anticipate the calamity that was soon to overwhelm European Jewry. The following extract is taken from his editorial, 'Wear the Yellow Badge with Pride!', a title which became a slogan of German Jewry, especially its youth.

The first of April, 1933, will remain an important date not only in the history of German Jewry, but in that of the entire Jewish people. For the events of the boycott day have not only their political and economic but their moral and spiritual aspects....

We live in a new time. A whole world of ideals and concepts has crashed to ruin. That may give pain to many. But none will be able to sustain himself from now on who shirks realities. We are in the midst of a complete transformation of our intellectual and political, social and economic life. Our gravest concern is this: how does Jewry react?

The first of April, 1933, can be a day of Jewish awakening and Jewish rebirth. If the Jews will it so! If the Jews have the inner maturity and magnanimity. If the Jews are not as their enemies represent them. Embattled Jewry must affirm itself....

In the midst of all the bitterness that fills us at the reading of the National-Socialist calls to boycott our people and at the false accusations contained therein, for one regulation we are not ungrateful to the boycott committee, which states in paragraph three: 'It goes without saying that we mean business concerns owned by members of the Jewish race. We are not concerned with religion. Jews who have submitted to Catholic or Protestant baptism or have seceded from their religious community remain Jews within the meaning of the order.'

That is a sound reminder to all *our* traitors. He who slinks away from his community in order to improve his personal position shall not earn the reward of his treason. In this attitude towards our renegades there may be the faint beginning of a clarification. The Jew who denies his Judaism is no better a citizen than he who affirms it uprightly. To be a renegade is shameful enough. So long as the world seemed to reward this shame it seemed profitable. The profit is swept away. The Jew is rendered recognizable as such. He wears the yellow badge.

That the boycott committee ordered shields 'showing on a

black background a yellow spot to be attached to the shops in question,' is a terrific symbol. For this shield was supposed to brand us and to render us contemptible in men's eyes. Very well. *We accept the shield and shall make of it a badge of honour.*[5]

Exclusion by legislation

7 April 1933. The Nazis introduced their first anti-Jewish law, the Restoration of the Professional Civil Service Act, providing for the arbitrary dismissal from Civil Service positions of 'non-Aryans' and opponents of the regime. This measure affected scientists, school and university teachers and all government employees. A 'non-Aryan' who fell liable to the terms of this regulation was defined (in a decree passed four days later) as anyone with one Jewish parent or grandparent – a purely racial definition. Various protests, including that from President Hindenburg, resulted in exceptions being made for war veterans and their close relatives. On that same day another law was passed prohibiting 'non-Aryans' from practising law. Thereafter, documentary 'proof' of 'Aryan' pedigree had to be furnished by all applicants to the Civil Service and, in time, in the case of all public appointments.

Over the subsequent months laws were passed barring 'non-Aryans' from practising as doctors and dentists in state-run hospitals and institutions; they were also forbidden to act as judges, jurors, tax consultants, publishers or editors. Jews, it seemed, were to be eliminated occupationally from the public arena.

25 April 1933. The Law against the Overcrowding of German Schools and Institutions of Higher Learning established the principle of a quota (upper limit) for the admission of 'non-Aryan' students. Later that same day a special decree fixed this limit at 1.5 per cent. From that time onwards Jews would be induced to educate their children in their own schools – part of a de-Germanization (and re-Judaization) strategy for Jews. In effect, the Nazis were imposing on the Jews a form of cultural segregation – in South Africa it is known as apartheid (separate development) – which represented a complete reversal of the integrationist trends of German–Jewish history during the previous 150 years.

In the final period of the Weimar Republic Nazi anti-Jewish

rhetoric had been comparatively restrained, preferring to emphasize the struggle against Marxist–Bolshevist forces as more likely to win middle-class and conservative votes. Now, however, Hitler's racial and anti-semitic philosophy could be given a higher profile. The anti-Jewish enactments unquestionably aroused disquiet and bewilderment among sections of the German population, but they also enjoyed an increasing measure of popular support.

10 May 1933. This day saw the obscene expression of a campaign of harassment against disaffected writers, academics and intellectuals. Goebbels had organized a public burning of 'un-German literature' which was carried out by student leaders in Berlin. Consigned to the flames was any book written or published by a Jew, living or dead, or any book which dealt sympathetically with a Jew or Jewish theme. Many other works – plays, poetry, novels and historical and philosophical tracts – whose liberal and humanistic ideas offended the regime, were consumed in this grotesque ritual. One of the authors whose work was destroyed in this fashion was the nineteenth-century German-Jewish poet, Heinrich Heine. One of his lines, composed with chilling and prophetic irony, reads: *'Those who begin by burning books end by burning people.'*[6]

14 July 1933. A law was passed providing for the cancellation of citizenship of any German who had been naturalized after September 1918. This enactment principally targeted the 100,000 Jews who had taken refuge in Germany from the postwar pogroms in eastern Europe (see Chapter 3).

29 September 1933. The Reich Chamber of Culture was established bringing all the country's cultural activities under central party control. One of its objectives was to ensure that 'non-Aryans' would be quite unable to participate in German artistic, literary and cultural life. On the same day a decree was passed restricting inheritance of farms solely to 'Aryans' who were obliged to 'prove' that they possessed no Jewish blood as far back as the year 1800.

Other measures introduced before the comprehensive Nuremberg Laws of September 1935 were essentially aimed at widening the social and psychological gulf between Germans and Jews. For example, Jews were forbidden to enter public swimming pools, to own dogs, to visit health spas, or to go into public parks.

21 May 1935. To underline just how unfit Jews were to serve the Fatherland, the Defence Law was passed making all 'non-Aryans' ineligible for military service. Although this may seem as much of a blessing as a penalty, this measure thoroughly demoralized those Jews who continued to feel, on many levels, intensely patriotic and inescapably German. They had tried to preserve their own sanity by drawing a distinction between the Germany they still loved and the Nazi regime they hoped was a passing nightmare. This was especially true of those German Jews who had been decorated during the First World War; it was among this group that the suicide rate rose to unprecedentedly high levels during the first two years of Hitler's reign.

The cordoning off of German Jews was elevated to new heights of legal absurdity and cruelty in September 1935 with the passing of the Nuremberg Laws. Until then the legislation had been extremely damaging and discriminatory, but measures were now to be taken which mirrored more clearly the racist objectives of National Socialism.

The Nuremberg Laws

15 September 1935. At the Reichstag's annual Nazi Party Congress, convened at Nuremberg, two momentous laws were passed. The first stripped all Jews of their citizenship, putting an end to Jewish emancipation. The second outlawed marriage and sexual relations between Jews and those of 'German or related blood'. An implementing decree of 14 November 1935 defined more precisely the terms 'Jew' (anyone with three or more Jewish grandparents), 'Aryan' and *Mischling* (one of mixed parentage). Christians whose parents or grandparents were Jewish could now be considered as full Jews for all purposes. The Nuremberg Laws effectively institutionalized Nazi racism and served as the basis for many further anti-Jewish regulations and pronouncements. According to the London *Times* (17 November): 'Nothing like the complete disinheritance and segregation of Jewish citizens now announced has been heard since medieval times.' (Excerpts from the two Nuremberg Laws of 15 September 1935 and the Implementing Decree of 14 November 1935 can be found in Appendix E.)

The party's image

Against a background of steady economic and industrial expansion, massive rearmament and the consequent radical reduction in the level of unemployment, Nazi propaganda developed the image of a party and a Germany that were benevolent, innovative, patriotic and muscular. The Nazi Party appeared genuinely to combine the interests of middle- and lower middle-class Germans with those of powerful landowners and industrial magnates. The policy of controlled terror was directed against relatively few people – its impact was not felt by the overwhelming majority. And, in any case, their lives were immeasurably improved. If progress could only be achieved at the expense of a minority – those whom their leaders described as the enemies of the Reich – then so be it!

The party's intense hostility towards communists and Jews was balanced by its warm and heartening embrace of the ordinary German: for every Jewish vice, so its propaganda went, there was a stout, respectable German virtue. This appeal to middle-class values is very evident in the following 'upright' piece which was widely disseminated by the Nazis. It was written by one of their most revered mentors, Theodor Fritsch, the late-nineteenth-century antisemitic politician. Today it is sometimes referred to as 'The Racists' Ten Commandments':

1. Be proud of being a German and strive earnestly and steadily to practise the inherited virtues of our people – courage, faithfulness and veracity – and to inspire and develop these in your children.
2. Thou shalt know that thou, together with all thy fellow Germans, regardless of faith or creed, hast a common implacable foe. His name is Jew.
3. Thou shalt keep thy blood pure. Consider it a crime to soil the noble Aryan breed of thy people by mingling it with the Jewish breed. For thou must know that Jewish blood is

everlasting, putting the Jewish stamp on body and soul unto the farthest generations.

4. Thou shalt be helpful to thy fellow German and further him in all matters not counter to the German conscience, the more so if he be pressed by the Jew. Thou shalt at once take into court any offence or crime committed by the Jew in deed, word or letter, that comes to thy knowledge, lest the Jew abuse the laws of our country with impunity.

5. Thou shalt have no social intercourse with the Jew. Avoid all contact and community with the Jew and keep him away from thyself and thy family, especially thy daughters, lest they suffer injury of body and soul.

6. Thou shalt have no business relations with the Jews. Never choose a Jew as a business partner, nor borrow nor buy from him, and keep your wife, too, from doing so. Thou shalt sell nothing to him, nor use him as an agent in thy transactions, that thou mayest remain free and not become slave unto the Jew nor help increase his money, which is the power by which he enslaves our people.

7. Thou shalt drive the Jew from thy own breast and take no example from Jewish tricks and Jewish wiles, for thou shalt never match the Jew in trickery but forfeit thy honour and earn the contempt of thy fellow Germans and the punishment of the courts.

8. Thou shalt not entrust thy rights to a Jewish lawyer, nor thy children to a Jewish physician, nor thy children to a Jewish teacher lest thy honour, body and soul suffer harm.

9. Thou shalt not lend ear nor give credence to the Jew. Keep away all Jewish writings from thy German home and hearth lest their lingering poison may unnerve and corrupt thyself and thy family.

10. Thou shalt use no violence against the Jews because it is unworthy of thee and against the law. But if a Jew attacks thee, ward off his Semitic insolence with German wrath.[7]

Consolidation of the SS state

All other political parties and trade unions had been declared illegal. Upon Hindenburg's death in August 1934, Hitler had amalgamated the roles of party chief and head of state under the title of Führer (supreme leader). From that point on there was to be blind and unquestioning obedience. Little more than one month earlier, on 30 June 1934 – 'the Night of the Long Knives' – the assassination of Captain Ernst Röhm, the leader of the SA, together with many of his supporters, had paved the way for the expansion and strengthening of the SS.

The SS were originally considered Hitler's own elite guard. Under the leadership of Heinrich Himmler, the SS took over most of the police functions of the state, including those of the Gestapo (Secret Police); they were placed in charge of the concentration camps (and later the extermination camps); and they also developed several military units – the Waffen SS – which were intended to act as a model, epitomizing the ideals of National Socialism which they would instil into the rest of the German army. The size of the Waffen SS was limited to 5 per cent of the total German armed forces in order to preserve its unique and special qualities. Anyone who wanted to join the SS had to be able to 'prove' that he possessed no Jewish blood as far back as 1750.

The extent to which the SS was infused with the ideas of racial purity can be gauged from the following excerpt from a speech given by Himmler to a group of SS officers on 7 September 1940:

> I have had one aim in mind for the eleven years in which I have been Reichsführer SS: to create an Order of Pure Blood for the service of Germany. This order will go into action with unshakeable determination, without sparing itself, knowing that the heaviest losses will not weaken its vitality because it is continually renewing itself. I want to create an Order which will disseminate the idea of Nordic Blood so widely that we shall attract all the Nordic blood in the world to our cause, shall keep it from our opponents, shall make it so much a part of ourselves that never again – speaking now on the level of high politics – will Nordic blood fight against us in any quantity, on any scale. We must make it our own – the rest of the world must have no share in it.[8]

Of the manic racial ingredients in Nazism, a prominent American Jewish historian made these observations:

> Over and above everything else the Nazi programme demanded that Germany 'Aryanize' itself, guard itself from 'blood poisoning' by the 'Jewish race'. The doctrines of the nineteenth-century racists were swallowed whole and reasserted with unprecedented intensity. The lewd, lascivious and pornographic antisemitism which pictured the Jew lying in wait to ravish the naive, blonde Aryan maiden became one of the

most effective images in the Nazi racist arsenal. It was propagandized by Hitler and his colleagues, provided with pseudo-scientific rationale by Goebbels, theorized by [Alfred] Rosenberg and [Walter] Darré, and depicted graphically in cartoons, drawings and public posters (the Jew was invariably the bogeyman with a great hooked nose) by Julius Streicher, Hitler's specialist in incendiary journalism.[9]

The Nuremberg Laws had supplied the basis for an 'Aryanized' legal, social and political system. Yet until 1937 the Jews were still able to engage at some level in commerce and industry. Many Jews believed that, as long as they were in a position to make a positive contribution to the German economy, the Nazis would tolerate a measure of official commercial freedom. This optimism was given a boost when, in 1936, shortly before the Olympic Games were held in Berlin – with the eyes of the world even more firmly upon them – the Nazis relaxed the intensity of their anti-Jewish propaganda and some of the restrictions. Some Jews were even allowed to compete in the games themselves.

Towards the end of 1936, however, Germany began to make military preparations and her economy was placed on a war footing. At the same time the campaign to remove the Jews from German economic life began again in earnest and in 1937 the Nazis formally introduced a policy of 'Aryanization' of businesses. Jewish assets were 'transferred' to Aryans, especially to those associated with the party. These 'transfers', though maintaining the semblance of legality, were almost always compulsory, the prices paid being laughably small.

Jewish emigration – from 1933 to the start of 1938

During the first five years of Hitler's rule, approximately 150,000 of Germany's Jews had emigrated. Most had sought refuge in neighbouring countries, such as Holland, France, Belgium and Switzerland, but these countries were themselves bedevilled by economic depression and unemployment. Jewish would-be immigrants were often perceived either as unproductive drains on their dwindling resources or as sources of unwelcome competition with their own populations. Moreover, the Nazis' projection of anti-Jewish stereotypes had, without doubt, penetrated other parts of western Europe, antisemitism being by no means an exclusively German phenomenon.

Principally because of obstacles to their gaining admission to other European countries and to the United States, many German Jews now turned in desperation to British-controlled Palestine. During the first three years of Hitler's regime, the British government allowed virtually unrestricted access to Palestine, though not to Britain itself. This policy would change dramatically on the eve of the Second World War, when considerations of state rather than of humanitarianism would come to dominate British thinking.

At first, there was clearly a coincidence of interests – though not, of course, of motives – between the international Zionist movement, which wanted as many European Jews as possible to migrate to Palestine, and the Nazi authorities, who at that time wanted German, and later Austrian Jews to leave their sphere of influence. A 'transfer' agreement (*Ha'avara*) was concluded between Palestine-based Jewish organizations and the Nazi Economic Ministry. This arrangement made it possible for German Jews to move part of their capital to Palestine in the form of German goods, thus enabling many thousands of German Jews to emigrate to Palestine. The agreement itself met with intense opposition from certain Jewish bodies outside Germany, in particular from the World Jewish Congress (WJC), which had been established in 1936 expressly to coordinate a boycott of all German goods. The WJC argued that its work would be undermined by the continued operation of this 'transfer' arrangement which it claimed was inflicting damage on German Jewry's long-term interests.

Despite the high rate of emigration, at the start of 1938 well over two-thirds of German Jews remained in Germany. They had weathered the Nazi storm and simply refused to believe that matters could grow worse. In addition, it was becoming progressively more difficult to gain entrance to other countries. Western nations were alarmed at the prospect of opening their doors, not only to the Jews of Germany but to the much larger Jewish communities of countries such as Poland and Romania. The latters' antisemitic stance was so notorious that it was feared they might relish the opportunity to export their own Jews. Chaim Weizmann, who was to become the first President of the State of Israel in 1949, had said of this impasse:

There are in this part of the world [i.e Europe] six million people doomed to be pent up in places where they are not wanted, and for whom the world is divided into places where they cannot live and places where they cannot enter.[10]

In the face of Nazi persecution, discrimination and exclusion, the German Jewish community was forced to become increasingly self-reliant. A national Jewish body had been established under the inspirational leadership of Leo Baeck, the Chief Rabbi of Berlin. Its principal aims were to assist in the organization and financing of emigration and to make its own educational provisions for distressed Jewish children, many of whom had been unable to cope with the harassment of party-appointed teachers or to withstand the taunts of fellow pupils in the general school system. Independent Jewish artistic and cultural associations were set up to provide employment for Jewish musicians and other artists who had been barred from public performance. Needless to say, the Jews of Germany were being slowly condemned to impoverishment, despair and humiliation.

CHAPTER 6

Nazi Europe, 1938–41: From *Kristallnacht* to Ghettoization in the East

The year 1938 was to prove a critical turning-point in terms of both Hitler's foreign and domestic policies. To most Germans and outsiders everything must have seemed to be going exactly as planned. There was every reason for Hitler to be satisfied. Germany's economy had been catapulted into a dynamic phase that, only five years earlier, would have been inconceivable. After the exceptionally high levels of unemployment in the early 1930s, full employment had virtually been restored.

Germany had already succeeded in getting away with several flagrant and menacing violations of the terms and spirit of the Treaty of Versailles: in October 1933 Hitler had withdrawn Germany from the League of Nations, which had been established to safeguard international peace – a contemptuous, inflammatory act which won the approval of over 90 per cent of the German people who voted in a plebiscite. Germany had engaged, almost unchallenged, in a massive rearmament programme; in May 1936 her army had re-entered the demilitarized Rhineland; and in 1937 both Germany and Italy had given considerable military support to General Franco's Fascist forces in the Spanish Civil War. These defiant and provocative attempts to overturn the humiliating First World War Settlement were seen by many Germans as evidence of the resurrection of their national and military pride. But they did not want war.

Hitler might have stopped there, had he been content merely

with achieving a Fascist state along the lines of Mussolini's Italy. But he wanted to go beyond this and to keep the German nation in a state of constant – if not permanent – revolution, working towards his racial and expansionist pan-German objectives.

The needs of the German people were, for the most part, being fulfilled. They were happy and generally content and, though many neither welcomed nor appreciated it, they were prepared to put up with the constant exposure to self-congratulatory government propaganda and to ritualized ideological hectoring. Very few understood the totalitarian context in which they found themselves. Still fewer had even the faintest notions of the cataclysmic events that would unfold during the next seven years.

Hitler believed that stagnation, complacency and decay were to be avoided at all costs. What followed, therefore, was a renewal and intensification of his anti-Jewish policy, which, in his mental world, was utterly central to the Nazification of German social, political and educational reality.

Nazi takeover of Austria

On 12 March 1938 Hitler's troops had advanced into Austria (the Anschluss). This invasion, the first major step in Hitler's plan to reunite all peoples of Germanic language, culture and 'race', met with hardly any opposition, either from within Austria or from other countries. Germany's Foreign Minister, Ribbentrop, had assured Berlin by telephone from London of Britain's unwillingness to intervene. Originally it had been Hitler's intention merely to proclaim a union between the two countries, but he and his troops were given such a rapturous welcome in Vienna that he decided to go further and to annex Austria. This involved the complete absorption of his own native country into Germany – an act which received an almost unanimous vote of approval from the citizens of Austria.

The takeover of Austria brought a further 180,000 Jews into Hitler's direct sphere of influence. In many respects they had a more traumatic experience than their German counterparts, since they were immediately subjected to the full rigour of Germany's social and legal discrimination. The public humiliation of the Jews of Vienna was openly reported in the world's press, including alarming photographs of prominent Jews cleaning the city's pavements with nail-brushes to the clear satisfaction and amusement of jeering Austrian onlookers. A central Office of Emigration was swiftly established in Vienna, under the leadership of Adolph Eichmann, a rising member of the SS, in order to hasten and systematize the departure of Austrian Jews from German-controlled territory. In effect 'voluntary emigration' gradually became little more than bureaucratic expulsion. By the outbreak of the Second World War it is estimated that approximately 110,000 Jews had left Austria. As a consequence of his successful 'experiment' in Vienna, Eichmann acquired a reputation for expertise in Jewish affairs and would later be made Head of the Jewish Section in the Reich Security Main Office.

Intensification of anti-Jewish measures

On 26 April 1938 the Decree Concerning the Reporting of Jewish Property was promulgated, ordering all Jews to register the value of their entire domestic and foreign property by 30 June of that year. This was the first in a series of regulations that would end in the expropriation of all Jewish property. In July those Jewish doctors still practising in the private sector had their licences revoked. On 17 August a law was passed forbidding Jews to take 'Aryan' names; the forbidden names were contained on published lists. In addition, all Jewish males were forced to adopt the extra name of Israel and all women that of Sarah. This regulation made it much easier to identify Jews in official documents and passports; it also anticipated the compulsory wearing throughout Nazi-occupied Europe of armbands and badges bearing the Star of David. In September it became impossible for any Jewish lawyer to practise his profession.

All of these measures may seem inconsequential compared with what was to follow, but their combined effect was to prove indispensable to the creation of a climate of social, occupational and psychological isolation that would make possible the 'Final Solution'.

The Evian Conference – an opportunity lost?

An international event which undoubtedly contributed to the circumstances and thinking that led to the Holocaust of 1941–5 was a conference held at Evian, France, in July 1938 (more than one commentator has pointed out that Evian is 'naive' spelt backwards). Though they did not and could not know it at the time, the United States, Great Britain and other Western democracies probably had it in their power to save Europe's beleaguered and doomed Jewish communities.

The Evian Conference, convened at the request of President Franklin D. Roosevelt, was attended by the representatives of 32 governments. They included 20 Latin American republics, Great Britain, France, Belgium, Switzerland, Sweden, Norway, the Netherlands, Denmark, Canada, Australia, New Zealand, South Africa and the United States. The conference was held ostensibly to address the plight of Jewish refugees from persecution. However, as an internal American State Department memorandum declared, the purpose of this American initiative was 'to get out in front [of liberal opinion] and attempt to guide the pressure [to increase Jewish immigration] primarily with a view to forestalling attempts to have the immigration laws liberalized'.[1] As Arthur Morse reflected:

> On this noble note the Evian Conference was born. It would be months in planning, would silence the critics of apathy and, if all worked well, would divert refugees from the United States to the other co-operating nations.[2]

Hitler responded tellingly to news of the proposed conference. In his speech at Königsberg he exclaimed:

> I can only hope and expect that the other world, which has such deep sympathy for these criminals, will at least be generous enough to convert this sympathy into practical aid. We, on our part, are ready to put all these criminals at the disposal of these countries, for all I care, even on luxury ships.[3]

In the event, both the United States and Britain rejected the possibility of taking in substantial numbers of Jews. The United States' unwillingness to alter its own immigration policy sent an unmistakable message to the other nations assembled at Evian. They, too, would be justified in closing their doors. According to Helen Fein, 'Interested and disinterested spectators alike saw the Evian Conference as an exercise in Anglo-American collaborative hypocrisy.'[4]

Holland and Denmark, both soon to be occupied by the Nazis, were the only European countries to agree to a limited increase in the number of refugees. The Dominican Republic in Central America also agreed to allow the entry of 100,000 immigrants, though this offer – essentially a piece of bombastic rhetoric – came to nothing.

It was not only the refusal by most of the participants at Evian to relax their immigration restrictions that encouraged Hitler in his treatment of the Jews. The Australian delegate informed the conference that his country had no racial problem and had no desire to import one, while the Canadian representative was reported to have said of the number of Jews his country would accept: 'None is too many!' The British representative at Evian, Lord Winterton, subsequently informed the cabinet that the Americans 'had wanted [to include] some clause of a denunciatory character towards the German government, but the British delegation under instructions from the Secretary of State for Foreign Affairs, have resisted this successfully'.[5]

Even more gratuitous support was given to Hitler by a memorandum drafted by the Evian Committee and sent to the German Foreign Office in October 1938. The memorandum stated that none of the nations gathered at Evian challenged the right of the German government to introduce measures affecting its own subjects, because such rights fell only within the province of state sovereignty. This memorandum, it should be noted, preceded *Kristallnacht* (see below, pp.141–2) by only one month.

The prevailing mood of appeasement is not the only explanation for the reluctance of certain governments to render assistance. For instance, what is one to make of the following statement attributed to Roger Makins of the British Foreign Office: 'The pitiful condition to which German Jews will be reduced will not make them desirable immigrants.'?[6]

The one practical achievement of the Evian Conference was to set up the Intergovernmental Committee on Refugees

(IGCR) which was to negotiate the release of Jews directly with the Nazi government. However, the protracted negotiations – often concerning how much of the emigrants' property the Nazis could extort – and the impossibility of finding countries prepared to absorb large numbers of Jews, meant that the IGCR's efforts were largely ineffectual.

The legacy of Evian

The Evian Conference, in failing to ease the rigorous immigration restrictions on German and Austrian Jewry, not only helped to incarcerate them within Nazi-controlled borders but – much more crucially – may have triggered a change in Nazi policy towards their Jewish subjects. The 'removal' of Jews from Germanic life, it was becoming increasingly apparent, could no longer be accomplished through a policy of exporting Jews, since, as Goebbels is reported to have put it, 'Nobody wants the scum!'

In effect, the Evian Conference may have justified and reinforced Nazi anti-Jewish ideology and helped move it on towards its monstrous climax – the decision to implement the 'Final Solution'. Certainly, the eventual policy of comprehensive annihilation, enacted in the period after the Nazi invasion of the Soviet Union of June 1941, would represent a marked change of direction from the policy that had characterized Nazi treatment of Jews in the period 1933–8. The lessons of Evian, as learnt by the Nazi leadership, may well have been decisive in altering Hitler's policy thinking on the Jewish question.

In exploring the link between Evian and Nazi anti-Jewish policy, we are certainly in the realm of unintended consequences. No one should accuse the governments involved of *direct* moral responsibility for the Holocaust, which in 1938 was an unimaginable crime. Nevertheless, there is more than a modicum of truth in Helen Fein's verdict: 'The problem in the United States and Great Britain was not inadequate resources in relation to the numbers pleading for escape but a lack of commitment to life-saving.'[7]

In her autobiography, Golda Meir, Prime Minister of the State of Israel between 1969 and 1974, described her feelings as an observer at Evian:

Sitting there in that magnificent hall and listening to the delegates of 32 countries rise, each in turn, to explain how much they would have liked to take in substantial numbers of refugees and how unfortunate it was that they were not able to do so, was a terrible experience. I don't think that anyone who didn't live through it can understand what I felt at Evian – a mixture of sorrow, rage, frustration and horror.[8]

Hitler's foreign policy

For much of September the world anxiously awaited the outcome of the Czechoslovak crisis. In his most warlike tone, Hitler had demanded the surrender to Germany of parts of western Czechoslovakia (Sudetenland), where a preponderance of ethnic Germans lived. In response to claims that this would be his last territorial demand, Britain's Prime Minister, Neville Chamberlain, desperate to avert another European war, agreed to the sacrifice.

In reality, this did not merely represent the first stage in the disintegration of Czechoslovakia – once the western powers had adopted what Hitler saw as a weak-kneed and gullible stance. It also served as a preliminary exercise of military force and threats, in pursuit of his dreams of expansion within Europe and ultimately into the Soviet Union; for throughout eastern Europe, racial 'inferiors' could be subordinated to the 'Aryan' master race.

One legendary, if controversial historian, A.J.P. Taylor, pronounced his verdict as follows:

Eastern expansion was the primary purpose of his policy, if not his only one. … There was nothing original in this policy. The unique quality in Hitler was the gift of translating commonplace thoughts into action. He took seriously what was to others mere talk. The driving force in him was a terrifying literalism. Writers had been running down democracy for half a century. It took Hitler to create a totalitarian dictatorship. … Again there was nothing new in antisemitism. It had been 'the Socialism of fools' for many years. Little had followed from it. Seipel, Austrian chancellor in the 1920s, said of the antisemitism which his party preached but did not practise: 'Das ist für die Gasse.' (That is for the street – or perhaps the gutter). … Many Germans had qualms as one act of persecution succeeded another … But few knew how to protest. Everything which Hitler did against the Jews followed logically from the racial doctrines in which most Germans vaguely believed. It was the same with foreign policy. Not many Germans cared passionately and persistently whether Germany again dominated Europe. But they talked as if they did. Hitler took them at their word. He made the Germans live up to their professions, or down to them – much to their regret.[9]

It would, however, be an error to regard Hitler's racial policy as separate from his foreign policy. Hitler's gaze was fixed on the east precisely because he wanted to carry the racist-ideological war into those parts of Europe which he regarded as the 'natural' living space for those whose blood was superior. The peoples of the east, who were on the bottom rung of the ladder of humanity, were to be enslaved. As for the Jews, they were not located on the ladder of humanity at all. They were a non-race or anti-race, and their densest concentrations of population were in Poland and the western provinces of the Soviet Union. The German historian, Klaus Hildebrand, has expressed this connection most forcefully:

> Antisemitism in Nazi Germany was not, as in the rest of Europe, a mere instrument of social and political integration: rather it was the dominant motif and purpose of Hitler's foreign policy and that of the regime.[10]

It is hardly surprising, therefore, that at this time of triumphant muscle-flexing and open contempt for the pacifism of Britain and France, the Nazis should step up the war against the Jews within their own borders.

Kristallnacht

By the beginning of November 1938, the Nazi leadership was becoming increasingly aggressive and confident. Himmler told his SS officers that their Führer was on the point of creating the most powerful empire the world had ever known. Hitler informed the national press that Germany had to be psychologically prepared for war; they should, therefore, stop writing on the desirability of peace. It was against this background of intensive preparations for war that the Nazis launched an unprecedented nationwide pogrom against the Jews.

In October 1938, several thousand Jews of Polish origin who resided in Germany were brutally expelled *en masse*. They were taken to the border but refused entry by a Polish government which was already antagonistic to its own Jewish citizens. They were consequently obliged to set up a makeshift camp under the most primitive conditions in a narrow strip of no-man's land that lay between the two countries. Among the Jewish families abused in this fashion was a couple named Grynszpan, whose teenage son, Herschl, was then studying in Paris. When he learned the fate of his parents, he went to the German Embassy and, in his desire for vengeance, shot Ernst vom Rath, the Third Secretary.

Though there was at this juncture no agreement within the Nazi leadership on the advisability of an *open* physical onslaught against the Jews in Germany, certain key figures in the Nazi hierarchy – chief among whom was Goebbels – had clearly been waiting for an international incident of this sort. Without properly consulting his colleagues, Goebbels decided to use this 'foul' murder of a loyal German as the justification for 'punishing' the Jews. The Nazi propaganda machine whirred into action and Grynszpan's act was condemned as part of a world-wide Jewish conspiracy aimed at the heart of Germany – always an appealing and prominent theme in antisemitic stereotyping. Under the guise of a 'spontaneous' outburst of popular indignation, Goebbels put into operation a plan which had been meticulously prepared.

On the night of 9/10 November, in a plainly orchestrated campaign, throughout the length and breadth of Germany gangs of SA thugs, other party members and hooligans roamed the streets in an orgy of violence. The operation took the form of the destruction or burning of synagogues, the ransacking of Jewish shops and warehouses and the terrorization, beating up and murder of Jewish individuals. According to the Nazis' own reports, 91 Jews were killed, more than 7,000 Jewish-owned shops destroyed and approximately 300 synagogues razed to the ground. The Nazis were apparently impressed by all the broken glass from the synagogue windows and named this violent night *Kristallnacht* ('The Night of Shattered Glass').

Reactions to Kristallnacht

The reaction abroad was predictably outraged. And even among ordinary Germans, the general response was far from supportive of, and at worst indifferent towards, their own government's measures at this time. Certainly the Nazis never again perpetrated such unbridled and passionate violence against the Jews in full view of their own citizens. They realized that it would not be condoned. The principal lesson of *Kristallnacht* for the Nazis was that the level of antisemitism in Germany was sufficiently high to tolerate the anti-Jewish excesses of the government, but only if its actions were largely invisible. It offended many Germans to *see* the results of their elected government's policy.

The American consul in Leipzig described the event and the public reaction to it in these words:

> The shattering of shop windows, looting of stores and dwellings of Jews. ... was hailed subsequently in the Nazi press as a 'spontaneous wave of righteous indignation throughout Germany' ... So far as a high percentage of the German populace is concerned, a state of popular indignation that would lead to such excesses, can be considered as non-existent. On the contrary, in viewing the ruins and attendant measures employed, all of the local crowds observed were obviously benumbed over what had happened and aghast over the unprecedented fury of Nazi acts that had been or were taking place with bewildering rapidity. ...
>
> At 3 a.m. on 10 November 1938 was unleashed a barrage of Nazi ferocity as had had no equal hitherto in Germany, or very likely anywhere else in the world since savagery began. Jewish buildings were smashed into and contents demolished or looted. In one of the Jewish sections an eighteen-year-old boy was hurled from a three-storey window to land with both legs broken on a street littered with burning beds and other household furniture and effects from his family's and other apartments. ... It is reported ... that among domestic effects thrown out of a Jewish building, a small dog descended four flights on to a cluttered street with a broken spine.
>
> Three synagogues in Leipzig were fired simultaneously by incendiary bombs and all sacred objects and records desecrated or destroyed, in most cases hurled through the windows and burned in the streets. No attempts whatsoever were made to quench the fires, the activity of the fire brigade being confined to

playing water on adjoining buildings. ...

Tactics which closely approached the ghoulish took place at the Jewish cemetery where the temple was fired together with a building occupied by caretakers, tombstones uprooted and graves violated. Eyewitnesses considered reliable the report that ten corpses were left unburied at this cemetery for a whole week because all gravediggers and cemetery attendants had been arrested. ...

Having demolished dwellings and hurled most of the movable effects onto the streets, the insatiably sadistic perpetrators threw many of the trembling inmates into a small stream that flows through the Zoological Park, commanding horrified spectators to spit at them, defile them with mud and jeer at their plight. The latter incident has been repeatedly corroborated by German witnesses who were nauseated in telling the tale ... These tactics were carried out the entire morning of 10 November without police intervention and they were applied to men, women and children.[11]

Several members of the Nazi leadership were furious with Goebbels for 'jumping the gun', in particular Göring and, to a lesser extent, Himmler, whose SS had apparently not even been informed of the 'action'. It is even possible that Hitler, too, was unaware that the pogrom was to be unleashed that night (a view contradicted by the entry in Goebbels' own diary). Nevertheless, they sought to exploit the situation in order to quicken the process of confiscation of property and to terrorize the Jewish community into flight from Germany and Austria. In order to deal with this outbreak of 'lawlessness', Göring convened a conference of Nazi officials to determine what punishment should be meted out to the Jews for provoking the 'just wrath' of the German populace. It was decided to impose a punitive fine of 1 billion Reichsmarks – a sum equivalent to one-sixth of all the property owned by Jews in Germany – on the already impoverished, disenfranchised and thoroughly demoralized Jewish community.

Aftermath of Kristallnacht

Shortly after *Kristallnacht*, approximately 25,000 Jews were arrested (Himmler's SS now coming into their own) and sent to concentration camps at Sachsenhausen, Buchenwald and Dachau – the very first mass round-up and internment of Jews.

Within a few days new regulations were introduced finally eliminating Jews entirely from German economic life. All Jewish institutions and communal bodies were placed under the direct supervision of the Gestapo. And on 16 November the following decree was passed concerning Jewish pupils attending German schools:

> After the ruthless murder of Paris [i.e. Grynszpan's shooting of vom Rath], German teachers can no longer be expected to give instruction to Jewish pupils. It is also self-evident that German students find it unbearable to share classrooms with Jews.
>
> Racial segregation in schools has been carried out in general during the past years, but a small number of Jewish pupils have remained, who can no longer be permitted to attend schools together with German boys and girls. ... Reich Minister of Education Rust has decreed the following which goes into effect immediately.
>
> 1. Jews are forbidden to attend German schools. They are permitted to attend Jewish schools only ... all Jewish school boys and girls still attending German schools are to be dismissed immediately.
>
> 2. Paragraph 5 of The First Decree to the Reich Citizenship Law of November 14, 1935, specifies who is Jewish.
>
> 3. The regulation extends to all schools under the supervision of the Reich Minister of Education, including continuation schools.[12]

Although the Nazis persevered in their aim to put pressure on the Jews to emigrate, the policy was not consistent – an incoherence that has caused some confusion among historians. There was quite plainly a struggle taking place within the Nazi bureaucracy. On the one hand, there were those who wanted to humiliate the Jews and drain them of their resources – which would logically have made it much more difficult for them to gain admission into other countries – and, on the other, there were those who wished to allow Jews to sustain a 'reasonable' economic level, if only to give other countries a realistic incentive to receive them.

Nazi assessment of Jewish policy

How the Nazis themselves weighed up their Jewish policy and its central significance in the drama of 1938 can be assessed in a revealing memorandum from the German Foreign Ministry on 'The Jewish Question', dated 25 January 1939. (A lengthy extract from this memorandum can be found in Appendix F). Here the Jewish question is described as 'both the pre-condition and consequence of the events of 1938'. At this stage, the declared 'ultimate aim' of Germany's anti-Jewish policy is 'the emigration of all Jews living in German territory'. At the same time, there is the stated desire for a 'splintering' of the Jewish population overseas and not the concentration of Jews in their own homeland in Palestine, which might create a potential anti-German Jewish power base. For 'the realization that Jewry will always be the implacable enemy of the Third Reich forces us to the decision to prevent any strengthening of the Jewish position. A Jewish State would give world Jewry increased power in international law and relations.' Rather the aim was to scatter German and Austrian Jewry in an impoverished and degraded condition throughout as many lands as possible, so that other countries, discomforted by the influx of these unwanted and undesirable immigrants, would reach the natural conclusion that Nazi Germany's assessment of the Jewish menace was correct. As the memorandum concludes:

> The aim of this German policy is a future international solution of the Jewish question, dictated not by false pity for a 'Jewish religious minority that has been driven out' but by the mature realization by all nations of the nature of the danger that Jewry spells for the national character of the nations.[13]

Precisely when the Nazi leadership started seriously to contemplate a major change in policy towards the Jews – from one of forced emigration to a more drastic solution – is unclear. Certainly the Second World War would provide the geographical and psychological context – particularly on the eastern front – for a more brutal and 'rational' concentration and, finally, elimination of this 'enemy' of the Reich.

Hitler threatens 'annihilation' of Jews

Hitler's dream of a Europe 'purified' of Jews was expressed in a surprisingly open and threatening way in a speech he delivered to the German parliament on 30 January 1939:

In connection with the Jewish question I have this to say: it is a shameful spectacle to see how the whole democratic world is oozing sympathy for the poor tormented Jewish people, but remains hard-hearted and obdurate when it comes to helping them. ...

The world has sufficient space for settlements but we must once and for all get rid of the opinion that the Jewish race was only created by God for the purpose of being ... a parasite living on the body and the productive work of other nations. The Jewish race will have to adapt itself to sound constructive activity as other nations do, or sooner or later it will succumb to a crisis of an inconceivable magnitude.

One thing I should like to say on this day which may be memorable for others as well as for us Germans: in the course of my life I have very often been a prophet, and have usually been ridiculed for it. During the time of my struggle for power it was in the first instance the Jewish race which received my prophecies with laughter when I said that I would one day take over the leadership of the State, and with it that of the whole nation, and that I would then settle the whole Jewish problem. The laughter was uproarious, but I think that for some time now they have been laughing on the other side of their face. *TODAY I WILL ONCE MORE BE A PROPHET: IF THE INTERNATIONAL JEWISH FINANCIERS IN AND OUTSIDE EUROPE SHOULD SUCCEED IN PLUNGING THE NATIONS ONCE MORE INTO A WORLD WAR, THEN THE RESULT WILL NOT BE THE BOLSHEVIZATION OF THE EARTH, AND THUS THE VICTORY OF JEWRY, BUT THE ANNIHILATION OF THE JEWISH RACE IN EUROPE!*[14]

Few of those who listened to Hitler's chilling speech took him literally. The argument has been put forward by several scholars that, at this stage, Hitler himself had no idea how or when he would translate this threat into reality; some have even described this speech as 'pure rhetoric' intended to frighten pro-Jewish elements abroad into desisting from anti-German activities. The Jews of Germany and Austria were to be held as hostages, guaranteeing the good behaviour of the rest of the world.

Czechoslovakia dismembered

Hitler's contempt for that 'other world' was made plain on 15 March 1939 when, in fulfilment of the first stage of his plans for European conquest and in open violation of treaty agreements, German troops marched into Prague. Czechoslovakia, castigated in Nazi propaganda as an 'aircraft carrier for the Soviet Union', was dismembered and utterly crushed. The German Protectorate of Bohemia and Moravia was established and the 'independent' territory of Slovakia turned into a client-state. Tens of thousands of Czech Jews were exposed to immediate danger and, in the longer term, were destined for a horrible fate.

This act of aggression against Czechoslovakia – in clear breach of promises given earlier at Munich – began to swing public opinion in Britain against the policy of appeasement. Neville Chamberlain's government felt obliged to offer a formal guarantee of protection to Poland, which, as 1939 wore on, had increasingly become the main target of Hitler's warlike noises. This move by Britain was intended more as a strong deterrent to Hitler's continued eastward expansion than as a serious and determined commitment to wage war with Germany. But Hitler's conviction that Britain would not take up arms again so soon after the First World War, would prove a colossal miscalculation.

The course of the Second World War

On 1 September 1939 the Germans launched an invasion of Poland. Two days later the Second World War started when, much to Hitler's surprise, Britain and France, remaining faithful to their undertaking to Poland, declared war on Germany. Nevertheless, within three weeks Germany had completely crushed Poland in a Blitzkrieg, a lightning military campaign coordinated between air and ground forces.

Most significantly, one week before the assault on Poland, Hitler had negotiated a secret non-aggression treaty with Stalin (the Molotov–Ribbentrop Pact, so named after the respective Foreign Ministers of the Soviet Union and Nazi Germany). For the fourth time in its history Poland was divided between Russia and Germany. The western and northern districts were annexed to the Greater German Reich, the eastern provinces ceded to the Soviet Union, as previously agreed in the Molotov–Ribbentrop Pact. The central section around Lublin, Cracow and the Polish capital Warsaw, became a German colony, known as the 'General Government'.

After several months of military inactivity, the German armies conquered and occupied one country after another in rapid succession: Denmark and Norway (April 1940), Holland and Belgium (May 1940) and France (June 1940). Defeated France was split into two regions: the larger, northern territory was ruled directly by Germany; the southern sector was unoccupied and known as Vichy France. Germany's inability to overcome stout British resistance, despite massive and intimidating aerial bombardment, led Hitler to turn his attention to the east and to prepare for the invasion of the Soviet Union. This, in tandem with his objective of ridding Greater Germany of the Jews, had always been his major ideological objective, as he makes clear in *Mein Kampf.*

In the spring of 1941 the German army under General Rommel captured much of North Africa, while in the Balkans they overran both Greece and Yugoslavia. Everywhere the German army was triumphant and seemingly invincible. The countries of south-eastern Europe – Bulgaria, Romania and Hungary – became German satellites, while Italy was, at first, Germany's principal European ally.

With Britain alone holding out, Hitler then made a blunder that was to prove fatal to his ambitions for sustained European domination. On 22 June 1941, he tore up his treaty with Stalin and attacked the Soviet Union with all his might. By October his forces had reached the gates of Moscow and Leningrad and, by the end of 1941, had taken extensive areas of Russia's western empire, including most of the Ukraine. The freezing Russian winter, however, severely hampered the progress of his offensive.

On 7 December 1941, Germany's eastern ally, Japan, mounted a surprise – and, as it turned out, extremely rash – attack on the American naval base at Pearl Harbor in Hawaii. Thus the United States, with her enormous military and industrial capacity, entered the conflict, with both Germany and Italy declaring war on her on 11 December 1941.

Two turning-points in the conflict occurred in 1942/3, which heralded the start of a fundamental change in the course of the war to the advantage of the anti-Nazi Allies. In January 1943, Soviet troops counterattacked to break the siege of the city of Stalingrad and won a decisive victory over seemingly indestructible German forces. Similarly, in the North African desert, in a victory that was just as psychologically crucial, the British under the command of General Montgomery destroyed Rommel's army in the battle of El-Alamein.

By the end of November 1943, the Allies had taken possession of southern Italy. In 1944, while the Russians were advancing westwards into Poland and Romania, British and American troops landed on the beaches of Normandy (6 June – D-Day) and began the liberation of France and Belgium.

With Allied armies advancing into Germany on two fronts, the frenzied defence of Berlin became the backdrop for the eventual suicide of Adolf Hitler at the end of April 1945. Germany surrendered on 7 May. The war in the Pacific, however, continued and only after the dropping of two atomic bombs on Hiroshima and Nagasaki did the Japanese capitulate. They surrendered unconditionally on 14 August 1945. The Second World War was over.

A new racial order

Before the tide of the war turned in 1942, it appeared that the Nazis would achieve their dream of creating a 'New Order' in a vanquished Europe. This 'New Order' was perceived not only in terms of territorial conquests but of the introduction into all Nazi-dominated lands of a social, political and philosophical system that in large measure stemmed from Nazi racial ideology. This would guide their moral conduct during the war – particularly their treatment of subject peoples and prisoners of war in the east, where 'inferior' Slavs lived. From the moment the Nazis conquered Poland, the Polish population fell victim to an inhuman policy of mass deportation and the wholesale confiscation of property. Poles were thrown out of their homes and workplaces in order to accommodate German 'Aryans' who were resettled there. It is estimated that over 6 million Poles were despatched to Germany as slave-workers. The Polish spiritual and intellectual leadership was decimated not only by the Nazi invader but also, during the period 1939–41, by the Russians in the eastern sector.

Above all, in an atmosphere of general barbarity and isolation, the war in the east steadily created the physical and emotional conditions which would make possible the radicalization of the Nazis' anti-Jewish campaign. Extreme conditions demanded extreme solutions. The push into Poland and the progressive subjugation of surrounding societies would bring millions of 'unwanted' Jews into the Nazi sphere of influence. Moreover, the Nazis could turn to their advantage the deeply ingrained antisemitism endemic in the increasingly brutalized European populations already under their sway.

The war and the sheer numbers of Jews it encompassed made it almost impossible to rely on methods previously employed for their 'removal'. The period from 1939–41, therefore, represents a transition from the previous policy of forced migration to one of mass extermination (or 'Final Solution', as the Nazis themselves called it) which would be implemented after the invasion of the Soviet Union in the years 1941–5 (see Chapter 7).

The occupation of Poland

During the weeks of fighting and the initial period of Nazi occupation, tens of thousands of Polish Jews escaped to the Soviet sector of Poland in the east of the country. Thousands were then arrested and imprisoned by the Soviets – usually on the grounds that they were spies – and subsequently deported eastwards, away from the very areas that would later be invaded by the Nazis. This had the paradoxical and quite unintended effect of saving many Jewish lives.

However, the overwhelming majority, some 2 million, remained in the Nazi-held regions of Poland. There the constraints that had kept Nazi behaviour within reasonable limits in Germany itself gave way to a savagely repressive regime. A series of economic measures robbed the Jews of any means of livelihood. An unrelenting policy of humiliation, discrimination and persecution was introduced, accompanied frequently by physical abuse and sporadic murder. Religious Jews, conspicuous in their traditional clothing, were a special target – they were publicly degraded, often by having their beards and sidelocks shorn or cruelly ripped off. Freedom of movement was denied and at first Jews could be hunted in the streets like animals and press-ganged into service for the German war effort. Later, regulations were passed controlling the number of Jews to be requisitioned for forced labour.

Towards a solution of the Jewish question – ghettoization

Reinhard Heydrich, Head of the Reich Security Main Office and of the Security Police and close associate of Heinrich Himmler, Head of the SS, was entrusted with the responsibility for devising a systematic interim method of dealing with the Jews in occupied Poland until a more permanent solution could be found. On 21 September 1939 Heydrich issued instructions to the leaders of the *Einsaztgruppen* (special task forces of the Security Police which operated behind the German front-line troops. They would later play a murderous role in shooting to death over 2 million civilians, including an estimated 1.5 million Jews in territory taken from the Russians).

The subject of his directive was 'the Jewish question in the occupied territory' of Poland and it established the basis for the organization, concentration and ghettoization of Jews that would define Jewish life in Poland until the death camps were ready to receive them:

> I refer to the conference held in Berlin today, and again point out that the *planned total measures* (i.e. the final aim) are to be kept *strictly secret*.
> A distinction must be made between:
> 1. the final aim (which will require extended periods of time) and
> 2. the stages leading to the fulfilment of this final aim. ...
> The planned measures require the most thorough preparation with regard to technical as well as economic aspects.
> It is obvious that the tasks ahead ... cannot be laid down in full detail. ...
> For the time being, the first prerequisite for the final aim is the concentration of the Jews from the countryside into the larger cities. This is to be carried out speedily. ... In this connection it should be borne in mind that only cities which are rail junctions, or are at least located on railroad lines, should be selected as concentration points.
> On principle, Jewish communities of less than 500 persons are to be dissolved and transferred to the nearest concentration centre. ...

Councils of Jewish Elders

1. In each Jewish community a Council of Jewish Elders is to be set up which, as far as possible, is to be composed of the remaining authoritative personalities and rabbis. ... The Council is to be made *fully responsible*, in the literal sense of the word, for the exact and prompt implementation of directives already issued or to be issued in the future.
2. In case of sabotage of such instructions, the Councils are to be warned that the most severe measures will be taken.
3. The Jewish Councils are to carry out an approximate census of the Jews in their areas. ...
4. The reason to be given for the concentration in the cities is that the Jews have taken a decisive part in sniper attacks and plundering.
5. ... the concentration of the Jews in the cities will probably call for regulations in these cities which will forbid their entry to certain quarters completely and that ... they may, for instance, not leave the ghetto, nor leave their homes after a certain hour in the evening, etc.[15]

Even though this document makes reference to the 'final aim', Heydrich clearly sees the establishment of ghettos merely as an interim measure. It is extremely unlikely that the decision had already been taken to annihilate every Jew in Nazi-occupied Europe. Indeed, in Germany and Austria emigration was possible – though not easily effected – right up to 1941. In the view of many historians, the long-range policy at this stage was to set up a Jewish 'reservation' in the Lublin district of Poland into which all Jews were to be transferred. Later, in 1940, but before the invasion of the Soviet Union was under serious consideration, there was a Nazi plan to ship all the Jews under their control to the island of Madagascar, off the east coast of Africa. Madagascar had previously been a French possession; this plan, however, proved impracticable when it became obvious that Britain was not going to negotiate a peace treaty. More significantly, the Madagascar plan was over-taken by events when the assault on the Soviet Union was being envisaged – an assault that, if successful, would bring many more millions of Jews into Nazi hands. Whether the Lublin or Madagascar schemes would have led to a different outcome for

European Jewry – or merely a different context for their massacre – is impossible to say.

Shortly after the occupation of Poland, the Nazis introduced a policy of deportation of Jews which sometimes involved the uprooting of whole communities. Jews were deported into occupied Poland (the General Government) from annexed territories of western Poland and also from regions of Austria and Sudeten Czechoslovakia which had been incorporated into the Greater German Reich. These eastward transportations were the forerunners of the later movement of millions, from all parts of Europe, to the death camps of Poland.

Conditions for Polish Jewry

In November 1939, all Polish Jews were ordered to wear a white armband with a Star of David. In accordance with Heydrich's instructions, ghettos were eventually established within the slum districts of major Polish cities during 1940 and 1941. These ghettos were mostly crude reconstructions of the walled-off parts of towns to which Jews had been confined in certain regions of Europe during the late medieval period (the first ghetto had been established in Venice in the early part of the sixteenth century). In keeping with their racial philosophy, the Germans aimed at the total separation of the Jewish people from their non-Jewish Polish environment; they were also to be deprived of any contact with other Jewish ghettos in Poland and with the various welfare organizations which Jewish communities in the free world had set up to assist their hapless brethren. The Allied governments, it must be said, were also reluctant to allow communication of any kind with Nazi-occupied lands; the shipment of food, clothing or money to Jews and other peoples subjected to Nazi terror and deprivation was viewed as giving resources to the enemy. Nevertheless, some aid – though pitifully inadequate – did reach the Jews inside the ghettos, thanks to ingenious methods of smuggling improvised by the Jews in their struggle for survival.

The Nazis sought to create inhuman conditions in the ghettos, where a combination of obscene overcrowding, deliberate starvation (the Germans controlled the rations of food) and outbreaks of typhus and cholera would reduce Jewish

numbers through 'natural wastage'. Any Jew caught attempting to escape was to be shot on the spot. In addition, any Jew
between the ages of 14 and 60 was liable to be conscripted for
forced work to special labour camps. The first major ghetto was
established in Lodz in the spring of 1940, and the largest in
Warsaw in the autumn of 1940. Warsaw's ghetto originally
contained 550,000 souls. By the time of its destruction 18
months later, there would only be 45,000 left alive.

The horrific implications of Nazi rule for the Jews of Poland
were understood in the following way by a contemporary
Warsaw Jewish chronicler, Chaim Kaplan. Yet, he also
believed, quite prophetically, in the indomitability of the Jewish
spirit:

> The gigantic catastrophe which has descended on Polish Jewry
> has no parallel, even in the darkest periods of Jewish history.
> Firstly – the depth of the hatred. This is not hatred whose
> source is simply in a party platform, invented for political
> purposes. It is a hatred of emotion, whose source is some
> psychopathic disease. In its outward manifestation it appears as
> physiological hatred, which sees the object of its hatred as
> tainted in body, as lepers who have no place in society. ...
> It is our good fortune that the conquerors failed to understand
> the nature and strength of Polish Jewry. Logically, we are
> obliged to die. According to the laws of nature, our end is
> destruction and total annihilation. How can an entire
> community feed itself when it has no grip on life? For there is no
> occupation, no trade which is not limited and circumscribed for
> us.
> But even this time we did not comply with the laws of nature.
> There is within us some hidden power, mysterious and secret,
> which keeps us going, keeps us alive, despite the natural law. If
> we cannot live on what is permitted, we live on what is
> forbidden. ...
> The Jews of Poland – oppressed and broken, shamed and
> debased, still love life, and do not wish to leave this world before
> their time. Say what you like, the will to live amidst terrible
> suffering is the manifestation of some hidden power whose
> nature we do not yet know. It is a marvellous, life-preserving
> power. ... The fact that we have hardly any suicides is worthy of
> special emphasis.
> We have remained naked. But as long as that secret power is
> concealed within us, we shall not yield to despair. The strength
> of this power lies in the very nature of the Polish Jew, which is
> rooted in our eternal tradition that commands us to live.[16]

The Jewish Council

In conformity with Heydrich's earlier directive, Jewish Councils (*Judenräte*) were established in each ghetto. They performed administrative functions that were, on the one hand, vital to the preservation of life and order – but, as Heydrich clearly intended, they also served the real German purpose. For the Jewish leadership was progressively induced to tie the nooses around the necks of their own people. They assumed responsibilities which touched on every aspect of the lives of the inhabitants: the deployment of workers, negotiation with the external German authority, the distribution of the meagre food rations allowed by the Germans, provision of clothing, education, burial, the maintenance of a Jewish police force and ghetto lawcourt and finally (as we shall see in Chapter 7), the making of life-and-death decisions about who was to be handed over to the Germans for deportation to the camps.

The Jewish Council as 'collaborator'?

The role of the Jewish Council is one of the most painful and controversial among writers and historians of the Holocaust years. Much of the early generalized thinking tended to view Jewish behaviour everywhere as passive, submissive, even lemming-like, involving wholesale cooperation and even collaboration in their own destruction. The part played by the Jewish council was seen as perhaps the ultimate expression of what Hannah Arendt called the complete 'moral collapse' which 'Nazism caused in respectable European society – not only in Germany but in almost all countries – not only among the persecutors but also among the victims'.[17]

In evaluating the role of the Jewish Council the case for the prosecution was made by the historian, Raul Hilberg.[18] According to Hilberg there were at least four ways in which the Jewish Councils satisfied the Nazi objective. Firstly, the Jewish Council became integrated into the bureaucratic machinery of destruction; Jews themselves actually provided the Germans with the administrative personnel who would keep the overall social, civil and 'Final Solution' machine ticking over.

Secondly, the Jewish Councils undermined a sense of communal solidarity by introducing a privileged power structure that, given human nature, inevitably led to corruption and self-serving activity. They exercised the power of life and death, with the result that the anger of the Jews was very often directed not at the Germans – the real enemy – but at the Jewish Councils. That is, of course, exactly what Heydrich had intended when ordering their establishment in September 1939.

Thirdly, Jewish Councils introduced self-delusion into the Jewish response; by having clandestine schools, social, religious and cultural activities, there was a lulling of the community into a false – and ultimately fatal – feeling of normality. Jewish Councils, Hilberg argues, lost sight of and helped others shut out the overall reality.

The fourth allegation is that the Jewish Councils were responsible for the Jewish police who physically rounded up deportees, pushed them on to trains and thus participated in the actual Jewish self-destruction process. Moreover the *Judenrat* police were the very young men who might otherwise have formed the nucleus of an organized armed resistance movement.

Hannah Arendt strengthened the indictment as follows:

> The whole truth was that if the Jewish people had been disorganized and leaderless, there would have been chaos and plenty of misery but the total number of dead would hardly have been six million.[19]

However, more recent research and thinking reveals that there is a colossal danger of overgeneralization and of the passing of simplistic moral judgements. When the whole range of Jewish Council responses is investigated and the unprecedented moral dilemmas they faced taken into account, no simple pattern of behaviour emerges. There was, in fact, among the Jewish Council leaders every conceivable human reaction – from compliance and submission at one extreme to attempted subversion and armed resistance at the other. (For an analysis of the different reactions of Jewish victims to the Nazi onslaught, see Chapter 8.)

The agony of the Warsaw ghetto

Conditions in the Warsaw ghetto in 1941 can be gauged from the following two documents. The first (a) appeared in a monthly field report in May from the German Army Headquarters in the Warsaw district; the second (b) is a lengthy and distressing entry in the diary of Stanislav Rozycki, a Polish visitor to the ghetto:

(a) The situation in the Jewish quarter is catastrophic. Dead bodies of those who collapsed from lack of strength are lying in the streets. Mortality ... has tripled since February. The only thing allotted to the Jews is 1.5 pounds of bread a week. Potatoes, for which the Jewish council has paid in advance of several million, have not yet been delivered. The larger number of welfare agencies created by the Jewish council are in no position to arrest the frightful misery. The ghetto is growing into a social scandal, a breeder of illnesses and of the worst subhumanity. The treatment of the Jews in the labour camps, where they are guarded solely by Poles can only be described as bestial.

(b) ... The majority are nightmare figures, ghosts of former human beings, miserable destitutes, pathetic remnants of former humanity. One is most affected by the characteristic change one sees in their faces: as a result of misery, poor nourishment, the lack of vitamins, fresh air and exercise, the numerous cares, worries, anticipated misfortunes, suffering and sickness, their faces have taken on a skeletal appearance.
   The prominent bones around their eye sockets, the yellow facial colour, the slack pendulous skin, the alarming emaciation and sickliness. And, in addition, this miserable, frightened, restless, apathetic and resigned expression like that of a hunted animal. I pass my closest friends without recognising them and guessing their fate. Many of them recognise me, come up to me and ask curiously how things are 'over there' behind the walls – there where there is enough bread, fresh air, freedom to move around, and above all freedom. ...
   On the streets children are crying in vain, children who are dying of hunger. They howl, beg, sing, moan, shiver with cold, without underwear, without clothing, without shoes, in rags, sacks, flannel which are bound in strips round the emaciated skeletons, children swollen with hunger, disfigured, half conscious, already completely grown-up at the age

of five, gloomy and weary of life. They are like old people and are only conscious of one thing: 'I'm cold.' 'I'm hungry.' They have become aware of the most important things in life that quickly. Through their innocent sacrifice and their frightening helplessness the thousands upon thousands of these little beggars level the main accusation against the proud civilization of today. Ten per cent of the new generation have already perished: every day and every night hundreds of these children die and there is no hope that anybody will put a stop to it.

There are not only children. Young and old people, men and women, bourgeois and proletarians, intelligentsia and business people are all being declassed and degraded. ... They are being gobbled up by the streets on to which they are brutally and ruthlessly thrown. They beg for one month, for two months, for three months – but they all go downhill and die on the street or in hospitals from cold or hunger or sickness or depression. Former human beings whom no one needs fall by the wayside: former citizens, former 'useful members of human society'.

I no longer look at people; when I hear groaning and sobbing I go over to the other side of the road; when I see something wrapped in rags, shivering with cold, stretched out on the ground I turn away and do not want to look ... I can't. It's become too much for me. And yet only an hour has passed. ...

For various reasons standards of hygiene are terribly poor. Above all a fearful population density in the streets with which nowhere in Europe can be remotely compared. ... And then the lack of light, gas and heating materials. Water consumption is also much reduced; people wash themselves much less and do not have baths or hot water. There are no green spaces, gardens, parks: no clumps of trees and no lawns to be seen. For a year no one has seen a village, a wood, a field, a river, or a mountain ...To speak of food hygiene would be ... regarded as mockery. People eat what is available, however much is available and when it is available. Other principles of nutrition are unknown here. Having said all this, one can easily draw one's own conclusions as to the consequences: stomach typhus and typhus, dysentery, tuberculosis, pneumonia, influenza, metabolic disturbances, the most common digestive illnesses, lack of vitamins, and all other illnesses associated with the lack of bread, fresh air, clothing and heating materials. Typhus is systematically and continually destroying the population. There are victims in every family. On average up to a thousand people are dying each month. In the early morning the corpses of beggars, children, old people, young people and women are lying in every street – the victims of the hunger and the cold. ... The shortage of the necessary medicines in sufficient quantities makes it impossible to treat the sick. Moreover, there is a shortage of food for the sick. There is only soup and tea. ...

While this cruel struggle for a little bit of bread, for a few metres of living space, for the maintenance of health, energy and life is going on, people are incapable of devoting much energy and strength to intellectual matters. In any case, there are German restrictions and bans. Nothing can be printed, taught or learnt. People are not allowed to organize themselves or exchange cultural possessions. We are cut off from the world and from books. It is not permitted to open libraries and sort out books from other printed materials. We are not allowed to print anything, neither books nor newspapers; schools, academic institutions etc. are not permitted to open. There are no cinemas, radio, no contacts with world culture. Nothing reaches us, no products of the human spirit reach us. We have to smuggle in not only foodstuffs and manufactured goods, but also cultural products. For that reason everything which we achieve in that respect is worthy of recognition irrespective of how much there is or what it consists of.[20]

Yet, however harsh and unendurable conditions for Jews were during this intermediate phase of ghettoization and internment, nothing – either in the previous 3,500 years of Jewish history or even in the first eight years of Hitler's reign – had prepared them for the next, unthinkable stage in the Nazi onslaught against them. For during the first months of 1941, while the invasion of the Soviet Union was being prepared in earnest, an unspeakable plan was simultaneously taking shape. Hitler's war on the Soviet Union was to be an ideological assault on 'Jewish Bolshevism'. Nazi theory and practice were about to flow together in a methodical and concerted frenzy of mass destruction: the Nazi hierarchy and SS leadership would soon be committed to killing every single Jew on the continent of Europe.

CHAPTER 7

The Holocaust, 1941–5: From Dehumanization to Annihilation

I believe in the sun even when it is not shining.
I believe in love even when feeling it not.
I believe in God even when He is silent
From an inscription on the walls of
a cellar in Cologne, Germany,
where Jews hid from Nazis

The context of war

The twentieth century, with its highly sophisticated tech-nology and communications systems, has proved the era in which undreamed-of possibilities in all fields have become realities. It has also been the century of unrestrained global warfare in which the value of individual human life has been alarmingly cheapened: it is now estimated that more people have been killed in this century alone than in all previous history.

The First World War of 1914–18 inflicted such massive casualties on all sides, and with such remarkable pointless-ness, that the continent of Europe became desensitized as never before to mass human destruction. The First World War, therefore, represents a watershed of huge significance for understanding the moral and psychological mechanisms that made the Nazi Holocaust a possibility. Under cover of that war, in 1915, the Ottoman Turks massacred over a million Armenians in the century's first systematic genocide (see Chapter 1), a monstrous crime in urgent need of thorough investigation (the world still waits, 79 years later, for an official Turkish admission of guilt).

The Second World War was, in almost every sense, a child of the First. As this second war progressed towards its third year, the Nazis' seeming invincibility strengthened their arrogant belief that nothing could stand in the way of their establishing the 'Thousand Year Reich' Hitler had promised them. The brutalizing theatre of war, which they now intended to carry into the Soviet Union, could provide them with the context in which their most ugly theories and fantasies of racial domination could be put into practice. As Joseph Goebbels, the Nazi Propaganda Minister, wrote in his diary:

> If we did not fight the Jews, they would destroy us. It's a life-and-death struggle between the Aryan race and the Jewish bacillus. No other government and no other regime would have the strength for such a global solution as this. Here, once again, the Führer is the undismayed champion of a radical solution.... Fortunately a whole series of possibilities presents itself to us in wartime which would be denied us in peace. We shall have to profit by this.[1]

The decision

Important questions, however, remain unanswered: when and how did the Nazi government decide upon a policy of comprehensive extermination of Europe's Jewish population? Who actually made the decision to begin the process of systematic annihilation?

That no written document survives, containing specific orders for the start of the massacres, should not surprise us unduly, since this operation was to be kept top secret; even close to the war's end, it was generally referred to by means of obscure and mysterious euphemisms. Perhaps the Nazi leadership did not wish to provide written evidence that might subsequently incriminate them. After all, the precise treatment of Jews was a subject they had for years felt obliged to conceal from the majority of their own population. Or, as is much more probable, did Hitler, who committed very few important directives to paper, simply give the order orally? Most historians who understand the internal workings of the Nazi government and, particularly, Hitler's style of leadership favour this latter view. (Those following a different line include a handful of malevolent cranks who believe that the absence of a written order 'proves' that Hitler was entirely ignorant – and therefore presumably innocent – of the 'Final Solution'!)

The transition to a policy of extermination

An examination of Hitler's writings and speeches, and those of other leaders, shows that certain remarks were made – some quite explicit – which could be interpreted as threatening an awful end for the Jews of Europe. However, the 25 Point Programme of the Nazi Party (1920) did not call for extermination of Jews, but merely for their exclusion from all areas of Germanic life. Until 1941 Nazi policy in the west continued to facilitate emigration, especially after the Austrian Anschluss of March 1938. Indeed, two out of every three Austrian Jews and one out of every two German Jews had made their way abroad before 1941.

Once war broke out, Germany had hoped to complete the process of Jewish emigration by negotiating a peace treaty with Britain and arranging to transport millions of Jews to Madagascar (a French possession). In the event, no peace with Britain emerged and, with the prospect of the invasion of the Soviet Union, Nazi Germany would soon be involved in a war on two fronts. The whole basis of the Madagascar plan was thus undermined and the scheme allowed to lapse, it being impracticable to export European Jewry beyond Germany's direct control.

During the past decade, the whole question of the causes and origins of the Final Solution – the actual decision to murder every Jew in Europe – has been the subject of an intense debate which has split historians into two broadly distinct camps. On the one hand, there are the so-called 'Intentionalists'.[2] They contend that from very early on Hitler intended the Final Solution to be implemented at the earliest possible moment – and that this came about in 1941 when the bulk of east European Jewry could be exterminated under the camouflage of an enormous, brutal war against the Soviet Union. They maintain that it is Hitler – his rabid antisemitism, his obsessive personality, his irresistible style of leadership, his earlier unequivocal statements of intent in both speeches and writings – who is the key to the decision to murder all the Jews of Europe. It is unthinkable, they argue, that such a significant process could have got under way without his personal authorization.

Another group of historians, often described as the 'Functionalists',[3] assert that the decision to embark upon the Final Solution, far from being the logical product of a desire to translate deep-seated intention into policy, was haphazard, improvised and even 'blundered into', after the alternatives of emigration had been exhausted. Hitler, they argue, was a remote leader whose vision, ideology and charisma often created a very general theoretical framework within which others would devise the policy details. It has even been suggested that, because there is no piece of paper testifying to Hitler's direct instruction to carry out the Final Solution, agencies lower down the SS hierarchy may have dreamed up this mass extermination in order to compete for favour and reward in Hitler's eyes and to extend their own personal power base in competition with other Nazi departments.

What is clear, however, is that by mid-1941 the Nazi leadership knew that they would be fighting, in the immediate future, a racial/ideological war involving a planned policy of 'depopulation' of Slavs, Russians and Jews. The aim of this policy was to plant new 'Aryan' settlements of warrior-farmers along the borders of Germanic civilization and to ensure that never again would ethnic Germans be subjected to the domination of racial 'inferiors'.

The path to extermination

Eight key developments seem to have led progressively, if not inexorably, to the the decision (or decisions) which came to be known as the 'Final Solution of the Jewish Question'. They chart a meandering and inconclusive path (intensely frustrating for those historians and students who believe that history must necessarily lend itself to uncomplicated and clear-cut explanations of 'causes'): from the comparatively unsystematic, even haphazard, 'liquidations' in the front-line Baltic states during the early stages of the war with the Soviet Union, to the methodical extermination processes which were to apply to all Jews in countries under direct German occupation:

1. 6 March and 6 June 1941

Agreement was reached between the army and SS Reich Security Main Office for rules of conduct when the eastern front became active. Specifically, mobile killing squads (*Einsatzgruppen*) would operate in the rear of the forward line with the aim of 'liquidating' potential partisan fighters, since 'in the fight against Bolshevism it is *not* to be expected that the enemy will act in accordance with the principles of humanity or international law'. The Reichsführer SS (Himmler) was empowered to act 'independently and on his own responsibility' in the execution of this task.

The army's acceptance of the presence and role of the SS so close to the fighting zone in the Soviet Union was crucial to the eventual success of the policy of wholesale slaughter of Jewish and other civilian elements. Whatever the individual soldier's reservations about the killings may have been, his duty was made evident in such instructions as this Order of the Day, issued by Field Marshall von Reichenau on 10 October, by which time the fighting and massacre of civilians were well under way:

> In the Eastern sphere the soldier is not simply a fighter according to the rules of war, but the supporter of a ruthless racial ideology. ... For this reason, the soldier must show full understanding of the necessity for the severe but just atonement being required of the Jewish subhumans.[4]

2. 2 July 1941

Heydrich issued guidelines to the higher SS and police leaders in the occupied territories of the Soviet Union concerning the actions of the *Einsatzgruppen*, of which the following is an extract:

> 4. Executions
>
> All the following are to be executed: Officials of the Comintern (together with professional Communist politicians in general); top and medium-level officials and radical lower-level officials of the Party, Central Committee and district and sub-district committees; People's Commissars; Jews in Party and State employment, and other radical elements (saboteurs, propagandists, snipers, assassins, inciters, etc.).[5]

Although this document refers only to the execution of 'Jews in Party and State employment', Heydrich had already, according to one eye-witness, given an oral order in Berlin to the *Einsatzgruppen* leaders to exterminate *'all* Russian Jews'. Apparently he had wished to 'soften' the order on paper in case objections were raised in Berlin. Certainly the *Einsatzgruppen* commanders in the field, after some initial inconsistencies, seem quickly and unequivocally to have interpreted the order as giving them licence to liquidate *all* Jews, including women and children.

3. 31 July 1941
Five weeks after the killing squads began their operations in the Baltic states, Göring, as second in command to Hitler, issued the following instruction to Heydrich:

> As supplement to the task which was entrusted to you in the decree dated 24 January, 1939, ... I herewith commission you to carry out all necessary preparations with regard to organizational, substantive and financial viewpoints for a total solution of the Jewish question in the German sphere of influence in Europe....
> I further commission you to submit to me promptly an overall plan showing the preliminary organizational, substantive and financial measures for the execution of the intended final solution [*Endlösung*] of the Jewish question.[6]

In effect, Heydrich was to be given responsibility for overall control of the murder of millions; for inventing the most sophisticated and economical means of accomplishing this aim; and for coordinating the railway, finance, foreign office and police departments. It is important, too, to note the deliberate use of Nazi euphemisms that helped to keep the programme secret and to distance Nazi bureaucrats from a frank appreciation of the consequences of their desk-bound activities.

4.   Summer 1941 (precise date unknown)
Heinrich Himmler, Head of the SS, instructed Rudolph Hoess to start preparing Auschwitz in Upper Silesia, Poland, as a death camp of considerable size and importance. (Hoess was to become the commandant of Auschwitz and relates in his autobiography that Himmler told him in Berlin that 'The

Führer has given the order for the final solution of the Jewish question').

5. September, 1941

The euthanasia programme at special German institutes was halted after the murder there of over 90,000 elderly, handicapped, 'incurably insane' and 'socially defective' people. Some were killed by lethal injection, but the majority were gassed to death with carbon monoxide fed into trucks or vans. The programme was stopped as a result of protest by members of the public, including representatives of the various churches in Germany. SS Major Christian Wirth was consequently released from his duties as administrative head of a euthanasia centre and, because of his expertise in mass extermination by this method, was assigned to take over the supervision of Chelmno, the first of six death camps in Poland to become operational. Later he was placed in charge of the death camps of Sobibor, Treblinka and Belzec.

6. Autumn 1941

The first experiments were conducted on Soviet prisoners of war with Zyclon B gas (hydrogen cyanide), an industrial cleansing and fumigation agent used to remove pesticides. The results of these experiments were to have fatal implications for millions of Jews throughout Europe.

7. October 1941

The first deportations of German, Austrian and Czech Jews to Riga and Kovno (in territory captured from the Soviet Union) took place, after which they were ghettoized or shot *en masse* – a move which foreshadowed the transportation eastwards of Jews from all over western and southern Europe. It marked the end of what remained of the Nazis' policy of emigration for the Jews of Greater Germany and signalled the extension westwards of the policy of mass annihilation already directed against the Jews of the Soviet Union.

8. 20 January 1942 – The Wannsee Conference

A conference was convened beside Lake Wannsee in Berlin. Its purpose was to coordinate the activities of all bodies and organizations whose participation would be needed for the

Final Solution. Although the key decisions had clearly already been reached at the highest levels of government, this conference is highly significant because Heydrich (who chaired the meeting) was able to gain unchallenged administrative supremacy for the SS in all matters relating to the implementation of Holocaust policy. Seated at this meeting were highly educated and cultivated Germans from many different branches of government – the cream of the German leadership. They calmly and deliberately listened to plans for the annihilation of an entire people.

A copy of the minutes of the conference, prepared by Adolf Eichmann, has survived intact. It constitutes one of the most important documents on the history of the Holocaust. The following is an excerpt:

In view of the dangers of emigration in war-time, and the possibilities in the East, the Reichsführer SS and Chief of the German Police [Himmler] has forbidden the emigration of Jews.

Emigration has now been replaced by evacuation of the Jews to the East, as a further possible solution, with the appropriate prior authorization of the Führer.

However, this operation should be regarded only as a provisional option; but it is already supplying practical experience of great significance in view of the coming final solution of the Jewish question.

In the course of this final solution of the European Jewish question approximately 11 million Jews may be taken into consideration, distributed over the individual countries as follows:

Country	Number
A. Germany	131,800
Austria	43,700
Eastern Territories	420,000
General Government (i.e. central Poland)	2,284,000
Bialystok	400,000
Protectorate of Bohemia and Moravia	74,200
Estonia – free of Jews	
Latvia	3,500
Lithuania	34,000
Belgium	43,000
Denmark	5,600
France: Occupied territory	165,000

France: Unoccupied territory		700,000
Greece		69,600
Holland		160,800
Norway		1,300
B. Bulgaria		48,000
England		330,000
Finland		2,300
Ireland		4,000
Italy, including Sardinia		58,000
Albania		200
Croatia		40,000
Portugal		3,000
Rumania, including Bessarabia		342,000
Sweden		8,000
Switzerland		18,000
Serbia		10,000
Slovakia		88,000
Spain		6,000
Turkey (European portion)		55,500
Hungary		742,800
USSR		5,000,000
Ukraine	2,994,684	
White Russia,		
without Bialystok	446,484	
Total:		over 11,000,000

[A: Countries already conquered by Nazi Germany

B: Neutral countries or countries either allied to, or still fighting against, Nazi Germany.]

The Jews are to be utilized for work in the East in an expedient manner in the course of the final solution. In large (labour) columns, with the sexes separated, Jews capable of work will be moved into those areas as they build roads, during which a large proportion will no doubt drop out through natural reduction. The remnant that eventually remains will require suitable treatment; because it will without doubt represent the most (physically) resistant part, it consists of a natural selection that could, on its release, become the germ-cell of a new Jewish revival (witness the experience of history).

Europe is to be combed through from West to East in the course of the practical implementation of the final solution. ... The evacuated Jews will first be taken, group by group, to so-called transit ghettos, in order to be transported further east from there.[7]

Although the language used in the minutes was euphemistic (since they would have been circulated beyond the confines of the meeting), no one at the conference would have been under any misapprehension about the intentions of those who had concocted the 'final solution'; nor would they have needed to ask the meaning of the term 'evacuation to the East'; nor did anyone present question the end towards which they would all be working. No objections were registered, no surprise expressed, though they requested clarification of such hairsplitting detail as the precise definition of 'half-Jews' and 'quarter-Jews' and the question of whether such categories would share the fate of 'full' Jews.

This document makes it abundantly clear that the Nazis were, by the beginning of 1942, unswervingly committed to killing every single Jew (according to their estimate 11,000,000) on the continent of Europe, including those living in countries that were neutral – for example, Eire, Sweden, Switzerland and Spain – or not yet conquered and occupied – e.g. Great Britain and the central and eastern regions of the Soviet Union.

The course of the Final Solution

During the four-year period from the Nazi invasion of the Soviet Union in June 1941 to the German surrender in May 1945, the Jewish people were the helpless victims of a campaign of relentless humiliation, starvation, torture, persecution and slaughter. Jews were generally murdered either in mass shootings or in the specially designed gas chambers and crematoria of death camps in Poland. Hundreds of thousands of Jews also perished through overwork, malnourishment, disease, on forced marches and, in some cases, through sheer despair. The carnage only came to an end when Poland and eventually Germany itself were overrun by Allied, particularly Soviet, forces. Even after liberation many Jews succumbed to the longer-term effects of their physical wounds and mental trauma.

Extermination strategy

The Holocaust, the actual mass annihilation, essentially took two forms:

1. Mobile killing operations in the Soviet Union which, though devastating, lacked the consistency, single-mindedness and methodical organization of later deportations.
2. Systematic deportation from all parts of Europe under Nazi occupation or influence to extermination camps on Polish soil (this stage is usually referred to by the Nazis' own terminology, 'The Final Solution').

In addition, ghettoization (described in Chapter 6) and the internment of Jews in a vast network of concentration and labour camps would end the lives of countless thousands through overwork, starvation and epidemic without the need for 'evacuation to the East'.

Mobile killing operations in the Soviet Union –
the Einsatzgruppen *death squads*

Mobile killing occurred as part of Operation Barbarossa, Germany's attack on the Soviet Union, and took place over a very wide area, from the Baltic down to the Ukraine. The SS Action Groups *(Einsatzgruppen)* were divided into four – Groups A, B, C and D – and operated just behind the advancing troops. Their primary targets for elimination were Jews, Soviet officials and gypsies – but, above all, Jews.

The killing of Jews began during the first days of the invasion. The pattern was usually the same. Immediately after the German army had subdued an area, the commander of the Action Group would enter a town or village. He would then send for the rabbi and demand that his community assemble for despatch to a Jewish region.

The reason why the majority of Jews generally obeyed such orders is that they did not have the faintest suspicion of the fate that awaited them. Since entering into his pact with Hitler two years previously, the Soviet leader, Stalin, had allowed very little negative information about Nazi behaviour towards civilian populations to reach his citizens. Ironically, the

Germans had also inherited a good reputation from the First World War in their dealings with the East European Jewish population. The Jews had learned from their own recent historical experience that it was from the Russian rather than the German army that they could expect harsh treatment. Had they been told that they were all going to be shot, they would scarcely have found it believable.

When the Jewish community had assembled, the Action Group, often with the help of locally recruited Lithuanian and Ukrainian militia, would usually transport the Jews by truck to a nearby ravine or wood where they were forced to dig a trench or pit. The whole Jewish population – men, women and children – would then be ordered to strip. They were then driven into the trench, machine-gunned, or shot individually by rifle or pistol, and buried immediately.

Such 'actions' were carried out repeatedly as the German army advanced. The most notorious single case occurred at Babi Yar, on the outskirts of the Ukrainian city of Kiev, where it is estimated that over 33,000 Jews were murdered in one or two days and then buried in a local ravine.

In towns and villages throughout the occupied territories of the Soviet Union – in eastern Poland, Latvia, Estonia, Lithuania, Byelorussia, Ukraine and the Crimea – the same dreadful picture emerged. The figures issued by Action Group A (*Einsatzgruppe A*) under the heading 'Executions up to 15 February 1942', speak for themselves:

Total	Jews	Communists	Together
Lithuania	80,311	860	81,171
Latvia	30,025	1,843	31,868
Estonia	474	684	1,158
White Russia	7,620	–	7,620
	118,430	3,387	121,817[8]

From such statistics it can be calculated that over 1,300,000 Jews were shot to death by the *Einsatzgruppen* within 18 months of the invasion of the Soviet Union. At the Nuremberg Trials of 1945 the following graphic account of one such massacre was given by a German builder, Hermann Gräbe:

A few lorries were parked in front of the mounds from which people were being driven by armed Ukrainian militia under the supervision of an armed SS man. The militia provided the guards on the lorries and drove them to and from the ditch. All these people wore the prescribed yellow patches on the front and back of their clothing so that they were identifiable as Jews....

I could now hear a series of rifle shots from behind the mounds. The people who had got off the lorries – men, women and children of all ages – had to undress on the orders of an SS man who was carrying a riding or dog whip in his hand. They had to place their clothing on separate piles for shoes, clothing and underwear. I saw a pile of shoes containing approximately 800–1,000 pairs, and great heaps of underwear and clothing. Without weeping or crying out these people undressed and stood together in family groups, embracing each other and saying goodbye while waiting for a sign from another SS man who stood on the edge of the ditch and also had a whip. During the quarter of an hour in which I stood near the ditch I did not hear a single complaint or plea for mercy. I watched a family of about eight, a man and a woman, both about fifty-years-old with their children of about one, eight and ten, as well as two grown-up daughters of about twenty and twenty-four. An old woman with snow-white hair held a one-year old child in her arms singing to it and tickling it. The child squeaked with delight. The married couple looked on with tears in their eyes. The father held the ten-year old boy by the hand speaking softly to him. The boy was struggling to hold back his tears. The father pointed a finger to the sky and stroked his head and seemed to be explaining something to him. At this moment, the SS man near the ditch called out something to his comrade. The latter counted off some twenty people and ordered them behind the mound. The family of which I have just spoken was among them. I can still remember how a girl, slender and dark, pointed to herself as she went past me, saying, 'twenty-three'.

I walked round the mound and stood in front of the huge grave. The bodies were lying so tightly packed together that only their heads showed, from almost all of which blood ran down over their shoulders. Some were still moving. Others raised their hands and turned their heads to show they were still alive. The ditch was already three quarters full. I estimate that it already held about a thousand bodies. I turned my eyes towards the man doing the shooting. He was an SS man; he sat, legs swinging, on the edge of the ditch. He had an automatic rifle resting on his knees and he was smoking a cigarette. The people, completely naked, climbed down steps which had been cut into the clay wall of the ditch, stumbled over the heads of those lying there and stopped at the spot indicated by the SS man. They lay down on top of the dead and wounded; some stroked those still living and spoke quietly to them. Then I heard a series of rifle shots. I looked into the ditch and saw the bodies contorting or, the heads already inert, sinking on the corpses beneath. Blood flowed from the nape of their necks. I was surprised not to be ordered away, but I noticed three postmen in uniform standing nearby. Then the next batch came up, climbed down into the ditch, laid themselves next to the previous victims and were shot....

I am making the above statement in Wiesbaden, Germany on 10 November 1945. I swear to God it is the whole truth.[9]

After the war, Gräbe was subjected to poisonous criticism by some of his fellow Germans and emigrated to California. In 1966 he received the Righteous Gentile award in the State of Israel.

Deportation to the east and extermination

Despite the staggering numbers of Jews murdered in mass shootings on the Russian front, the Nazis experienced problems with this method of extermination. Firstly, there were panicky memoranda sent from the *Einsatzgruppen* commanders to Berlin, complaining of the demoralizing effects the shootings were having on their men. Some could only cope with the 'assignment' by consuming large quantities of alcohol. It was not that they had any moral objection to killing large numbers of Jewish civilians; it was simply too messy a business – even the most battle-hardened drunkard could be squeamish about shooting thousands of women and children at close quarters. Secondly, it was far too public an operation. The shootings were often conducted in the presence of unauthorized civilians (see document above), and occasionally prompted clashes between the SS and members of the regular German army who did not regard such atrocities as being worthy of the glorious German military tradition. (Nevertheless, by 1941 such atrocities on the Russian front did in fact have the active participation of considerable numbers of regular German soldiers, many of whom volunteered to assist the SS in their murderous activities.)

Once the decision had been reached to kill *all* the Jews of Europe, not only those in distant Russia – a decision in all probability hastened by unexpected difficulties and reverses in the campaign against the Soviet Union – a more discreet method of extermination had to be devised; and one that protected the perpetrators from too close an involvement in the actual physical process of destruction. In this way the problem of demoralization of 'good Germans' could be overcome. Himmler himself, according to one eye-witness, had nearly passed out when he visited the site of a mass shooting in Minsk in August 1941. According to witnesses, he had later remarked on the need to find a more 'humane' (i.e. for the perpetrators) and 'rational' method of mass killing.

All of these 'problems' were to be resolved in the next decisive stage of the 'Final Solution' – the establishment of a network of annihilation camps. It is believed that the order for the construction of these camps was issued during the late summer of 1941. This excerpt is taken from the recollections of Rudolf Hoess, first commandant of Auschwitz:

In the summer of 1941 – I cannot remember the exact date – I was suddenly summoned to the Reichsführer SS ... Contrary to his usual custom, Himmler received me without his adjutant being present and said in effect:

'The Führer has ordered that the Jewish question be solved once and for all and that we, the SS, are to implement that order.

'The existing extermination centres in the East are not in a position to carry out the large actions which are anticipated. I have therefore earmarked Auschwitz for this purpose, both because of its good position as regards communications and because the area can easily be isolated and camouflaged. ... It is difficult and onerous and calls for complete devotion notwithstanding the difficulties which may arise. ...

'You will treat this order as absolutely secret, even from your superiors. After your talk with Eichmann you will immediately forward to me the plans of the projected installations.

'The Jews are the sworn enemies of the German people and must be eradicated. Every Jew that we can lay our hands on is to be destroyed now during the war, without exception. If we cannot now obliterate the biological basis of Jewry, the Jews will one day destroy the German people.'[10]

Location of death camps

Poland was chosen as the location for these camps for several reasons: firstly, it had by far the largest concentration of Jews in Nazi-occupied territories; secondly, it was located at a sufficient distance from prying German and other western eyes, yet was close enough to make feasible the transport of millions of Jews from other parts of Europe; thirdly, the Nazis had such deep contempt for the Poles that it was not considered unacceptable for Polish soil to be drenched in human blood – indeed the Polish nation, too, lost 6 million people during the Second World War, including the 3 million Polish Jews; and, lastly, the Nazis believed – as events turned out, with more than a little justification – that the level of religious and racial antisemitism among the ordinary Polish population was sufficiently high to suggest that they would remain aloof and indifferent to the Holocaust that was to be perpetrated in their own back yard.

In Poland the SS used slave-labour to construct highly sophisticated gassing installations. In these annihilation centres, the SS turned mass murder into a streamlined, cost-effective and labour-efficient industry. The techniques of killing by carbon monoxide gas and then disposing of the bodies in crematoria had previously been tried and tested on tens of thousands of victims during the 'euthanasia' programme of 1939–41, until pressure from German public opinion shut the operation down. 'Euthanasia' experts, such as Christian Wirth, were transferred to senior positions to administer the Final Solution. Experiments with a new, more economical gas, Zyclon B, had been conducted, using 'disposable' Russian prisoners of war as guinea pigs. SS participation in the horrendous process and aftermath of death was to be reduced to an absolutely tolerable minimum – the Jews themselves and other prisoners were, as far as possible, to be induced into carrying out all the truly loathsome tasks.

The six extermination factories were sited in Poland. They were all located near major cities with which they had excellent railway links. *Treblinka* was close to Warsaw; *Chelmno* to Lodz; and the camps of *Belzec*, *Sobibor* and *Majdanek* to the city of Lublin. The camp at *Auschwitz*, a small town in Galicia in south-west Poland, was chosen to exterminate longer-distance deportees from western, central and southern Europe and was adjacent to a major railway artery from Vienna to the Polish city of Crakow.

The annihilation camps

Chelmno was the first death camp to be put into operation. Between December 1941 and the spring of 1943, it is estimated that over 200,000 Polish Jews and tens of thousands of Soviet prisoners and gypsies were murdered there, in trucks converted into gas chambers. The second camp to become operational was Belzec, where approximately 500,000 Jews were exterminated by carbon monoxide gas between March 1942 and May 1943.

Sobibor was the scene of the slaughter of about 250,000 Jews, transported from many different parts of Europe. They died, as did countless non-Jewish civilians and prisoners of war, in the more sophisticated gas chambers – disguised as shower and disinfection installations – between May 1942 and October 1943.

Treblinka was the camp that 'serviced' the Jews of Warsaw, among others. There some 800,000 Jews cruelly lost their lives between July 1942 and August 1943. These camps had no purpose other than to kill their inmates; there was no possibility of surviving as slave-labourers and virtually all Jews were murdered instantly upon arrival. The only ones to cling precariously to life in these camps were those needed by the Nazis to help with the gruesome tasks associated with the ritual of deception, murder, disposal of corpses and endless sorting of the personal belongings of the dead. During 1942 and 1943, an additional 130,000 Jews perished at the concentration and extermination camp at Majdanek, established near the Polish city of Lublin.

The number of Jews murdered at the largest camp, Auschwitz, between January 1942 and November 1944, is now estimated to have been in the region of 1,250,000. Auschwitz was in fact a complex of camps, combining the very different functions of labour, internment and extermination. Auschwitz I was a 'normal' concentration centre. Auschwitz II, known also as Birkenau, was the most ambitious, extensive – and today the most notorious – of all the death camps. Auschwitz III, known also as Buna, was a huge labour camp, serving the German war economy. According to the most reliable estimates, the Jewish victims constituted the vast majority of all those murdered at Auschwitz and Birkenau.

Europe-wide operation

The Jews who perished at Auschwitz/Birkenau came from a bewildering variety of countries – from Holland, Greece, Germany, Poland, Russia, France, Belgium, Hungary, Romania, Bulgaria, Norway, Austria, Slovakia, Croatia, Italy and Yugoslavia. These victims, entirely unaware of the fate that awaited them, had generally endured the indescribable torment of long rail journeys, during which they were crowded into cattle trucks and deprived of air, food and water. These were journeys on which many had died through suffocation and dehydration. Immediately upon arrival at Auschwitz, the majority were tricked into taking 'showers' or sometimes had to be driven with whips, savage dogs and bullets into the chambers; once naked inside these rooms, the doors were bolted and they were poisoned by hydrogen cyanide gas (Zyclon B).

All over Nazi-occupied Europe there were round-ups of Jews, followed by deportations. In some instances the round-ups were orderly and dignified, the Jewish victims genuinely believing they were being transferred to work-camps in the east. In other cases the Jews were hunted down and literally dragged off to transit camps to await their deportation. The Nazis went to extraordinary and successful lengths to starve the Jews of information and to conceal the true meaning of the camps. To strengthen the deception, on 11 July 1943 Hitler officially banned all public references to the 'Final Solution of the Jewish Question'.

Deportation from countries which were not directly under German control posed difficulties for the Nazis. Their allies and satellites often put up the greatest resistance – in Hungary deportations only started in earnest after it was occupied in March 1944. Before then, Admiral Horthy had persistently refused to obey Hitler's demands that Hungarian Jews be handed over, even though his government had participated in the deportation of Polish and Russian Jews who fell into Hungarian hands during the military campaign in the Soviet Union. In 'independent' Slovakia, on the other hand, the government showed itself willing from the first to assist the Nazis in their genocidal actions against the Jewish population.

Italy, especially its armed forces, actively protected Jews in areas under its sway and, again, deportations from Italy proper only occurred after Mussolini's fall in October 1943 when the north of the country was occupied by German troops. Romania was a pro-German ally which afforded a measure of protection to Romanian Jews in its Regat heartland. However, it carried out a policy of brutal extermination in Southern Ukraine, culminating in the massacre of over 60,000 Jews from the city of Odessa in 1941. The Bulgarian authorities went to great lengths to protect their own Jews but were prepared to surrender Jews residing in those parts of Greece and Yugoslavia over which they had assumed control.

The overwhelming majority of the Jews of Greece were deported and murdered at Auschwitz. The astonishingly high number of Greek Jews who perished also reflects the harshness of the regime the Nazis imposed on the Greek population as a whole. In Yugoslavia the Nazis launched a relentlessly murderous onslaught against the Jews of Serbia; in the territory of Croatia a Fascist government (the Ustachi), obedient to the will of Hitler, was established: the Jews were consequently driven into concentration camps and either slaughtered there by their Croat captors or deported to the Nazi death camps. The minority of Yugoslav Jews who survived were fortunate enough to be in that part of Croatia which fell under Italian control. Once again, Italian officials defended the Jews by successfully resisting attempts to have Jews deported from their area of jurisdiction.

In all parts of western Europe there was a precarious balance between the degree of resistance shown to the Nazis by the indigenous population and the extent of local collaboration with the occupying German administration. Generally speaking, Belgium and Holland were reluctant to comply with Nazi demands for Jewish deportees, but since Germany held these countries in an iron grip, remarkably few Jews survived, despite the local population's sympathy. In Belgium, Catholic religious institutions made an heroic, if only partially successful, effort to rescue Jews, while in Amsterdam a general workers' strike, held as a demonstration of solidarity with the Jews of Holland, was ruthlessly crushed by the Nazis.

In France, ruled nominally by Pétain's Vichy government in the south, but totally occupied after 1942, Pétain's government introduced its own antisemitic laws and actively assisted in the round-ups of French Jews. Nevertheless, the incidence of Jewish lives being saved by individual French citizens and by the French Resistance was mercifully high. French Jews also enjoyed extraordinary protection in the small area of south-east France that was for a time under Italian authority.

In Norway, despite the collaborationist Quisling being in nominal control of the puppet government, many ordinary Norwegians and church officials defied Nazi requests for deportations. Indeed just under half of the Jewish population of Norway was smuggled to safety in neutral Sweden. But the outstanding example of successful rescue is that of Denmark, whose Jewish population was almost entirely saved. At virtually every level of Danish society, from the king downwards, the Danes made strenuous efforts to ensure that their Jewish population escaped deportation. At great risk to their protectors, the Jews were hidden and eventually transferred by boat to safety in nearby Sweden.

Statistics of death

Of all the Jewish dead during the Holocaust years, well over 3 million are thought to have died in the conveyor-belt slaughter of the extermination camps. About 1.5 million were shot to death by the mobile killing squads in the Soviet Union. Over 900,000 perished in the unimaginable squalor of the ghettos, and in the brutal conditions of concentration, transit and labour camps. Additional tens of thousands died in railroad cattle-trucks, on death marches towards the end of the war and in a host of other circumstances – too diverse and cruel to enumerate. [For numbers of Jews murdered in each country, see Appendix G.]

Part 3

Themes, Issues and Protagonists

CHAPTER 8

Perpetrators, Victims and Bystanders

The educational and moral lessons of the Holocaust have been summed up by the historian, Yehuda Bauer, in the following memorable three-point prohibition:

Do not be a perpetrator.
Do not be a victim.
Do not be a bystander.

In the view of many commentators, it was the interaction of these very elements – the implacable cruelty and irrationality of the Nazi perpetrator, the overwhelming passivity and compliance of the Jewish victim, and the inaction and indifference of much of the rest of the world – that made possible this unthinkable episode in human history. In this chapter we shall therefore explore some of the psychological and motivational forces at work in all three groups and, in doing so, challenge several of the myths and generalizations that may obscure our judgement.

THE PERPETRATORS

Everywhere the human soul stands between a hemisphere of light and another of darkness

Thomas Carlyle

The question has often been asked: how on earth was it possible for educated, cultured and 'professional' members of such a highly developed European society as Germany to apply

183

themselves so assiduously to the task of butchering an entire people? And not only that, but to regard what they were doing as morally correct and patriotic?

Dehumanization of the victim

Had Hitler ordered the destruction of all Jewish life within weeks or months of coming to power, such an undertaking would literally have been impossible to accomplish. By 1941, however, the process of 'dehumanization' of the Jews had gradually had its effect and progressively insinuated itself into the consciousness of many Germans – even among those who in normal times would have regarded themselves as law-abiding. The various legal measures had, over the years, reduced the Jews both in Germany and elsewhere to a pathetic group of paupers, utterly devoid of rights and dignity. To many Germans, the Jews now did more than merely resemble the grotesque and pornographic caricatures of the Nazi propaganda machine.

How effective this process of dehumanization had been was particularly evident once the war was under way. Whatever doubts may have existed concerning the assimilated Jews of Germany hardly seemed to apply to the culturally alien Jews of the east – the teeming, pestilential Jewish masses of Poland. That the physical deterioration of Jewish life was the direct consequence of Nazi policies of ghettoization, forced labour and starvation seemed entirely irrelevant. Such reservations did not apply at all to the Jews of Russia, once the invasion of the Soviet Union was in full swing. After all, in Nazi demonology, the Jew had been the principal architect of the Bolshevik Revolution and was the symbol of everything 'unclean' that Germany was pitted against in her righteous war of self-defence and purification.

To a small but decisive number of Germans and Austrians, the Jew in the east had become divested of most, if not all, of the attributes associated with human beings – qualities that would generally have invited a measure of identity, sympathy, gentleness and compassion. The Jew was no longer 'one of us'. He was the ultimate 'other'. He was both 'our most dangerous enemy' *and* contemptible, entirely expendable 'vermin'.

In one's behaviour towards the 'sub-human' Jew, therefore,

all moral restraints could be cast aside – particularly when the state ideology demanded it (whether one believed it or not), when the extremities of war sanctioned it, and when one's career advancement depended on it. Not only that, but the chain of command, the bureaucratic system of which one was part and the collective group to which one belonged appeared to absolve the individual of all responsibility. What was important was to do one's duty with skill and efficiency. That was true virtue. The individual member of the SS did not create the system, did not invent the rules. In time it was possible to grow accustomed to just about anything, especially if new styles of language and methods of implementation were devised which could help distance one from the horror, and even allow one to sustain a sense of moral purpose.

The cold cult of professionalism

As Jeremy Noakes and Geoffrey Pridham have pointed out, in the case of senior SS officials, it was

> above all, the quintessentially modern cult of professionalism ... [that] enabled them to make a sharp distinction between public and private morality. ...
> The often fairly primitive low-ranking SS men, on the other hand, were quickly corrupted by being given the power of life and death over people whom they were officially encouraged to regard as sub-human, even though they were aware that in practice many were of superior social background and culture to themselves.[1]

The motives, mentality and moral 'colour blindness' of the perpetrators are partially revealed to us through their own speeches at the time and, more significantly, in a few memoirs written after the war. A recurring motif is what can only be described as a kind of 'shut-off mechanism' which allowed them to become almost totally blind to the essential humanity of the victims and the reality of the pain they were inflicting.[2] Particularly illuminating and disturbing are the recollections of Franz Stangl, former Commandant of the Treblinka extermination camp, recorded by the journalist Gitta Sereny in 1971.[3]

Stangl appeared to have felt no genuine hatred towards

Jews and indeed to have possessed no noticeable commitment to Nazi ideology. He claimed that at first, as an Austrian policeman, he had been opposed to the Nazi take-over of his native country. In late 1940, largely to escape from an unpleasant boss, he accepted the opportunity to be transferred to the post of police superintendent at one of the Nazi euthanasia centres. There he overcame his initial revulsion at the mass gassing of the mentally and physically handicapped, and performed his duties with great efficiency and attention to detail. He soon discovered a world in which he was effective and in which his efforts were greatly appreciated. The pattern was set. He had found his niche.

So impressive was his performance that, after the euthanasia programme was forced out of business by German public opinion, he was eventually transferred to the position of Commander of the Sobibor extermination camp. Several months later, in September 1942, he had distinguished himself to such an extent that he was given command of the then largest death camp in Poland, Treblinka. There he won a reputation among his peers as a gentle-voiced, courteous and affable figure, who ran his camp with clockwork efficiency. So dedicated was he to the punctilious carrying out of his duties that he won a commendation, which described him as 'the best camp commander in Poland'. Quite simply, he seemed – like most of us – to take enormous pride in doing a job well and to be greatly motivated by the admiration and recognition of colleagues and superiors alike. He acknowledged that the job was in certain obvious respects distasteful, but he was able to get used to that. The truly loathsome tasks he could of course delegate to others, particularly the prisoners, who could thus 'buy' a little extra time on this planet.

In his interviews with Sereny he stated that he regarded the Jews as 'cargo' to be despatched. He hardly ever saw them as individual human beings, more as an amorphous horde:

> It was always a huge mass. I sometimes stood on the wall and saw them in the tube. But – how can I explain it – they were naked, packed together, running, being driven with whips.[4]

Later in the war (after the uprising at Treblinka and the camp's destruction), Stangl assisted in the systematic organization of SS 'actions' against Yugoslav partisans. Later still he supervised 500,000 Italian construction workers under German command.

After escaping detection for many years, he was finally extradited from Brazil to West Germany and in October 1970 was found guilty of joint responsibility for the mass murder of 900,000 Jews. At no stage, either during the interrogation, the trial, or in his interviews with Sereny in prison, did any marked ideological hostility towards Jews emerge. It seems that, in his working life, he would have done whatever was asked of him, provided, that is, that he respected the source of authority from which the instruction came. As long as he received the approval of his superiors, he would aim for and reach quite remarkable standards of proficiency. This kind of mentality, where devotion to duty becomes an end in itself without reference to the content of that duty, is very typical of 'Nazi morality'. But it is certainly not confined to the Nazi period; it is a syndrome that will perhaps be familiar to many who have worked in a bureaucratic organization.[5]

The medical 'experimenters'

Such cool and detached professionalism, insulating individuals from an honest confrontation with the moral implications of their work, is especially detectable in the behaviour of the SS doctors who performed grisly experiments on human guinea pigs in the camps. They tended to justify their endeavours as contributions to the advance of medical knowledge. Such 'medical' activity involved sterilization, castration, the removal of living foetuses at different stages of development, transplanting human organs, seeing how long a man could survive in freezing water and many other experiments besides. The following excerpt is taken from the diaries of SS Doctor Johann Kremer, Professor of Medicine at the University of Münster and assigned to Auschwitz for ten weeks:

> 2 September, 1942 – First time present at a special action at 3 a.m. Compared with this, Dante's Inferno seems to me a comedy. Not for nothing is Auschwitz called the 'extermination camp'!

> 5 September, 1942 – This afternoon present at a special action for prisoners in the female camp: horror of horrors. Dr Thilo is

right when he told me this morning that we are in the 'anus mundi'. In the evening, at approximately eight, I was again present at a special action for the Dutch. The men all want to take part in these actions because of the special rations they get, consisting of a fifth of a litre of schnapps, 5 cigarettes, 100g. of sausage and bread.

6 September, 1942 – Today, Sunday, excellent lunch: tomato soup, half a hen with potatoes and red cabbage (20 g. fat) sweets and marvellous vanilla ice.... in the evening at eight outside for a special action.

9 September, 1942 – This morning I got the pleasant news from my lawyer ... that I got divorced from my wife on the first of the month (Note: I see colours again, a black curtain is drawn from my life). Later on present at a corporal punishment of eight prisoners and an execution by shooting with small calibre rifles. Got soap flakes and two pieces of soap. ... In the evening present at a special action for the fourth time.

23 September, 1942 – Present last night at the sixth and seventh special actions. ... In the evening dinner in the commandant's house, ... a real banquet. We had apple pie, as much as we wanted, good coffee, excellent beer and cakes.

3 October, 1942 – Today we fixed living material of human liver, spleen and pancreas. ...

12 October, 1942 – Inoculation against typhoid, after that feverish in the evening. In spite of that, present at a special action during the night (1,600 people from Holland). Terrible scenes near the last bunker. The tenth special action.

13 November, 1942 – Living, fresh material of liver, spleen and pancreas taken from a Jewish prisoner of 18 years of age, who was very atrophic. First we took a photo of him. Liver and spleen fixed as usual in Carnoy and pancreas in Zenker (prisoner no. 68030).[6]

Crude prejudice: the 'justification' for mass murder

On a different motivational level, crude prejudice, naked fanaticism and bloodlust were often satisfied in those who formed part of the killing squads. What follows is an extract from a letter written by a German police-sergeant serving in an *Einsatzkommando* unit in the southern Ukraine:

We men of the new Germany must be strict with ourselves even if it means a long period of separation from our family. For we must finish matters once and for all and finally settle accounts with the war criminals, in order to create a better and eternal Germany for our heirs. We are not sleeping here. There are three or four operations a week. Sometimes Gypsies, another time Jews, partisans and all sorts of trash. ... We are not carrying on a lawless regime here, but when an action requires immediate atonement we contact the SD and justice takes its course. If the official judicial system were operating, it would be impossible to exterminate a whole family when only the father is guilty.

I do not know if you ... ever saw such frightful kinds of Jews in Poland. I am grateful for having been allowed to see this bastard race close up. If fate permits, I shall have something to tell my children. Syphilitics, cripples, idiots were typical of them. One thing was clear: they were materialists to the end. They were saying things like: 'We are skilled workers, you are not going to shoot us.' They were not men but monkeys in human form.

Ah well, there is only a small percentage of the 24,000 Jews of Kamenetz-Podolsk left. The Yids in the surrounding area are also clients of ours. We are ruthlessly making a clean sweep with a clear conscience and then ... the waves close over, the world has peace.[7]

The moral blindness of leadership

What of the mentality of the SS leadership itself? Himmler, who had almost fainted when he attended a mass execution at Minsk, was nevertheless able to deliver the following address to senior SS officers in Poznan on 4 October 1943. There are two emphases in his speech, first the need for absolute secrecy in this 'glorious' task and, second, his insistence that the 'honour' of the SS remain unsullied. Here we see in one and the same person the extraordinary co-existence of an almost puritanical morality – he is clearly obsessed with the need to eliminate petty misdemeanours from the ranks of his men – with an unswerving commitment to wholesale genocide, an undertaking to which he attaches no *moral* importance. Here the motivation closely resembles a common feature in most, if not all, genocides. The perpetrator, particularly at the highest bureaucratic and ideological level, justifies his action as a pseudo-religious duty. The 'holiness' of his mission against the dehumanized 'enemy' sanitizes his deeds and exempts him from all sense of moral blame.

I also want to speak to you here, in complete frankness, of a really grave chapter. Amongst ourselves, for once, it shall be said quite openly, but all the same we will never speak about it in public ... I am referring here to the evacuation of the Jews, the extermination of the Jewish people. This is one of the things that is easily said: 'The Jewish people are going to be exterminated,' that's what every Party member says, 'sure, it's in our programme, elimination of the Jews, extermination – it'll be done.' And then they all come along, the 80 million worthy Germans, and each one has his one decent Jew. Of course, the others are swine, but this one, he is a first-rate Jew. Of all those who talk like that, not one has seen it happen, not one has had to go through with it. Most of you men know what it is like to see 100 corpses side by side, or 500 or 1,000. To have stood fast through this and – except for cases of human weakness – to have stayed decent, that has made us hard. This is an unwritten and never-to-be-written page of glory in our history ...

The wealth they possessed we took from them. I gave a strict order ... that this wealth will of course be handed over to the Reich in its entirety. We have taken none of it for ourselves. Individuals, who have erred will be punished in accordance with the order given by me at the start that anyone who takes so much as a single Mark of this money is a dead man. A number of SS men – they are not very many – committed this offence, and they shall die. There will be no mercy. We had the moral right, we had the duty towards our people, to destroy this people that wanted to destroy us. But we do not have the right to enrich ourselves by so much as a fur, as a watch, by one Mark or a cigarette or anything else. We do not want, in the end, because we destroyed a bacillus, to be infected by this bacillus and to die. I will never stand by and watch while even a small rotten spot develops or takes hold. Wherever it may form we will together burn it away. All in all, however, we can say that we have carried out this most difficult of tasks in a spirit of love for our people. And we have suffered no harm to our inner being, our soul, our character.[8]

Obedience to a higher authority

A naive, unquestioning obedience, which often involved the complete neutralization of any moral dimension to their deeds, is evident in the motives and behaviour of even the highest echelons of the SS bureaucracy. The final documents we shall consider in this section are selected from the startling reminiscences, rationalizations and self-evaluation of Rudolf Hoess. For three blood-drenched years Hoess was the Commandant at Auschwitz, where he oversaw the slaughter of almost 2 million people. He was himself executed at Auschwitz in 1947:

> I must emphasize here that I have never personally hated the Jews. It is true that I looked upon them as the enemies of our people. But just because of this I saw no difference between them and the other prisoners, and I treated them all in the same way. I never drew any distinctions. In any event the emotion of hatred is foreign to my nature. But I know what hate is, and what it looks like. I have seen it and I have suffered it myself ...
>
> When in the summer of 1941 Himmler gave me the order to prepare installations at Auschwitz where mass exterminations could take place, and personally to carry out these exterminations, I did not have the slightest idea of their scale or consequences. It was certainly an extraordinary and monstrous order. Nevertheless the reasons behind the extermination programme seemed to me right. I did not reflect on it at the time.
>
> I had been given an order, and I had to carry it out. Whether this mass extermination of the Jews was necessary or not was something on which I could not allow myself to form an opinion, for I lacked the necessary breadth of view.[9]

When asked if he had ever regarded the Jews he butchered as guilty of any crime or in any way deserving of their fate, Hoess attempted to explain that the question was in some way inappropriate as he had been living in a totally different reality:

> Don't you see, we SS men were not supposed to think about these things; it never even occurred to us. And besides, it was something already taken for granted that the Jews were to blame for everything. ... We just never heard anything else. It was not just newspapers like the *Stürmer* but it was everything we ever heard.
>
> Even our military and ideological training took for granted that we had to protect Germany from the Jews. ... It only started to occur to me after the collapse that maybe it was not all quite right, after I heard what everybody was saying. But nobody had ever said these things before: at least we never heard of it. Now I wonder if Himmler really believed all that himself or just gave

me an excuse to justify what he wanted me to do. But, anyway, that really didn't matter. We were all so trained to obey orders without even thinking that the thought of disobeying an order would simply never have occurred to anybody and somebody else would have done just as well if I hadn't. ... Himmler was so strict about little things, and executed SS men for such small offences, that naturally we took it for granted that he was acting according to a strict code of honour....

You can be sure that it was not always a pleasure to see those mountains of corpses or smell the continual burning. But Himmler had ordered it and had explained the necessity and I really never gave much thought to whether it was wrong. It just seemed a necessity.[10]

THE VICTIMS

Let us therefore bravely look the truth straight in the face.
Jewish Combat organization, 4 December 1942

A painful and disturbing notion arose from the conclusions of some of the early commentators on these terrible events: that the Holocaust essentially involved the interaction of Nazi perpetrators and the Jewish victims themselves; that at virtually every stage of the process of annihilation the Jews had 'cooperated', in their own destruction or had gone, as the cliché put it, 'like sheep to the slaughter'. When asked, in so many countries, to register as Jews, they had complied; when asked to wear the yellow star, they had complied; when asked to form Jewish Councils and Jewish police forces that would facilitate the work of the Nazis, they had complied; when asked to report at railway stations for deportation to the east, they had complied; when asked to dig their own graves, they had complied; when asked to walk into the gas chambers, they had complied.

The questions almost screamed out at us: why did they appear to be so cringing, passive and acquiescent? Why did they *allow* themselves to be massacred? Why did they offer no concerted resistance?

Such judgements, though built on some small basis in fact, were in reality often facile assessments subconsciously linked to crude stereotypes that perhaps owed more to the guilt and shame of postwar thinkers than to detailed scholarship and genuine understanding. To demand to know why Jews did not mount widespread armed resistance and opposition to the Nazi regime not only employs the extravagant logic of hindsight but betrays a genuine failure to grasp the essential conditions – physical and psychological – under which the Jews subsisted in Nazi-occupied Europe. For unlike other peoples subjected to Nazism, the Jews were locked into a predicament of almost total isolation, powerlessness and choicelessness. All generalizations about the mass behaviour of human beings are notoriously unreliable. In the case of the victims of the Holocaust, there is an added problem: is any one of us today truly competent to judge their responses to dilemmas which our imaginations would fail to conjure up even in our most disturbed nightmares?

The scale of Jewish resistance

Recent research has shown that the incidence of Jewish rebellion was, in fact, much greater than had previously been thought, though it was limited, inevitably, in its scope and effectiveness. There were eight major factors which militated against the staging of an effective Jewish armed resistance: the intense secrecy of Nazi plans and the consequent dearth of information available; the sheer isolation of the victims; the fear of 'collective punishment'; the belief among certain Jewish leaders in their economic indispensability to the Nazi war effort; the prevailing psychological climate of despair and helplessness; the natural human tendency to block out unwelcome possibilities; the unimagined enormity of Nazi intentions; and the Jewish cultural tradition of passivity.

1. Lack of knowledge

The Nazis went to staggering lengths to deny the Jews access to knowledge of the true meaning of 'evacuation to the east'. To be sure, despite the obsessive secrecy and deceitful jargon surrounding the Final Solution, there were occasional leaks of information, rumours and eyewitness reports, particularly in connection with the mass shootings in the Soviet Union. But by and large the Nazis were alarmingly successful in misleading the Jews and in manipulating their expectations. It was always tempting for the Jews to dismiss outrageous reports of factories where Jews were being systematically murdered as unreliable gossip and scare-mongering. In the context of war, confusion, terror and starvation there were always wild rumours which usually turned out to have no foundation. For most Jews, who were already in a state of demoralization and physical exhaustion, the idea that they would all soon be the victims of irrational genocide, unless heroic action was immediately undertaken, required a leap of imagination and will that was beyond the realistic capacity of most.

2. Isolation of victims
The second factor concerns the impossibility the Jews faced in establishing proper communication with the outside world. Even if the Jews had fully appreciated that certain death awaited them, the practical difficulties of maintaining vital contact with Jews in other ghettos and camps, of equipping themselves with weapons and necessary supplies, provided either by the free world or by non-Jewish partisan and resistance groups, were insurmountable. This was especially true in eastern Europe where they were needed most. The isolation of the Jews was agonizingly effective.

3. Fear of collective punishment
There was at all times the overpowering and justified fear of collective punishment. Time and again the Nazis had demonstrated that even the smallest act of defiance would be met by an awesome show of retribution and cruelty. The ghetto of Vilna, in Lithuania, provides a typical example: there the Nazis decreed that if anyone tried to escape from a work-party outside the ghetto walls, the entire group would be shot together with their families. We have already seen, even before the war, the scale of retaliation the Nazis mounted in response to the Grynszpan shooting. A major rebellion at the Bialystok ghetto in 1943 led to the seizure and murder of 1,000 Jewish children by way of 'punishment'.

4. Belief in economic value to the Nazis
It is hardly surprising, therefore, in this intimidating environment, that the stiffest opposition to planned resistance often came from Jews themselves and, above all, from their own leadership. This leadership tended to have an almost

mystical belief that Hitler would eventually be defeated and that their primary task was to struggle by all available means to keep as many Jews alive for as long as possible. Those who resisted were invariably seen not as heroic champions of their people, but as traitors who were irresponsibly endangering the lives of their fellow-Jews. The primary strategy for survival adopted by several Jewish leaders was to prove to the enemy that Jews could be productive and therefore economically indispensable to the Nazi war effort; such a strategy involved compliance at virtually every stage and was in complete opposition to the option of physical resistance.

5. Despair and helplessness

The fifth factor explaining the comparative lack of resistance belongs to the realm of psychology. In the grotesque world which the Nazis created for them, Jews had to contend with the unrelenting fear, degradation, the constant loss of loved ones and, above all, what has been termed the 'normality of death' around them. Consequently, they all too easily lapsed into a state of helplessness and paralysis which, for most of them, made effective armed resistance a psychological impossibility. As the psychoanalyst Bruno Bettelheim has pointed out, the unresisting behaviour of the Jewish victims must be understood as the result of the dehumanizing effects of Nazi attitudes and policy towards them. By such means the Nazis had succeeded in turning the Jews into 'docile masses from which no individual or group act of resistance could arise'. They became 'people who were so deprived of affection, self-esteem, and every form of stimulation, so totally exhausted, both physically and emotionally, that they had given the environment total power over them'. The Nazi camps, according to Bettelheim, had robbed the Jews of all individuality and 'made it impossible to see themselves as fully adult persons any more'.[11]

That the victims felt they were being punished for no logical reason, that they were entirely innocent of blame, must also have worked against them and accelerated their sense of resignation and despondency. Furthermore, even when they contemplated resistance, their despair of any realistic hope of success must have been intensified by the knowledge that the forces they were pitted against were so heavily armed, so well organized and so inflexibly committed to their cause.

6. Blocking out the unpalatable

A sixth explanation lies in the human inclination to block out information that one does not *want* to receive; the self-defence mechanism that seeks to repress knowledge of the unpalatable; the tendency to rationalize the terrible, to convince oneself that things cannot get worse than *this*; the seeming inability to grasp reality if it is unwelcome and undesirable.

7. Incomprehensibility of the Nazi plan

Most significantly, the enormity and utter audacity of the Nazi design was, quite simply, beyond the comprehension of most. As Isaiah Trunk, who more than any other scholar has investigated the responses of Jews to the Nazi onslaught, has written:

> Even the greatest pessimists in their darkest fantasies could not imagine that the 'final solution of the Jewish problem in Europe' meant the total physical extermination of all Jews regardless of sex or age. That would have been a crime without precedent in the history of mankind, and sane and reasonable people were incapable of conceiving of such a possibility.... when [escapees] told of their experiences, they encountered disbelief from people who listened sympathetically but who treated the stories as products of sick imaginations and disturbed minds.[12]

8. Cultural tradition of passivity

Suffering may have been part of the Jewish cultural tradition, but so had *survival*. The Jewish historical experience had, to an extent, conditioned them to expect persecution, misery and degradation, but it had also taught them that, if they kept their heads down, they would always win through. They were, however, entirely unprepared for an enemy who wanted to kill every one of them without mercy and without exception. The anti-Judaism of the Middle Ages and the fatalism of the rabbis had induced a certain docility and passivity in their response; the primary reactions of Diaspora Jewry had consistently been those of compliance, compromise and adaptation. They could not simply unlearn all the lessons of their own long history, especially when the other opposing factors intervened, and accept that there could be no accommodation with this most deadly of all foes.

The world of the victim

When considering the behaviour of the victims, the Nobel Prize-winning writer Elie Wiesel, himself a survivor of the camps, put it thus:

Reduced to a mere number, the man in the concentration camp at the same time lost his identity and his individual destiny. He came to realise that his presence in the camp was due solely to the fact that he was part of a forgotten and condemned collectivity. It is not written: I shall live or die, but: *someone* – today – will vanish, or will continue to suffer; and from the point of view of the collective, it makes no difference whether that someone is I or another. Only the number, only the quota counts. Thus, the one who had been spared, above all during the selections, could not repress his first spontaneous reflex of joy. A moment, a week, or an eternity later, this joy weighted with fear and anxiety will turn into guilt. *'I am happy to have escaped death'* becomes equivalent to admitting: *'I am glad someone else went in my place'*. It was in order not to think about this that the prisoners so very quickly managed to forget their comrades or their relatives: those who had been selected. They forgot them quickly – trying to shut their eyes to the reproachful glances which still floated in the air around them.

Why did the Jews in the camps not choose a death with honour, knife in hand and hate on their lips? It is understandable that all of us should wonder why. Putting aside the technical and psychological reasons which made any attempt at revolt impossible (the Jews knew they had been sacrificed, forgotten, crossed off by humanity), to answer we must consider the moral aspects of the question. The Jews, conscious of the curse weighing them down, came to believe that they were neither worthy nor capable of an act of honour. To die struggling would have meant a betrayal of those who had gone to their deaths submissive and silent. The only way was to follow in their footsteps, die their kind of death – only then could the living make their peace with those who had already gone.

I attended the Eichmann trial, I heard the prosecutor try to get the witnesses to talk by forcing them to expose themselves and to probe the innermost recesses of their being: why didn't you resist? Why didn't you attack your assassins when you outnumbered them?

Pale, embarrassed, ill at ease, the survivors all responded in the same way: 'You cannot understand. Anyone who wasn't there cannot imagine it.'

Well I was there. And I do not understand. I do not

understand that child in the Warsaw Ghetto who wrote in his diary: 'I'm hungry, I'm cold; when I grow up I want to be a German, and then I won't be hungry any more.'

I still do not understand why I did not throw myself upon the Kapo, who was beating my father before my very eyes. In Galicia, Jews dug their own graves and lined up, without any trace of panic, at the edge of the trench to await the machine-gun barrage. I do not understand their calm. And that woman, that mother, in the bunker somewhere in Poland, I do not understand her either; her companions smothered her child for fear its cries might betray their presence; that woman, that mother, having lived this scene of biblical intensity, did not go mad. I do not understand her; why and by what right, and in the name of what, did she not go mad?

I do not know why, but I forbid us to ask the question.[13]

Armed resistance

And yet, despite the near impossible circumstances, there *were* acts of physical resistance. Many did not carry the genuine belief that, as rebellions, they would achieve anything of substance; rather, their actions were born of hopelessness and of the need for a heroic gesture of defiance. Indeed, the question that ought perhaps to be asked is this: how was it possible, given the extremity of their physical and psychological conditions, that the Jews offered as much resistance as they did, limited though it undoubtedly was in its extent and in its practical consequences?

Despite the perilous obstacles, not least the opposition of many Jewish leaders and rank-and-file members of their own communities, a Jewish underground continued its political activities throughout the war years. It was engaged in a desperate attempt to keep abreast of developments in the Nazi empire, to warn the Jewish community – through illegal publications – of the fate of their brethren elsewhere in Europe, to secure what few arms they could and to urge their people to rise up against their oppressors. Jewish armed resistance was of two main kinds: uprisings in the ghettos and camps; and Jewish participation in their own partisan movements and in the general resistance and partisan organizations of Europe.

1. Uprisings in the ghettos and camps

The armed struggle was instigated, in the main, by three politically conscious groups: the Zionists, the Jewish socialists (Bundists) and the Jewish communists. The underground activity in the ghettos took place in a most antagonistic and dangerous environment: anything short of total success brought the heaviest penalties: torture at the hands of the Gestapo and inevitable death.

(a) Warsaw Ghetto Uprising

Armed revolts broke out in at least 20 ghettos in eastern Europe but the largest and most remarkable uprising against the Nazis took place in the Warsaw ghetto. It also constituted the very first armed rebellion by any civilian group in occupied Europe.

Betty Merti provides the following graphic description of this revolt:

> By the time the ghetto dwellers took up arms, 90 per cent of the half-million Jews of Warsaw were already gone. Starvation and disease had killed at least 100,000. The rest had been deported to the death camps. The remaining 60,000 were the most able-bodied workers whom the SS always saved for last. Many were teenagers.
>
> The heart of Warsaw's fighters consisted of two main fighting forces of men and women: the 600-member Jewish Fighting organization, under the leadership of twenty-four-year-old Mordechai Anielewicz, and the National Military organization, composed of 400 fighters. However, as the battle progressed, all ghetto Jews were to join in the fighting.
>
> They faced monumental problems. Very few of the fighters had had military training. Even worse, they had no arms! But what these young Jews lacked in equipment and training, they made up for in courage and determination.
>
> Intense training sessions began. To store what little food and supplies they could get their hands on, they dug underground bunkers and passageways. Nor did they allow themselves to become discouraged when the local Polish resistance refused to give weapons to their emissaries who had stolen out of the ghetto. Returning almost empty-handed, the emissaries had only a few rusty guns and several rounds of dynamite and ammunition which they had somehow managed to gather from

other sources. But the Warsaw fighters didn't give up; they made their own Molotov cocktails, mines, and other weapons to trip Nazi feet.

When the SS entered the ghetto gates in January 1943 to round up another trainload of people for deportation, they were frightened out of their wits. Bombs, wild shooting and mine explosions ripped into dozens of them. Twenty lay dying.

Even the Resistance was impressed when they learned about this episode. They still refused Anielewicz's invitation to join in the fight against their common Nazi enemy, but they did hand over a small supply of weapons. Altogether, the Warsaw ghetto forces now had three machine guns, a few hundred guns and a small supply of hand grenades.

They were certainly no match for the German forces who came down on them in full force on April 18, 1943. On Himmler's orders, 3,000 troops under the command of Jürgen Stroop descended on the ghetto. At the same time, tanks and other heavy artillery surrounded the walls of Warsaw. As reinforcements, 8,000 more German soldiers were stationed throughout the city of Warsaw. Himmler had promised Adolf Hitler a birthday present: the complete liquidation of the Warsaw ghetto within three days!

Hitler didn't get his present on time. After several days of savage fighting, Commander Stroop was flustered. German tanks had been splintered with bull's-eye hits from Molotov cocktails. Mines exploded and machine-gun fire cut the German forces down every time they entered the ghetto. The puzzled Stroop couldn't figure out how the Jewish fighters were moving from place to place sight unseen. Nazi machine-gun sights had scrutinized the empty ghetto street to no avail.

Little did Stroop know that the ghetto fighters were travelling through the connected attics of the buildings.

Stroop's revenge turned black. He ordered new battle tactics: search dogs, airplane bombers and fire. Now German bombers careened in and hurled their explosives at the ghetto buildings. Then Stroop ordered the burning of the buildings block by block. Suspecting that Jews were taking shelter in underground sewers, his men unleashed gas and smoke bombs in the sewer systems. He was right. Choking and suffocating, Jews tried to hold on. Many who could not fit into the underground sewers remained in the burning buildings to be consumed by fire rather than surrender to their Nazi tormentors. Those who jumped from the windows of burning buildings at the last minute became shooting targets for the Nazi gunners.

On May 8, after twenty-one long days in this living hell, the Nazis surrounded the hide-out of Jewish commander Mordechai Anielewicz and eighty other brave fighters. All eighty-one died in battle. By now the entire Warsaw Ghetto was aflame. Yet the few Jewish fighters who remained refused to surrende:. They fought on for another week!

On May 16, the ghetto was rubble. Over 15,000 Jews had died in battle. More than 50,000 had been captured and shipped off to death camps.[14]

(b) Defiance at Vilna

The following proclamation, calling for resistance, had been issued much earlier (January 1942) in the ghetto of Vilna, Lithuania, by the Jewish Pioneer Youth Group:

Jewish youth, do not be led astray. Of the 80,000 Jews in the 'Jerusalem of Lithuania' [Vilna] only 20,000 have remained. Before our eyes they tore from us our parents, our brothers and sisters. Where are the hundreds of men who were taken away for work by the Lithuanian 'snatchers'? Where are the naked women and children who were taken from us in the night of terror of the 'provokatzia'?

Where are the Jews (who were taken away) on the Day of Atonement?

Where are our brothers from the second ghetto?

All those who were taken away from the ghetto never came back.

All the roads of the Gestapo lead to Ponary.

And Ponary is death!

Doubters! Cast off all illusions. Your children, your husbands and your wives are no longer alive.

Ponary is not a camp – *all* are shot there.

Hitler aims to destroy all the Jews of Europe. The Jews of Lithuania are fated to be the first in line.

Let us not go as sheep to slaughter!

It is true that we are weak and defenceless, but resistance is the only reply to the enemy!

Brothers! It is better to fall as free fighters than to live by the grace of the murderers.

Resist! To the last breath.[15]

In the summer of 1943, many young Jewish fighters succeeded in escaping from the Vilna ghetto, formed Jewish partisan units (see p.203) and contributed to the eventual liberation of their city. There was a similar uprising at that time in the ghetto at Bialystok.

(c) Death camp revolts

There were even revolts in the death camps themselves: In Auschwitz about 12 prisoners blew up one of the crematoria and killed several of the SS guards. Although they were all later captured and executed, they had succeeded in reducing the destructive capacity of this most busy factory of death. In Treblinka there was a much bigger uprising involving several dozen prisoners. Only 12 survived, but the rioters had scored a great blow against the Nazis' feeling of invulnerability. In Sobibor several hundred prisoners stormed the gates; the majority were cut down in a hail of bullets or perished in the minefield on the perimeter of the camp, but so much damage had been inflicted that two days later the camp was permanently shut down. In this single most effective rebellion, it is thought over a hundred escaped, many of them to join anti-Nazi partisan units in the forests.

Despite the hopelessness of most forms of Jewish armed resistance, what it meant to those who took part can be gauged from the following document. It is taken from the last letter written by Mordechai Anielewicz, the leader of the Warsaw Ghetto Uprising:

> It is impossible to put into words what we have been through. One thing is clear; what happened exceeded our boldest dreams. The Germans ran twice from the ghetto. One of our companies held out for 40 minutes and another for more than 6 hours. ... Several of our companies attacked the dispersing Germans. ... Y[echiel] fell. He fell a hero, at the machine gun. I feel that great things are happening and what we dared do is of great, enormous importance. ...
>
> It is impossible to describe the conditions under which the Jews of the ghetto are now living. Only a few will be able to hold out. The remainder will die sooner or later. Their fate is decided. In almost all the hiding places in which thousands are concealing themselves it is not possible to light a candle for lack of air.
>
> With the aid of our transmitter we heard a marvellous report on our fighting. ... The fact that we are remembered beyond the ghetto walls encourages us in our struggle. Peace go with you,

my friend! ... The dream of my life has risen to become fact.
Self-defence in the ghetto will have become a reality. Jewish
armed resistance and revenge are facts. I have been a witness to
the magnificent, heroic fighting of Jewish men in battle.

Ghetto, April 23 1943[16]

2. *Partisan and general resistance activity*

Despite the uniqueness of their position as members of a group
that had been condemned to death, and despite the
extraordinarily difficult circumstances and generally hostile
environment in eastern Europe, tens of thousands of Jews
participated throughout Nazi-occupied Europe in the various
partisan or resistance movements. Sometimes they operated
as part of the general national or multinational guerrilla
struggle against the Nazis, sometimes in necessarily separate
Jewish contingents. For all the reasons outlined above, the
numbers involved were inevitably small when compared with
the millions of their brethren caught in the Nazi trap.

In western and southern Europe, generally speaking Jews
were less incapacitated by the hostility of the indigenous
population and, in addition to forming their own independent
units, were able to join the various resistance movements in
France, Belgium, Holland, Italy, Yugoslavia and Greece. In all
of these countries they made a valuable and heroic
contribution to military engagements with the German army
and their allies. They were also able to render life-saving
assistance to Jewish individuals on the run from the Gestapo.
In Slovakia, for all their vulnerability, Jewish groups were in
the vanguard of the formation of the anti-Nazi partisan
organization, which by 1944 grew into an all-out national
uprising. Two Jewish labour camps were actually liberated
during this rebellion and the freed prisoners swelled the ranks
of the insurgents.

In eastern Europe, however, most notably in Poland,
Lithuania, the Ukraine and Byelorussia, Jews frequently met
bigotry and animosity not only from ordinary inhabitants of
the countryside but even from the anti-Nazi partisan groups
who were themselves infused with antisemitism. The Jews
were consequently obliged – in many cases they actively
wanted – to form separate Jewish units. In 1944, however,
when the Russian army had established direct contact with

partisan groups in these territories, the Soviets did not tolerate autonomous Jewish units and they were mostly incorporated – often uneasily and warily – into the mainstream multinational partisan commands.

Two memorable focal points for Jewish resistance activity were in the Vilna and Bialystok regions. After uprisings in these ghettos, the surviving Jewish partisans continued their struggle in the forests. The fighting Jewish Brigade was formed in the forests of Rudnik near Vilna in four battalions under the leadership of Abba Kovner. Survivors of the Kovno ghetto, too, succeeded in making their way to these same forests. Elsewhere, the Jews of Minsk also featured prominently in the general partisan movements under Soviet control.

Spiritual resistance

Armed revolt was perhaps the obvious way of defying the enemy but it was by no means the only form of opposition. An increasing number of historians and other writers have extended the definition of resistance during the Holocaust period to include types of non-violent and 'spiritual' resistance. Since the Nazis were trying to destroy not only Jewish life but all vestige of Jewish dignity, any deed which the victim performed which was life-affirming – and which, in particular, proclaimed his Jewishness and sense of individual identity – would have run counter to the intentions and expectations of the enemy.

Cultural survival

Spiritual resistance included attempts by ghetto inhabitants to preserve – in unbearable conditions of deprivation – Jewish cultural, educational and religious activities. The holding of illegal wedding and Bar Mitzvah (confirmation) ceremonies, musical concerts and Hebrew language classes may well appear to us now as utterly irrelevant to the main business of staying alive. But such preoccupations did much to enrich whatever remained of life and, in the face of an omnipotent, remorseless enemy, should not be underestimated as examples of stubborn, even valiant resistance.

Acts of defiance

Other important acts of defiance included the smuggling of food, radios, newspapers and periodicals; the producing of drawings and paintings depicting life in the ghettos and camps; the taking of photographs and the keeping of diaries and other records – now such an important source of knowledge to historians. When, in December 1941, the renowned Jewish historian, Simon Dubnow (then 81 years old), was being dragged away by SS murderers in Riga, his last words – typical of the man – were: '*Yidn, shreibt un farschreibt!*' ('Jews, write and record!'). Even if he was not to survive, the most sacred act of resistance was to ensure that later generations be informed of the catastrophe overwhelming east European Jewry.

Commitment to physical survival: the 'sanctification of life'

In Jewish tradition, any Jew who was killed for his or her faith was considered to have died a martyr's death and to have achieved 'sanctification of the Name' (of God; Hebrew *Kiddush Hashem*). Indeed, this belief may account for the development of a passive, fatalistic attitude towards persecution for countless centuries. In the Holocaust period, however, there also emerged many instances of what has since been termed 'sanctification of life' (Hebrew *Kiddush Hachayim*), that the very act of clinging to and enriching life in the most desperate conditions, rather than succumbing supinely to one's enemy, was itself an expression of spiritual resistance. The following extract, taken from the Warsaw ghetto diary of Avraham Levin, demonstrates not only the intrinsic importance of recording and remembering but – in such tragic circumstances and against all the odds – the intensity of the Jewish commitment to life and survival:

One of the most surprising side-effects of this war is the clinging to life, the almost total absence of suicides. People die in great numbers of starvation, the typhus epidemic or dysentery, they are tortured and murdered by the Germans in great numbers, but they do not escape from life by their own desire. On the contrary, they are tied to life by all their senses, they want to live at any price and to survive the war. The tensions of this historic world conflict are so great that all wish to see the outcome of the gigantic struggle and the new regime in the world, the small and the great, old men and boys. The old have just one wish: the privilege of seeing the end and surviving Hitler.

I know a Jew who is all old age. He is certainly about 80. Last winter a great tragedy befell the old man. He had an only son who was about 52. The son died of typhus. He has no other children. And the son died. He did not marry a second time and lived with his son. A few days ago I visited the old man. When I left – his mind is still entirely clear – he burst out crying and said: 'I want to see the end of the war, even if I live only another half an hour!'

Why should the old man wish so much to stay alive? There it is: even he wants to live, 'if only for half an hour' after the last shot is fired. That is the burning desire of all the Jews.[17]

THE BYSTANDERS

One of the most painful aspects of being in the camp was the sensation of being totally abandoned.

A survivor, 1980

In my opinion, a disproportionate amount of time is wasted on dealing with these wailing Jews.

British Foreign Office memorandum, 7 September 1944

The history and literature of the Nazi Holocaust have understandably concentrated upon the perpetrators and their victims. Yet in the work of a growing number of scholars, attention has also fallen on the role of the 'passive accomplices' to Nazi brutality. To a greater extent than had previously been imagined, it is argued, the savage destruction of European Jewry was aided and abetted by the inaction and indifference of members of various groups – the peoples of Nazi-dominated Europe, the various churches, neutral countries, the International Red Cross and even those nations fighting against the Nazis. Jewish communities in the free world, particularly in the United States and Palestine, have also been criticized for not being vigilant enough in defence of their European brethren. This sentiment has been expressed very strongly by Simon Sibelman:

Those who stood by in utter indifference to what they saw somehow appear less human. To commit acts of sadistic barbarity is tragically a human characteristic. To suffer the indignities of persecution, to become a victim of senseless hatred and pain likewise forms part of the human condition. But to remain perfectly indifferent, to choose to impose a degree of selective amnesia and to adopt a role of total passivity is a denial of human responsibility.[18]

On the other hand, to many observers, the inclination to be aloof and detached from the problems of others – particularly when those problems are not actually witnessed – is all *too* recognizable and 'human'. The tendency to shut out of our consciousness and consciences all kinds of horrors which today fill our newspapers and television screens is only too familiar – though no less excusable for being so. During the Second World War, despite the constant flow of rumours and information about the Final Solution, the conception of what the Jews were actually experiencing was deeply influenced by what Walter Laqueur describes as 'the denial of reality, the psychological rejection of information which for one reason or another is not acceptable'. Even American newspaper editors, who ran stories about the 'extermination' programme, admitted that they were unable to digest the meaning of their own headlines. Words were simply not adequate to convey such reality. This inability to absorb and comprehend was, in many instances, combined with an undercurrent of anti-Jewish feeling, which made it easier to dismiss and disregard such stories.

How – and indeed whether – to pass judgement on onlookers who, by their inaction, connive at the commission of crimes by others is a question that has exercised the minds of philosophers, theologians and jurists for many centuries. One thing, however, is certain. If the universal lessons of the Holocaust are to be grasped and genocide prevented in the future, we must try to understand how it happened, in terms not only of the killers and the killed, but of the bystanders as well.

We shall briefly consider the roles of three groups: the ordinary people of Germany under Nazi sway; the Anglo-American Allies; and the Churches of Europe.

German bystanders

It can be asserted with a fair degree of certainty that the Holocaust was not perpetrated by an isolated criminal elite acting alone; nor, as a contrary notion, was the Holocaust a 'popular' war of extermination against the Jews. Rather the Holocaust was perpetrated by an ideological clique in power which relied upon the deep-seated but largely 'passive' antisemitism of much of the population in Germany itself (in eastern Europe – especially in the Ukraine, Lithuania and Poland – the antisemitism was generally more active). In the end the Nazis successfully quarantined their victims by cutting the normal channels of social interaction and by constructing a wall of isolation behind which the Jewish community could be slaughtered with most of the non-Jewish population reduced either to unawareness or indifference.

The *Kristallnacht* of 1938 had demonstrated to the Nazi leadership the futility of trying to win popular approval for a violent campaign against the Jews *inside* Germany. The German population as a whole was *not* ideologically Nazi and, with the exception of the youth educated under the new regime, there was little racial consciousness. There was, however, a deep and ancient gulf between gentile and Jew which was still further widened by such prewar measures as the official removal of occupational and social contact, the creation of Jewish housing zones, the cutting off of telephones and the imposition of curfews and restrictions on the use of public transport. With less and less communication, with greatly increased segregation and, as we have seen, with the progressive dehumanization of the victim in the eyes of all, the twin image of the Jew as both danger and parasite was reinforced to strengthen these existing isolationist attitudes.

During the war, the occasional Allied radio broadcasts which focused on the persecution and massacre of Jewish and other civilian populations in Nazi-occupied Europe, were generally dismissed by the German public as gross exaggerations associated with anti-German propaganda. These allegations of barbaric behaviour could all the more easily be shrugged off by a population which was in any case disinclined to feel sympathy or empathy towards the Jewish people, especially that most 'alien' of groups, east European Jewry.

We can hardly escape the conclusion that in both Germany itself and in other European countries the Nazis succeeded in exploiting huge reservoirs of what has been called 'static' antisemitism, essentially a legacy of Christian, religious antisemitism, to enable modern 'dynamic' racial antisemitism to pursue its goals unimpeded. As the historian Ian Kershaw has written:

> Popular opinion, largely indifferent and infused with a latent anti-Jewish feeling, further bolstered by propaganda, provided the climate within which spiralling Nazi aggression towards the Jews could take place unchallenged. ...
> The road to Auschwitz was built by hate but paved with indifference.[19]

(For a more detailed examination of the attitudes of ordinary Germans to the treatment of Jews during the 12 years of Nazi rule, see Chapter 9.)

The Anglo-American Allies

In the case of the western Allies, who undoubtedly fought not only in their own interests but in defence of civilized humanity, the following questions have been posed: what did they know of the death camps and when did they receive their information? How did they respond to the knowledge they received? Could anything more have been done to save lives? Was the lack of intervention by the Allies a contributory factor to the direct criminality of the perpetrator? And – most difficult of all – to what degree, if any, can they be held morally accountable for the deaths of millions? (These questions are seldom asked of the Soviet Allies, presumably because they were preoccupied with the agonizing struggle to defeat the Nazi aggressor, in the course of which they lost many more lives – both civilian and military – than did any other country. Another reason may be that we tend to judge Stalin's Russia, itself a most brutal regime, according to different moral standards. Stalin's genocidal policies towards the Kulaks, in the period 1929–32, is estimated to have claimed up to 14 million lives.)

On such a highly charged emotional theme as the Holocaust, the historical and the hysterical can sometimes become confused. Yet there does seem abundant evidence in the works of Martin Gilbert,[20] Bernard Wasserstein,[21] David Wyman[22] and others that the Anglo-American Allies, most notably certain individuals in the US State Department and the British Foreign Office, for a multiplicity of reasons – disbelief, expediency, incompetence, apathy and downright prejudice among them – were in possession of the requisite knowledge but were either unable or unwilling to intervene.

So was it, in fact, indifference that prevented the Allies from taking measures to rescue civilians destined for mass annihilation? Certainly ignorance could not be used as an excuse for inaction. The first detailed account of mass murder reached the west in May–June 1942. Not unnaturally it took time for such information to be internalized. It was not until 17 December 1942 that the Americans and British gave this and subsequent information sufficient credence to announce that the Nazis were indeed systematically murdering the Jews of Europe.

The question of whether the Allies were truly in a position to save Jewish lives is extraordinarily complex militarily, politically and logistically. Such a question can only be properly tackled within the global context of the Second World War. Certainly no easy charge should be levelled against those whose priorities were determined by the life-and-death struggle in which they themselves were engaged. What remains an undisputed fact, however, is that the Allies did not make any genuine attempt to rescue Jews.

Assessing Allied non-intervention

There are several considerations that should be borne in mind when weighing Allied behaviour. Firstly, the Allies were generally disinclined to intercede on behalf of victimized civilian populations inside enemy territory; they claimed a prior need to defeat the enemy militarily, an objective to which all potential distractions should be subordinated. On the other hand, they did make allowances for those 'valiant allies-in-arms' who, having been defeated, were worthy of further support while under occupation, such as the citizens of Greece.

Secondly, it is difficult to imagine how the Allies could have prevented the slaughter of well over a million Jews by the

Einsatzgruppen murder squads in the Soviet Union in 1941–2. Nor could they realistically have prevented the deaths – through overwork, starvation and disease – of tens of thousands of Jews in the ghettos of Poland.

Thirdly, the principal method whereby the Allies might have made an effective intervention was by precision bombing of death camps and their railway systems. The explanation given for the Allies' failure to consider bombing Auschwitz during the first two years of its murderous activity was that Auschwitz's real purpose remained a secret until mid-1944 – an admission revealing just how woefully defective Allied intelligence was in respect of civilian populations inside Nazi Europe. Only after the arrival of information provided by three escaped prisoners was the true nature and function of the Auschwitz complex revealed; it had been known of since 1940 as a Polish concentration camp and was identified later as a synthetic oil plant, but this seems only to have further confused the Allies.

The first request for bombing, therefore, came as late as July 1944, but was not acted upon because of resistance from the Air Ministry and other British bureaucrats. Winston Churchill, who has generally received a good press on most matters relating to the Holocaust, does not appear to have had sufficient interest in the project to push it through. Despite the timing of the request, and even though between May and July 1944 nearly 400,000 Hungarian Jews had already been deported to Auschwitz, a successful bombing operation could still have saved up to 250,000 remaining deportees.

In his book dealing with the response of the United States government to the Jewish question, David Wyman states:

Most likely, it would not have been possible to rescue millions. But without impeding the war effort, additional tens of thousands – probably hundreds of thousands – could have been saved.[23]

A second line of approach by Allied governments *was* actually used successfully in Hungary earlier in 1944, before the Nazis assumed direct control of that country's internal affairs. Allied pressure was applied to Nazi Germany's satellites and allies to discourage compliance with German requests to hand Jews over for deportation. Since 1943 it was clear to most countries that Germany was about to lose the war and the threat of Allied retribution was becoming a more realistic possibility as each day passed. In certain respects this threat was already beginning to bear fruit by 1943 and may partially explain why countries such as Italy, Hungary, Romania and Bulgaria – perhaps somewhat surprisingly – refused to 'evacuate' many of their Jews, except when under direct German occupation. Nevertheless, David Wyman argues that this pressure could and should have been stepped up by the United States and the other Allies.

Wyman further suggests that the United States should have funded and encouraged neutral countries – Spain, Portugal, Turkey, Switzerland and Sweden – to take in refugees on a temporary basis. More permanent and distant reception camps could have been set up in North Africa. At the very least, he adds, wartime visa quotas could have been filled for entry into Palestine and the United States.

Britain, it must be stressed, despite possessing incontrovertible evidence of the slaughter of the European Jews (though not its extent) remained unshakeably committed to her earlier policy of drastically limiting the number of Jews admitted to Palestine. For in order to assuage Arab anger and thus win Arab support in Britain's conflict with Hitler, the average annual number of Jewish entries to Palestine had been restricted to a mere 15,000 under the terms of the White Paper of May 1939 – a quota rigorously enforced right through the war years. David Ben-Gurion, the leader of the Jewish settlement in Palestine, had responded in sheer disbelief:

> We must assist the British in the war as though there were no White Paper, and we must resist the White Paper as if there were no war![24]

The Jews of Europe, who were so desperate for a sanctuary, were to be cut off – in the interests of power politics – from their most obvious haven.

An additional charge made against the Allies is that they ought to have broadcast into occupied Europe more information about the Nazis' true intentions towards the Jews. This might have broken the powerful spell of deception to which the Jews and other members of the population had fallen prey. As

Rudolf Vrba, the Czech Jew who escaped from Auschwitz, put it:

> Would anyone have got me alive to Auschwitz if I had had this information? Would thousands and thousands of able-bodied Jewish men have sent their children, wives, mothers to Auschwitz from all over Europe, if they knew?[25]

As it was, the cloak of secrecy, intimidation and terror which had descended on Jews and non-Jews alike, enabled the Holocaust to take place against a backcloth of silence, ignorance and evasion of truth.

Excuses for Allied inaction

There were several standard Allied excuses for not launching rescue attempts on behalf of Jewry, some more convincing than others. The first was that the necessary shipping required for such an undertaking was simply not available. Second, they feared the presence of foreign agents among Jewish refugees, which might seriously have undermined the war effort. The third factor which discouraged Allied intervention was the application of the principle of non-discrimination. The American State Department and British Foreign Office refused to acknowledge the special case of the Jews, given that others – Poles, Ukrainians, Russians and White Russians – were also being butchered in their millions.

Fourthly, there was a fear in both Britain and the United States of an economic, antisemitic backlash at home, if there was a large influx of Jewish refugees. This attitude certainly prevailed before the war, as we have seen at the time of the Evian Conference of July 1938, but it also persisted well into the war years.

Fifthly, there was the overriding concern that nothing should detract from military priorities. Consequently, there was opposition to the investment of time, energy and resources in rescue attempts that might slow down the conduct of the war itself. The overall campaign to overthrow the Hitler tyranny as speedily as possible was considered to be the most valid and effective means of assisting *all* suffering civilian groups in Europe. As a Foreign Office communiqué put it: 'By ridding Europe of the present German regime, we hope to render a supreme service to the Jewish people.'

The sixth factor, as we have seen, was British anxiety about reverberations in Palestine. The designation of Jewish refugees as potential emigrants to Palestine acted as a barrier to British help, since they continued to dread the loss of Arab support in the region. This fear was particularly strong before 1943, while the war in North Africa was still in the balance. This helps to account for aggressive British action towards ships carrying Jewish refugees in their desperate bid to reach the Palestine shore. Several were simply turned back to the European mainland. The most shocking, tragic and unnecessary episode involved the *Struma*, a boat with 769 Jewish refugees aboard, including 260 women and 70 children. The British refused to let it proceed beyond Turkish waters, even though the official Palestine quota would have permitted their entry. Eventually the boat was torpedoed (probably by a Soviet submarine patrolling the Black Sea) and on 24 February 1942 everyone – with the exception of one refugee – was drowned.

Lastly and most decisively, the Jews were simply not perceived as a legitimate allied nationality worthy of help. As Bernard Wasserstein concludes: 'One of the most depressing features of British policy towards the Jews ... [was] their peculiarly ungenerous treatment.'[26] Other defeated allies were given help on a large scale – over 100,000 Poles, Greeks and Yugoslavs were evacuated after 1942; and the Allies supplied much of the food needs of the Greek population between 1942 and 1945. The Jews, on the other hand, were viewed neither as a nationality nor as an ally.

Conclusions

What we are left with are some important but ultimately unanswerable questions. Was it in fact within the Allies' power to have exerted a meaningful influence on events deep inside enemy territory? Even if we conclude that intervention might have yielded positive results, is it reasonable to assume that the Allies could have known this then? Can we fairly claim that their priorities, at such a time of national and international emergency, ought to have coincided with ours today? Were the Allies morally obliged to take measures to alleviate the suffering of any and all of the victims of Nazi brutality?

Or – on the contrary – did this inaction on the part of the Allies, in fact, represent the triumph of national self-interest over conscience and morality? Did the decision-takers and civil servants in London and Washington feel any real sympathy for the Jews and, for that matter, for the gypsies and other 'remote' victims of Nazism? Was there any semblance of an emotional or political interest in the destiny of Europe's Jewish population?

It can further be asked whether the complacency of the Allies was of the same order as the indifference of the European bystanders. Or is it our own want of imagination that makes us expect, say, British bureaucrats to have understood the hell of Auschwitz from the comfort of Whitehall? Quite clearly, Britain and the United States did not consider it their duty to initiate action that went beyond their mainstream strategy for ensuring the defeat of Nazi Germany. But are these excuses mere rationalizations? Did the 'superior' prejudice and xenophobia of a British or American civil servant neatly dovetail with the manic Jew-hatred of Nazi ideology to prevent any escape?

The Church

Strictly speaking, any serious evaluation of the part played by the Church in the history of the Nazi Holocaust must have, as its starting-point, the contribution over a period of 1,500 years of Christian theology and demonology to the development of negative stereotyping about Judaism and the Jewish people. In this section, however, we shall confine our enquiries to the public stance adopted by the various Churches throughout Europe during the Hitler years and particularly during the period 1941–5. (For an examination of religious anti-Judaism and its transformation into racial antisemitism during the nineteenth and twentieth centuries, see Chapter 3.) While it is desirable to avoid generalizations in such a delicate area as this, it is quite impossible to assess the extent of activity by individual church functionaries who were doubtless working 'behind the scenes' in the fight against Nazi racism and genocide.

The Catholic Church

(a) The Vatican

Much of the debate on the role of the Church in Nazi-occupied
Europe – and in particular the accusation of callous
insensitivity to the plight of the Jews – has been focused upon
the behaviour of the Pope and the Catholic Church as a whole.

During the war the Vatican, which enjoyed – as it does today
– political and diplomatic independence, was officially neutral.
Like many neutral states, it felt extremely vulnerable to Nazi
aggression, especially since Hitler made it clear that he would
brook no opposition from the Church. So long as Germany
appeared likely to win the war, the official Catholic Church
tended to adopt, at best, a silent posture and, at worst, an
apparently pro-German stance. After all, one of Germany's
principal foes was the Soviet Union, and the Vatican was
intensely anti-communist. However, after Germany's military
reverses at Stalingrad and El Alamein, and with her defeat an
ever increasing probability, the Vatican – preoccupied (in
common with other neutral countries) with survival and no
doubt with an eye on its postwar reputation – danced less
cravenly to the Nazi tune.

The principal accusation levelled against Pope Pius XII is
that, in the face of countless appeals, he consistently refused to
speak out against the Nazis' policy of annihilation, a policy
described by Winston Churchill in the summer of 1944 as
'probably the greatest and most horrible crime ever committed
in the whole history of the world'. This silence was even
maintained while – in his own back yard – 8,000 Jews of Rome
were being hunted down for deportation to the death camps.
Why, it has been asked repeatedly, did the Pope not utter a
solemn denunciation of this crime against the Jews and
against humanity? His moral authority was so great that, had
he publicized the true purpose behind deportation, he would
have been believed, whereas Allied broadcasts could always be
dismissed as propaganda. Why did he not threaten with
excommunication the many Catholics who participated in this
mass murder? Had he done so, it has been argued, it would
certainly have had no effect on nominal Catholics like Hitler
and Goebbels, but it might have deterred Polish complicity and

reduced the number of Catholic recruits to the SS in Lithuania, Austria and Germany itself.

Why, it has been demanded, did he not give a clear moral and spiritual lead to Catholic priests throughout Europe? In June 1941, when the Vichy French government introduced 'Jewish laws' closely modelled upon the Nuremberg Laws, the Pope responded to appeals from French bishops by stating that such laws were not in conflict with Catholic teaching. Later efforts by the British, Americans and Poles to persuade the Vatican to publish a specific condemnation of Nazi extermination of the Jews fell on deaf ears. The Pope, came the reply, could only issue a general denunciation of wartime atrocities.

A strong and openly voiced papal line might have silenced those Catholic bishops throughout Europe who actively and fervently collaborated with their Nazi masters. An example of the very worst of such enthusiastic clerical support for Nazi ideology – and a clear indication of the link between modern antisemitism and earlier expressions of Christian contempt and hostility towards the Jewish people – appeared in a paper published by the Bishop of Sarajevo, of the Croatian Catholic Church in Yugoslavia. The article, entitled 'Why Are the Jews Persecuted?' contains this extract:

> The descendants of those who hated Jesus, persecuted him to death, crucified him and persecuted his disciples, are guilty of greater sins than their forebears. Jewish greed increases. The Jews have led Europe and the world towards disaster – moral and economic disaster. Their appetite grows till only their domination of the whole world will satisfy it. ... Satan aided them in the invention of Socialism and Communism. There is a limit to love. The movement of liberation of the world from the Jews is a movement for the renewal of human dignity. Omniscient and omnipotent God stands behind this movement.[27]

(b) German Catholicism

In Germany the Catholic hierarchy restricted its expressions of sympathy towards victims of Nazi racism mostly to Jewish converts to Catholicism. Vague statements about 'unjust treatment' of foreign races were made by a few German bishops, but in such general terms that they had no effect either on public opinion or on government policy. One heroic exception was Father Bernhard Lichtenberg, who recited a daily prayer for the Jews and was subsequently arrested because of this public display of tenderness. In October 1941 he had the following announcement read from pulpits of all the churches in his diocese:

> An inflammatory pamphlet anonymously attacking the Jews is being disseminated among the houses of Berlin. It declares that any German who, because of allegedly false sentimentality, aids the Jews in any way, be it only through a friendly gesture, is guilty of betraying his people. Do not allow yourselves to be confused by this un-Christian attitude, but act according to the strict commandment of Jesus Christ: 'Thou shalt love thy neighbour as thyself.'

Father Lichtenberg died in November 1943, while being transferred to Dachau concentration camp.

While it is clear that the Church in Germany, including the minority Catholic Church, was desperate to avoid confrontation with the Nazi authorities, their failure to take a public stand in defence of Jewish lives must be placed in the context of the successful outcry against the euthanasia programme. In August 1941, after a similarly slow and hesitant response by a Church fearful of imperilling its pastoral and ecclesiastical position, the Bishop of Münster, Cardinal Clemens August von Galen, staged the most vigorous and dramatic opposition to the state-sponsored murder of the old, the crippled and the insane. This was by no means the only example of Church and public denunciation of euthanasia but it was the most decisive. Within three weeks Hitler had ordered a halt to the programme. A powerful precedent had been established: it had in fact proved possible for those with religious authority to deflect the Nazis from their seemingly irresistible course. When it came to the Jewish question, this precedent would be largely ignored.

(c) Catholic response in other countries

The moral cowardice of both the Vatican and the German episcopate stands in marked contrast to the behaviour of individual Catholic bishops and papal nuncios in other countries. In France, Belgium and Holland, senior Church dignitaries frequently used their pulpits to protest against Nazi deportation of Jews, to deplore the participation of Catholic police in round-ups and to urge Catholics to provide shelter and protection to Jews. In Romania, Hungary and Slovakia, satellite countries where it was easier to make representations to the government than in countries ruled directly by the Nazis, Catholic clergy, acting for the most part independently of the papal policy of non-intervention, went to the most courageous lengths to rescue Jews. (According to some commentators, the local Catholic nuncios were, in certain instances, under instructions from the Vatican to do what they could to save Jewish lives.)

Protestant and Orthodox Churches

(a) The Protestant Churches in Germany

The overall record of the official Lutheran Church of Germany is dismal and depressing. To be sure, there were isolated exceptions – instances where local clerics defied the prevailing attitudes and encouraged their congregations to protect Jewish victims of oppression. Undoubtedly many survivors owe their lives to individual acts of humanitarianism and compassion thus inspired. But the overwhelming impression is one of silence, fear and subservience to the dictates of the Nazi authorities. Such lack of concerted opposition can only have served to reinforce the general acquiescence of the population at large.

Nevertheless, one of the most remarkable figures from the entire Nazi period was Pastor Martin Niemöller, a Protestant minister and the guiding spirit of the anti-Nazi Confessional Church. He was twice arrested, found guilty of subversive attacks against the state and spent seven years in concentration camps. After the war, he coined this memorable and timeless message:

> They came for the communists, and I wasn't a communist,
>   so I didn't protest;
> They came for the socialists, and I wasn't a socialist,
>   so I didn't protest;

They came for the trade unionists but I wasn't a
trade unionist, so I didn't protest;
They came for the Jews, and I wasn't a Jew, so I
didn't protest;
Then they came for me, and there was no one left to protest.'

(b) Protestant and Orthodox Churches outside Germany

In occupied territories the response of Protestant leaders was
more heartening. In France, Holland, Norway and Denmark
official protests against deportation of Jews were lodged and
messages of support recited from church pulpits. In one quite
remarkable case the entire French village of Le Chambon-sur-
Lignon, inspired by its charismatic Protestant pastors (André
Trocmé and Edouard Théis), rescued about 2,000 Jews, either
by hiding them in ordinary villagers' homes or by smuggling
them out from under the very noses of the Gestapo.

Prominent leaders of the Greek Orthodox Church in Athens
and Salonica vigorously opposed the abuse of Jewish life and
the transportation of thousands of Jews to Auschwitz, but to no
avail. In Yugoslav Croatia, too, there is evidence that officials
of the Orthodox Church pleaded with the authorities to curtail
the vicious treatment meted out to both Orthodox Serbs and
Jews.

In Germany's satellites, Nazi policy towards the Jews was
sometimes challenged and blocked. In both Romania and
Bulgaria high-ranking members of the Orthodox clergy
objected in the most forceful way, intervening with their
respective governments and saving many Jewish lives. In the
Nazi puppet-state of Slovakia, too, the Lutheran Church
registered protests about the treatment of Jews. In Hungary,
however, bishops of the Lutheran and Reformed Churches
supported the introduction of anti-Jewish legislation in 1938
and 1939. Although they later protested – after the imposition
of direct German rule in 1944 – against mass deportations of
Jews, by then it was too late for them to influence the course of
events and the horrendous slaughter of their fellow-
Hungarians was allowed to proceed.

There is no record of any public protests at all from
non-Roman Catholic Churches in other countries of Nazi-
occupied Europe (i.e. Belgium, Italy, Finland, Poland,
Bohemia-Moravia, or Austria). In the neutral countries, the

Protestant Churches in Sweden and, rather belatedly, Switzerland also played a part in reducing the miserable plight of Jewish fugitives from Nazi terror. Most notably, the Swedes saved the majority of the Jews of Denmark by taking them in after a daring sea-borne operation. They also admitted many Norwegian Jews. The Swiss record is more chequered: they saved over 20,000 Jews – most of them late in the war when Hitler was clearly heading for defeat – but before 1944 they had also turned many thousands back to their doom.

In the free world, church leaders in the United States and Great Britain made an energetic contribution to their nation's cries of dismay and outrage. But in the final analysis, they were unable to persuade their governments or military establishments to take concrete steps towards the saving of lives.

CHAPTER 9

The Jewish Question:
Public Opinion in Nazi Germany

The one condition necessary for the triumph of evil is that
good men do nothing.

Edmund Burke

Public Reactions during the period 1933–9

One of the most crucial, yet puzzling areas of inquiry for the
student of the Holocaust concerns the feelings and attitudes of
ordinary Germans during the 12 years of Nazi rule. Any
attempt, however, to assess the pattern of responses by the
German public to anti-Jewish propaganda and policy in the
Third Reich poses serious difficulties for the historian. The
Nazi government's interference in people's lives and in the
formation of their opinions was so great – through an incessant
barrage of propaganda, indoctrination, rigged plebiscites, a
rigidly controlled media, the absence of opinion polls and the
constant fear of denunciation – that it is not at all easy to reach
accurate conclusions about the stance of different social
classes, political groupings and religious denominations. Nor
can we clearly identify which sections of the population
actively supported the regime, accepted its aims and willingly
joined in the antisemitic campaigns, which sections made
up the silent and complacent majority, and which sections, if
any, actively opposed the regime.

In spite of these formidable barriers, a number of broad
findings do emerge clearly from some of the available
documents and memoirs, especially the Nazis' own local

222

surveys of the mood of the general population. The use of such materials, compiled by loyal Nazis, poses obvious problems; nevertheless, since they were secret and intended only for internal consumption, such appraisals are less prone to distortion and form a *comparatively* reliable source of information.

Reactions to antisemitic propaganda

Antisemitic propaganda may have played a fundamental role in unifying the Nazi Party, but it certainly did not perform the same function with the public at large. There is striking evidence for this assertion from the autumn of 1934 when the anti-Jewish campaign was being stepped up. The Gestapo station's report at Potsdam for the month of September reads as follows:

> Undoubtedly the Jewish question is not the main problem of the German public. ... Utterances on the Jewish peril are dismissed as of no account and those engaged in enlightening the population are to a certain extent depicted as fools.[1]

The attitude so vividly sketched in this report is also characteristic of other regions, unconcern and indifference appearing to dominate the public response to antisemitic propaganda and indoctrination. This may account for the relatively small numbers of Germans (excluding party members and sympathizers) actually participating in concrete anti-Jewish activities – riots, physical attacks, destruction of property and similar acts of vandalism. Moreover, even if we cannot always identify perpetrators of anti-Jewish raids, it can be inferred from endless testimonies that they mostly belonged to Nazi organizations such as the Hitler Youth or the SA, whose savage character and hooligan behaviour were well known. The great majority of the population, meanwhile, preferred the role of passive spectators.

Even during the summer months of 1935, when the attacks reached an unprecedented height and swept frighteningly through the country, most of the population refrained from direct involvement. One illustration of this point is contained in the survey of July 1935 compiled by the Gestapo station at Kiel:

> It is noteworthy that whenever there are actions against the Jews, these emanate chiefly from members of the Party and its affiliated organizations, whereas the majority of the population hardly participates in the Jewish question.[2]

Furthermore, this report reflected conditions in the Protestant north – an area noted for its massive support for National Socialism – yet strongly suggests the sheer nonchalance of most of the population towards the antisemitic drive. In other regions the response was even less favourable. From a report surveying the public mood in the Rhineland – a Catholic region with more liberal traditions – we can deduce that a sizeable section of the population there completely rejected *Der Stürmer* (the party's antisemitic newspaper). They neither appreciated nor welcomed the rag's crude attempts to fan popular hatred by reviving the medieval Blood Libel (accusing the Jews of using Christian blood in their baking of Passover bread).

In rural areas there is strong evidence of the population's reluctance to sever relations with the local Jewish inhabitants. Bavarian peasants, for example, were anxious to continue their trade with Jewish cattle-dealers and were clearly irritated by the Nazi Party's unrelenting tirades against Jewish activities. In Bavaria, according to Ian Kershaw, 'peasant attitudes were determined almost wholly by material considerations and economic self-interest. Nazi propaganda played no part.' The local Gestapo described the peasants who supported Jewish economic activity as having 'no idea about the racial problem'. Similarly, the Gestapo in Munich, reporting on the continued relations between Jews and peasants, found 'shocking results'.

In urban districts it was widely believed that certain elements only joined in antisemitic activities in order to settle personal scores and to eliminate economic competition. The motives behind such participation were therefore often perceived as greed, envy and the satisfaction of private interests.[3]

Responses to the rioting and economic boycott

When anti-Jewish boycotts were organized, the general public did not seem to be willing collaborators with the party machinery. However, we should not conclude that reluctance to participate in anti-Jewish actions derived from principled opposition to state-sponsored discrimination. The German population were, in effect, helping to sustain a tough antisemitic policy by largely turning a blind eye. Nevertheless, at this early stage, they were inclined to resist its implementation through boycott and violence. For the most part they continued to patronize shops owned by Jews, despite the heavy pressures exerted by party activists to frighten off their customers.[4] The poorer segments of society were especially unresponsive to the call and carried on shopping in Jewish-owned stores. Similar conduct is detectable among other social categories: industrialists, for example, did not react favourably to the party's appeals. Once again, it was not the breach of any code of morality that lay behind their objections; they were chiefly concerned that anti-Jewish activities at home might damage Germany's economic interests overseas: they were wary of international retaliation which might take the form of anti-German boycotts organized by American and British Jews.[5]

Objections to the boycott and to violence increased when the public questioned the political wisdom of such actions, judging that their own interests might be jeopardized. The Gestapo of Kosslin, for example, reported that, while the local population was indeed antisemitic, they did not wish to be harmed by antisemitic policy.[6] Harburg's report for August 1935 reached similar conclusions: there the local Gestapo stressed that the public tacitly refused to show understanding for the attacks on Jews and even went so far as to condemn them vigorously.[7] The explanation for this reaction, the report stated, was that the public believed the maltreatment of Jews to be counterproductive because the victims would be turned into martyrs. There were also complaints that the damage done would have to be paid for by the state. Some disapproved, for instance, of the Nazis' smashing of plate glass because they were convinced that German insurance companies would inevitably be obliged to return its cost to the Jews.

That the public elevated their own economic wellbeing above loyalty to party doctrine is evident from a Gestapo survey in the district of Koblenz for the months of August and September 1935. A township in that district had actually requested that the level of antisemitic pressure be reduced; since the inhabitants earned their livelihood from a Jewish-owned medical institution, they argued that its closure would mean a radical loss of income for many family heads.[8]

For others it was not antisemitism that aroused criticism but its extent and degree. A report from Magdeburg for July stated that in the public view the antisemitic campaign had simply gone too far. From the survey for Cologne we learn that it was not persecution of Jews *per se* that upset the public but the brutal and vulgar *nature* of that persecution. A major concern frequently mentioned in these early reports was that of Germany's image abroad. As one Gestapo agent explained, the public voiced its reservations because anti-Jewish riots were felt merely to add fuel to the 'atrocity propaganda' spread outside Germany against the Third Reich. According to these reports, only very seldom was popular indignation rooted in humanitarian values, expressions of solidarity with the persecuted Jews being extremely rare.

Reactions to the legislation

As we have seen, the Nazis' very first law of 7 April 1933, the Law for the Restoration of the Professional Civil Service, established racial criteria for all public appointments and led to the dismissal of thousands of officials. In contemptuous disregard for the Weimar Constitution, it removed 'non-Aryans' from the Civil Service, alleging that the republic had filled the bureaucracy with incompetent functionaries. In reality, of course, the Nazis simply wished to purge state institutions of Jews and other 'undesirable' elements. Nazi radicals may have been unhappy with the relatively small scale of the purge, but the public seems to have accepted the legislation without much protest. The lack of opposition to this policy is grounded in various factors. Firstly, the extent of the purge had been deliberately restricted to minimize the level of disruption to bureaucratic activities – in Prussia it affected between 12.5 and 15.5 per cent of the administration, in other states much less (between 4.5 and 5 per cent). Secondly, the purge proved a welcome source of upward mobility, with many only too happy to take advantage of the dismissal of Jews from state, municipal and other public offices. Jewish judges and magistrates were retired, doctors discharged and teachers forced to relinquish their posts. In this way many fresh job opportunities were created, thus keeping the public happy.

The state's antisemitic legislation also featured a prohibition on conscription of Jews into the army when, at the end of February 1934, the law of 7 April 1933 was made applicable to the armed forces. Yet the army had, on its own initiative, already proposed, in December 1933, that the Aryan clause be observed in the appointment of all officer cadets. As this affected only a few dozen officers, it drew a minimal reaction, the structure of the military being left essentially unaltered. The few voices of protest in army circles were principally concerned with their growing loss of independence and gradual subordination to the party's ideology.

Reactions to the Nuremberg Laws

As we saw earlier (in Chapter 5), at the festive rally of the Nazi Party at Nuremberg in September 1935, two laws were adopted which radically affected the status of German Jews. The bulk of the population appears to have received these laws with a sense of approval and even relief. This acceptance did not merely represent conformity to the authority of the state as a law-making institution: that a law is a law simply because the state deems it so. It was rather a deep identification with the very spirit of the legislation, which met the need to institutionalize the concepts of racial separatism within the Reich, thus providing formal confirmation of the isolation and removal of the Jews from the midst of the German nation.[9] Secondly, and most significantly, the laws met with public approval because they curbed the apparently random and anarchic antisemitic violence, containing it securely within the framework of law and order.

The law annulling Jewish citizenship aroused little comment. Since it officially sanctioned an existing reality, it was accepted as an obvious and natural development. As for the Law for the Protection of German Blood and Honour, the population's acquiescence signified an increased readiness – to some extent – to embrace Nazi doctrine as well as the desire to be rid of the unpleasantness and uncertainty caused by anti-semitic terror. The public assumed that this law would fully pacify the streets and thus help to restore Germany's flagging image as a civilized nation.

The waves of terror which had preceded this legislation had filled the public with alarm and confusion. Individual acts of violence against Jews and Jewish property were seen as undermining public order. There were also fears that the violence might spread to non-Jewish groups, who were identified as targets. This included the various churches and any who maintained social or economic contact with Jews, or who were represented as doing so. The atmosphere of unbridled denunciation and public condemnation, which grew especially tense towards the middle of 1935, had engendered a sense of crisis which demanded a solution. As a report by the Gestapo in Berlin made clear, what disturbed the public was the absence of a clear and agreed policy towards the Jews.[10] It added that, since more and more complaints were being lodged about 'race defilement', it would be impossible to prevent the renewal of antisemitic riots by normal police methods. The population, it went on, expected a legal settlement of the question of race desecration. The laws plainly excited great enthusiasm because, in place of muddle and disarray, they had finally achieved – as the Gestapo agent put it – a clearly defined relationship between Jew and German.

Examples of unqualified reservations about these laws, because of their inherent immorality, are conspicuous by their rarity. Only among serious opponents of the regime were the laws challenged, whether on ethical or political grounds. Some churchmen roundly condemned the principle of racial discrimination – a criticism voiced, for example, in sermons given by Evangelical pastors who were hostile to the ideology of the Nazi Party. The racial legislation also raised an acute problem over the status of converts whose origins were Jewish. The Marxist underground censured the laws and issued a call to turn the struggle against antisemitism into a concerted struggle against the regime. Antagonistic remarks were also heard from certain members of the educated bourgeoisie and liberal intelligentsia, who objected on both moral and pragmatic grounds.

Some of the dissatisfaction over the Nuremberg Laws stemmed from self-interest and, once again, from fear of economic reprisals against Germany.[11] Individuals employed by Jews expressed their understandable dismay at being faced with the prospect of unemployment. In commercial circles, too, there were dissenting voices among those who believed that the Jews abroad would use this legislation as a pretext to whip up anti-German feeling. In addition, there was one specific item in the law which attracted opposition from a section of the population that felt singularly threatened: the clause prohibiting the employment by Jews of German maids under the age of 45 aroused the resentment of those Christian women who saw it as an assault on their livelihood.

Reactions to antisemitic radicalization in 1938

In 1938 the Jewish question was again placed to the fore of a virulent propaganda campaign, intensifying pressure to expel the Jews from Germany. During the winter and spring months, the Aryanization process was abruptly stepped up. At the same time, there was a new wave of antisemitic rabble-rousing, and a discernible increase in the number of violent attacks. In the summer this policy assumed even more serious dimensions: at the end of May, rioting broke out in Berlin, reaching its climax in the so-called *Juniaktion*, when large numbers of German Jews were arrested.

As for the overall public reaction to these events, there was no specific change in the now familiar attitudes that had crystallized during the preceding years. As this stage, too, despite the strength of traditional anti-Jewish attitudes, self-interest came before allegiance to party dogma. Although the public felt little sympathy for Jews, they did not refrain from shopping in Jewish stores where this was still possible.

The German population appears to have remained entirely consistent in their indifference towards persecution of the Jews, even when its level was severely increased during the summer of 1938. The 'socialist informer' from Schleswig tried to explain this lack of interest as a sign that the German public were too distracted by their own troubles, in particular by their fears of war breaking out. Besides, many simply failed to comprehend the logic of reviving the antisemitic drive since, in their view, the Jews had already been successfully driven out of the German economy.[12]

Reactions to Kristallnacht

It took the unprecedented nationwide pogrom of 9 November 1938 to provoke a major negative reaction in the German population. This seems to have been prompted by their dislike of overt signs of suffering. Their personal confrontation with a sight they had no wish to see persuaded many Germans that the bounds of acceptability had been breached. Up till then the acceptance of antisemitism as a social norm had undermined any resistance to the persecution of Jews in the Third Reich. The public had gradually grown used to an antisemitic reality and had generally taken no notice of it. Their toleration of 'mild' antisemitism had unquestionably paved the way for harsher measures. On the other hand, ordinary Germans clearly could not countenance actions which outraged their sense of decency, even if those actions were directed against a despised and stigmatized minority. For, as long as the Jews were merely segregated and, in most cases, rarely seen, the public could deny the reality of their misery. As long as the Germans could content themselves with abstractions about a mythical Jewish menace, they could sustain an indifferent stance.

The *Kristallnacht* pogrom, however, appears to have shaken them out of their complacency and made them rudely aware of the implications of supporting the Nazi regime. This explains why it was only then that many sections of German society registered their deep shock and revulsion at what they had witnessed on their city streets. Even within the upper echelons of the Nazi Party there were disagreements – as we have seen in Chapter 7 – about the wisdom and timing of such *open* and widespread physical abuse. However, although a critical tone is apparent in most of the sources, the dominant motif is by no means one of condemnation grounded in moral concerns. In most of the cases quite different feelings are revealed: shame at the act itself, alarm at its extent and, in particular, regret for the wasteful destruction to property. The most vehement objections came from those groups which feared they might be next in line for similar treatment, especially the Catholic minority and German intellectual circles.

The American consul in Leipzig recorded the reactions of the local German population to *Kristallnacht*:

> The shattering of shop windows, looting of stores and dwellings of Jews which began in the early hours of 10 November 1938 was hailed subsequently in the Nazi press as 'a spontaneous wave of righteous indignation throughout Germany ...'. So far as a very high percentage of the German populace is concerned, a state of popular indignation that would spontaneously lead to such excesses, can be considered as nonexistent. On the contrary, in viewing the ruins and attendant measures employed, all of the local crowds observed were obviously benumbed over what had happened and aghast over the unprecedented fury of Nazi acts that had been or were taking place with bewildering rapidity throughout their city.[13]

Reactions in wartime, 1939–45

Conditions for Jews

Before exploring German public responses during the war itself, it is important to bear in mind the conditions in which Jews lived in wartime Germany. A state of isolation had been systematically established; Jewish families were compelled to move to overcrowded communal quarters occupied exclusively by fellow-Jews. In the cities they were transferred from many different districts to Jewish neighbourhoods – a form of ghettoized environment – and were obliged to display a Star of David on their front doors. Administration of these houses was turned over to the Jewish community itself. Jews were not seen in cinemas, at concerts, in museums, libraries, or parks. They were barely visible in shops, since only the most meagre food ration was allowed to them; and they were compelled to buy all their provisions at clearly designated shops and only at certain fixed hours.

They were only very rarely glimpsed at work. For in order to extract the last ounce of work from them before their deportation from the Reich, all Jews between the ages of 16 and 65, fit and unfit, were drafted into forced labour, and usually into segregated companies. Those assigned to a particular factory were organized into a single group and put to work in such a way as to make contact with German workers almost impossible. In factory canteens, Jews were forbidden to take their meals together with other workers. Later on, they were barred from canteens altogether and ordered to eat in special kitchens organized by their own community inside the factory compound.

Eventually Jews were not seen in the commercial world at all. In the autumn of 1941, they were finally prohibited from engaging in any kind of business whatsoever. The exceptions to this rule were a handful of physicians, dentists and lawyers, granted special permission to continue practising. Even in these cases, however, they were not permitted to call themselves by the customary titles, but had to adopt special designations such as 'medical adviser', or 'legal adviser'. Those professionals allowed to remain in practice could only retain their Jewish clients. Conversely, non-Jewish doctors and lawyers were forbidden to provide services to Jews.

Jews seldom appeared on public transport, since they were forbidden to use street cars and could only travel on railways with a special permit which was rarely granted. A curfew was established for Jews alone which required them to be off the streets by 8 p.m. during the winter and by 9 p.m. during the summer. One of the paradoxical effects of this isolation was that it actually cut down the level of anti-Jewish violence; because Jewish ties with the German population had by now been almost totally severed, they were consequently less exposed to immediate physical danger.

German public response

According to a contemporary eyewitness, the general attitude towards Jews was neutral and reserved, most people giving precious little thought to their plight.[14] In the street and during rare encounters on public transport there was little harassment. Occasionally there were expressions of surprise that Jews were still around; sometimes there were uncomfortable and embarrassed looks. But the overwhelming impression is that long-term exposure to the unpleasant realities of Jewry's demeaned and institutionalized status had caused most people to become quite inured to their wretched condition. They had become just another fact of life and barely merited comment. The individual's sensitivity to his former neighbour had, to put it mildly, been dulled by daily immersion in a poisonous and corrupting racist environment.

It was by no means only the party that monitored and restricted contact with Jews. By this stage, many ordinary members of the public, too, endorsed the 'legal' persecution and insisted that unsettled issues of anti-Jewish policy be resolved. Indeed, there were numerous examples of public dissatisfaction with inconsistencies surrounding the Jewish question – in spite of the overwhelming indifference, there were regular criticisms of laxity in the implementation of anti-Jewish policy. Professional practitioners formally requested that Jews no longer receive pay for public holidays. A doctor protested that, in writing to a Jewish counterpart, he still had to address him by his title, as if he were a colleague; if a university professor became a criminal, he argued, his title would be taken away; why, therefore, should a Jew – an arch-criminal who had started the war – receive such courtesies? Some expressed their anger that Jewish children should continue to receive the same milk ration as German children or that some Jewish houses remained unmarked in defiance of the law. Others took exception to regulations regarding public transport: they complained that Jews, who travelled third class with their special permits, could still enter the same compartments as German workers and soldiers, who were thus unable to avoid contact with them. They suggested that Germany copy Slovakia by insisting that Jews travel in special wagons. There were also those who pleaded that Jews be barred altogether from public transport, except when travelling to work.

The restrictions on shopping hours for Jews also served as a source of complaint. Some urged that Jews should only purchase their products *after* regular hours, when Germans had finished their shopping, or that they be assigned to separate stores. Still others recommended that Jewish clothing be externally marked, as in Poland, so that they would not come to markets and so that 'Jewish-looking' Germans would face no threat of assault. Some argued that the overall antisemitic measures taken fell short of the desired state of affairs and that the best solution would be to evacuate the Jews immediately from Germany.

Sympathetic Germans

The preponderance, by this time, of extreme antisemitic dispositions casts into shadow the relatively few cases of benevolence shown towards Jews. There were, without doubt, examples of generous and compassionate attitudes displayed by individuals swimming against extremely powerful currents in German society. Some attempted to defy the authorities by providing Jewish families with items of food they were not allowed to buy, such as fruit, pastry and chocolate. A small minority of Germans – individuals who had been profoundly moved by the Jewish predicament – displayed a quite exceptional moral stature and proved willing to offer help for strictly altruistic reasons.

A Jewish woman from Stuttgart recalls in her diary how a few brave Germans came to her family's assistance:

> 1939 – My mother and I are forced to leave our flat. The beginning of the war – further restrictions and bans. However, these bans are not always respected by non-Jewish fellow-citizens. When the foodstuffs allocated to us begin to get scarce, a woman who is a complete stranger gives my mother a quarter of a pound of butter as she passes her in the street. Now and then we find a basket of vegetables, fruit and eggs in front of our door. Those are in short supply, particularly for us. Sometimes such things are brought to us in our flat by loyal people, to a flat which non-Jews should not have entered. But these are only glimpses of light in this gloomy hopelessness.[15]

A few, operating within small clandestine networks, provided Jews with food and clothing. Some extended help quite independently of any anti-Nazi organization, like the handful of anonymous Germans who brought provisions to Jews rounded up in assembly camps prior to deportation. To keep a sense of proportion, however, it must be emphasized that these acts of good will, while being in many instances noble and even heroic, represent but a tiny fraction of the overall public response. When viewed in that light, these deeds of kindness seem even more remarkable.[16]

The authorities' stance towards compassionate Germans

The authorities did everything they could to discourage such displays of individual compassion. In October 1941, for example, the Gestapo chief, Heinrich Müller, issued the following order:

> It has repeatedly come to our notice recently that persons of German blood continue to maintain friendly relations with Jews and appear with them in public in a blatant fashion. Since such persons of German blood apparently even now still show a lack of understanding of the most elementary and basic principles of National Socialism and since their behaviour must be regarded as a flouting of official measures, my orders are that in such cases the person of German blood concerned is to be taken into protective custody for educational purposes or in serious cases to be transferred to a concentration camp, Grade 1. The Jewish participant is invariably to be taken into protective custody and transferred to a concentration camp for the time being.[17]

Acts of humanity derived their inspiration from a variety of sources. Some were motivated by Christian ethics: this was true of members of the German Society of Friends, who sent parcels to deportees in Poland and were arrested for their pains. It also accurately portrays the intentions of the nuns who helped Jews in the convent outside Munich where the 'Jewish Ghetto' was created.

Actions which were sympathetic towards Jewish victims of Nazism tended to be wholly unrepresentative of general trends within German society and, in so far as they were almost always performed by unorthodox individuals, did not really call into question the overall antisemitic policy. In several instances it was a question of offering assistance to known acquaintances; there are even examples of quite prominent citizens appealing to high-ranking personalities to intercede on behalf of their Jewish acquaintances. Those who conducted themselves in this manner drew a distinction between their theoretical approval of a policy, on the one hand, and its implementation within their own social milieu on the other. For many, raising objections to the continued hounding of Jews was not grounded so much in a dislike of antisemitism, as in a wish to uphold the outward show of law and order which they felt was being violated by Nazi barbarity. Some, sorely shaken by the savagery, turned away from Nazism, especially after 1938 when they found the hooliganism and terror of *Kristallnacht* utterly abhorrent.

There was another kind of positive treatment of Jews, which rested neither on religious and humanitarian considerations, nor on a wish to maintain law and order. Quite simply, there were sometimes cynical material benefits to be gained, employers plainly having ulterior motives for treating their Jewish employees with comparative decency: they were only too glad to get workers who would do their jobs without any risk of distraction through military service or by the need to give time to Nazi Party rallies.

The churches and churchgoing public

Many of those who grasped the real meaning of Nazi policy towards the Jews, and who were well placed to attempt some form of organized rescue, chose to do nothing. This posture was highly characteristic of the German church hierarchy which generally opted to remain silent in the face of glaring inhumanity. For example, when the law forcing Jews to wear a yellow badge was issued in September 1941, some parishioners told their priests that they no longer wished to pray, or take communion with converted Jews. So, in order to encourage Germans to continue attending church, converted Jews wearing the yellow star were asked to stay away from services or to attend inconspicuously (i.e. to stand where nobody else could see them). Such incidents prompted the Confessing Church in Breslau to disseminate a leaflet throughout the Reich, urging Christians not to discriminate against converted Jews. It also suggested that former Jews be seated on special benches to protect them from violence and that trustworthy churchgoers sit next to them.

The position in Catholic communities was no different. In the large cities the idea was put forward by both members of the clergy and their congregations that a community of Jewish Christians with its own religious services be set up, to avoid giving offence to German Christians. When this came to the notice of Cardinal Bertram, he pronounced that any measures which might be hurtful to Jewish converts be avoided. He conceded, however, that if this approach posed problems, the Church should consider holding separate services.

These were the sentiments towards converts, who were supposedly fully integrated into German society. Indeed, the biographies of half-Jews and converts provide staggering pictures of what they had to endure, precisely because they still had, or wanted to have, contact with the surrounding society. They reveal the German public's deep entanglement in the Nazi web. It was certainly not the Nazi terror apparatus alone that was to blame. Personal accounts demonstrate how converted Jews were ostracized even by the churchgoing population. Christians flatly refused to kneel next to a former Jew or take communion with him. Even priests abstained from contact with converted Jews.

Personal diaries and recollections disclose how painful it was for these converts when people of their own persuasion and social grouping – the educated circles of civil servants – declared their contempt. These displays of antipathy were not exclusively anti-Jewish. Rather, they mirrored the pronounced racist tendencies of the German population towards Jews and other 'inferior' peoples. For example, many sources show that the issue of attending church with Polish slave-workers was also the subject of heated exchanges, as were the special services granted by the Catholic Church to foreign, mainly Polish, workers – a consequence of the refusal by German churchgoing population to pray with them.[18]

Reactions to the yellow star

When the compulsory wearing of the yellow star was introduced for Jews in September 1941, some protests were lodged but only in very small, inconsequential ways. For the overwhelming majority the theme was not important enough to transform criticism, if they had any, into full-blown opposition. Of those who took exception to the measure, some Catholic and middle-class Germans complained that it represented a reversion to medieval practices. For others this antisemitic regulation triggered off apprehensions that Germans in neutral and Allied countries – particularly in the United States – might suffer reprisals, perhaps being marked by a swastika in retaliation.

In response to previous antisemitic measures, many could hide behind their private lives and show no apparent interest. Labelling the victim with a yellow star, however, brought the issue out into the open as a symbolic reminder of what it meant to acquiesce in such a divisive system. The conscience of many ordinary Germans was, for the first time, disturbed by this public branding of the Jew. These feelings, however, did not seem to last long. As had happened with other measures, the sheer passage of time, combined with the penalties imposed for showing sympathy to Jews and, above all, mounting indifference to what had become a common sight brought increasing insensitivity. Acts of charity towards Jews, recorded by eyewitnesses, show that the labelling aroused dormant moral reflexes only in small segments of the population. Most Germans, however, would simply grow used to the branding of Jews. It was certainly easier to adjust to a criminal normality than to persevere as a non-conformist – all the more so when such acceptance earned the approval of one's peers and considerable economic benefit from the Aryanization and appropriation of Jewish property.

A Jewish woman recalls her feelings at having to wear the yellow star:

> Wearing the yellow star, with which we were branded from 1941 onwards as if we were criminals, was a form of torture. Every day when I went out into the street I had to struggle to maintain my composure.
>
> I had some bitter disappointments with acquaintances and colleagues. I was treated very badly by a doctor. I learnt then what it meant to be at the mercy of someone without compassion.
>
> In 1943 I took a train from Sillenbuch to my place of work and on the platform – it was forbidden for Jews to go inside the vehicle even if one had the travel permit issued by the Gestapo – I found myself among a group of teenage school children. They shouted: 'Throw the Jewess off.' They recognized that I was Jewish because of the yellow star. Throughout the journey through the Sillenbucher forest I could feel them pressing against my back. The pupils behind me (both boys and girls) shouted and abused me. Some boys were standing in front of me and I looked at them very calmly and seriously. They looked away in embarrassment and did not move. And then the others quietened down and nothing happened.[19]

Reactions to the deportations

What were the responses in 1941–3 to news of the deportations, when a large proportion of the population either knew or could surmise that a deportee was highly unlikely to return? Were the deportations warmly endorsed by the population or did they meet with protest or indifference?

The Jewish issue was certainly not a major factor in shaping public opinion in wartime Germany. Yet the circumstances surrounding the deportation policy heightened the public's awareness of what was taking place. For example, abandoned Jewish property and Jewish belongings put up for public auction were coveted both by official parties and by private individuals. Abundant documentation exists to suggest that, after the Jews were sent to the east, the question of who would profit from the plunder became hotly disputed.[20] Unscrupulous members of the public, anxious for a share of the spoils, grumbled that the best goods had been seized by party bosses and that the apartments of deported Jews had not been made available to them.

The deportations were significant enough to become a theme of discussion and debate among the various sections of the population most plainly affected by them. Those who gave voice to serious reservations came mainly from Church circles and the liberal intelligentsia – especially among the older generation. Since Nazi policy violated some of the fundamental principles of these groups, religious and liberal values played a greater part in the formation of their opposition. They objected to the deportations out of a combination of Christian humanitarianism, moral sensitivity and fear of retribution. Church leaders warned of divine punishment for sending Jews to their deaths, couching their disaffection in theological terms.

Committed Nazis naturally supported the deportations and greeted the imminent elimination of all German Jewry with enthusiasm. In other sections of society approval and dissent were interwoven. Some showed a readiness to object to the regime's policy, protesting not so much against the principle of deporting Jews as against a particular aspect of that measure; for instance, they were prepared to defend local Jews whom they held in esteem, while agreeing that others should all be deported. As long as anonymous Jews were persecuted, it seems that the population could remain free from emotional involvement, detached from the moral consequences of the infliction of pain their silence had helped to promote. Again, it would be wrong to conclude that such objections as there were were motivated by purely ethical or humanitarian considerations. Some undoubtedly were, but many smacked of undisguised self-interest. This was often the case with industrialists heading firms which employed Jews. As a result of conscription, manpower was scarce and the armaments industry constantly pressed for higher production. Consequently, industrialists asked that their Jewish workforce be spared, arguing that they were vital to production needs; the real attraction of Jewish workers, of course, was that they were an extremely cheap and totally unprotected source of labour.

Reactions to the extermination

> As far as the great majority were concerned, Jewish suffering affected beings in another galaxy rather than inhabitants of the same planet as themselves. ... basically the Holocaust was not a real event to most Germans, not because it occurred in wartime and under conditions of secrecy, but because Jews were astronomically remote and not real people.
>
> Richard Grunberger[21]

Once the Nazis started to implement a Europe-wide policy of extermination, refusal to believe and 'repression' were typical reactions of the Jewish victims, who naturally did not want to accept that what awaited them was inevitable death. But what was the response of the average German conformist, of the silent majority? After the war the common claim that the German people 'did not know' was often – though not always – an elaborate pretence in order to shrug off responsibility. During the war, however, many members of the public did sense the common guilt, since their perception of the killing operations exceeded mere suspicion.

From 1941 on, chilling stories and rumours circulated about what was really happening to the Jewish population in the eastern territories. Since soldiers on leave made no secret of the murderous activity of the *Einsatzgruppen*, their stories fuelled speculation about the fate awaiting deportees. In response the public, it seems, chose to bury the unpalatable truth about the mass killings – to suppress it in the belief that non-involvement in the Jewish question would dissociate them from collective guilt. Passivity and apathy were the outward appearances the public assumed perhaps to minimize discomfort and embarrassment. But behind the apparent insensitivity lurked a frightened consciousness. The population sensed the catastrophic end of the regime it had tolerated and in whose crimes so many had become implicated. Hence, despite ceaseless and strenuous efforts – conscious and unconscious – to hide the unpleasantness of the Jewish issue, it re-emerged when fears of reprisals fed feelings of guilt.

Such concerns were articulated as soon as the earliest whispers of the extermination reached the German population. The public may have tried their best to ignore the deportation and extermination programmes, but feelings of guilt and shame surfaced when they were confronted with the prospect of punishment (by the Allies). In appealing to, and attempting to reinforce, antisemitic feelings, the Nazis did not diminish the public's anxieties, but in fact achieved quite the opposite, highlighting the far-reaching moral implications of Hitler's extermination policy.

Up to this point the antisemitic campaign had been more or less tolerable, and never sufficiently outrageous to provoke more than a show of irritation – especially once the persecution of Jews bore the external mark of legality. Many may have disliked the physical persecution yet remained silent in the face of terror. At least in this way, it was thought, the Jews would be eliminated from Germanic life and order restored to the streets. It was an unfortunate but moderate price to pay to achieve a utopian racial community. Many ordinary Germans came to realize, however, that there was a huge difference between acceptable discrimination – even when 'emergency' terrorist tactics had sometimes to be employed – and the unacceptable horror of genocide. They recognized that there was a point beyond which they could not applaud the antisemitic mania; that to be receptive to fantastic arguments whose consummation was mass murder was to link themselves irrevocably with, and thus become accomplices to, the Final Solution.[22]

Conclusion

If *all* Germans had been solidly and undeviatingly behind Hitler – if they had *all* been rabidly committed to Nazi Jew-hatred – in a curious way that would have made the Nazi era in general, and the Holocaust in particular, a *less* frightening phenomenon. For had that been the case – if Germans had all thought and behaved as one – this twentieth-century episode could simply be dismissed as an utterly bizarre historical aberration, as though invaders had landed from outer space.

But the truth is that Nazi Germany did exist in the real world; Germans of the 1930s and 1940s – like any other set of human beings – embraced a whole range of different attitudes and sentiments. There were many who were democrats at heart; many who favoured socialism and liberalism; and many who were tolerant and gentle. Only a minority of the German electorate ever voted for the Nazi Party in free elections, and literally millions of Germans loathed everything Hitler represented and never wished to wage war on anyone. *And yet* the Nazi Party reigned supreme and succeeded in implementing the most ghastly parts of its unlikely programme.

This is what finally makes the Nazi era so horrifying: that so many Germans, who at no time embraced Nazi ideology, were capable – in relation to the Jews, at any rate – of suspending normal moral standards and of blocking out of their minds the horror they had indirectly promoted; they were certainly able to distinguish between right and wrong, yet could allow themselves to be dominated by such an evil philosophy. To state this alarming reality does little to resolve the vexed question of the 'responsibility' of the ordinary German. In the context of a totalitarian society such as Nazi Germany that entire issue remains open-ended, highly subjective and deeply problematic. But one thing is certain: the German people cannot pin *all* the blame on Adolf Hitler and a handful of his cronies.

CHAPTER 10

The Aftermath and Impact of the Holocaust

The toll

The Second World War brought carnage and devastation to many parts of the globe, on a scale never before experienced. It is neither easy nor, perhaps, desirable to set apart the calamity suffered by any one group; when the evidence is examined, however, the nature – if not the extent – of the Jewish experience appears strikingly different from that of any other group, whether combatant or non-combatant. It is this singularity which gives the Holocaust its distinctive character and unique identity.

Out of an estimated worldwide total of about 53 million dead (approximately 15 million military battle deaths, and approximately 38 million civilian deaths), some 6 million Jewish civilians had been murdered as part of a plan of comprehensive annihilation within the continent of Europe. In terms of statistics, the inventory of the dead is quite stupefying: more than one third of all the Jews in the world, more than one half of all the Jews in Europe and more than two thirds of all the Jews in the Nazi sphere of influence, had perished. And – perhaps just as significant – the great Jewish civilization of eastern Europe, the nerve-centre of Jewish cultural and spiritual life for many centuries, had been virtually extinguished. The Jewish population of Poland, numbering some 3 million in 1941, today adds up to a paltry few thousand. In a thoroughly drastic and revolutionary fashion, the centre of gravity in Jewish life has shifted to two different communities – one very new – to replace that of eastern Europe, namely Israel and the United States.

Not only were there 6 million Jewish dead, but we also have to take into account all the unborn children and grandchildren, all those generations of descendants who would now never draw breath, and who might otherwise have been granted the opportunity to perpetuate their culture. This is one of the most appalling, and often neglected, consequences of genocide. It is of course impossible, in the final analysis, to make any definitive assessment of the impact on the Jewish people and on the subsequent development of Jewish history of such a cataclysmic event as the Holocaust. What we can say is that much of Jewish life since the Second World War has been preoccupied, consciously or unconsciously, with making good the damage done – physically, politically and psychologically.

The arena of terminology

Those who have tried to grapple with the meaning of these events have sometimes expressed their struggle through the use of different terms to describe what happened. In the first 15 years or so after the war, no single expression was used, merely vague, often euphemistic, references to the 'catastrophe', 'disaster' or 'mass murders' in Europe. By the early 1960s, a definite – if not definitive – term came increasingly to the fore in the writing of scholars and commentators: 'Holocaust' – a Greek word meaning literally 'whole burnt offering', and possessing an undisguised sacrificial religious connotation. This term, by which the event is still most commonly known (and, for that reason alone, is included in the title of this book), has grown progressively less popular: in certain (particularly Jewish) circles, objections have sometimes been voiced to its implicit notion that the Jews were somehow chosen, or destined, according to some 'divine' plan, for this incomprehensible 'punishment' or 'sacrifice'. (The term 'Holocaust' also smacks of theological 'explanation' which many have found wholly unpalatable.)

Another expression that some writers applied was the Hebrew *Churban*, a word which the medieval rabbis had employed to describe the 'destruction' of the Jewish Temple, followed by the 'punishment' of exile. (For the impact on subsequent Jewish history of the destruction of their Temple, see Chapter 2.) Use of this latter term would enable the events of the Nazi period to be viewed very much through the prism of 'Jewish history', instead of separating it off as an entirely unrelated experience. In the past decade, the Hebrew term *Shoah*[1] (a biblical term literally meaning 'desolation') has been much favoured by those who have come to feel that 'Holocaust' (a very 'Christian' term anyway) has been devalued through overuse and misuse, a casualty of the general debasement of images, symbols and reference points that derive from the Nazi period. Another, even more recent term, which aims to capture the specificity of the slaughter of Jews, is 'Judeocide', coined by the American historian, Arno Mayer.[2]

The term 'genocide' has seldom been used expressly of the Nazi treatment of the Jews, because it is too closely associated with the experiences of other victim groups in human history. Through such a use, it is felt, the 'uniqueness' of the Jewish experience might be endangered, and so become lost in a wilderness of empty comparisons and meaningless universality. On the other hand, if a writer or teacher wishes to emphasize the educational and moral *relevance* of the Holocaust, it becomes critically important that a link be established between the Holocaust and other genocides, precisely so that its universal messages may be explored and absorbed. (For the possible links between the Holocaust and other cases of genocide, see Chapter 1.[3])

The Holocaust: an ambiguous legacy

Half a century may have passed since these terrible events, yet the Holocaust continues, in many ways, to have a profoundly ambiguous effect on the contemporary Jewish world and its relationship with the non-Jewish majority. So convoluted are its psychological links with almost everything connected with the State of Israel, that the Holocaust is sometimes used and, more often, misused by those occupying diametrically opposed political positions: on the one hand, it has been brandished as a weapon by opponents of Israeli government policy towards the Palestinian people, to demonstrate the savage irony of the victims of the Holocaust committing injustices against another people; within the literature and cartoons of anti-Israeli propaganda, grotesque Nazi imagery abounds – 'Israeli jackboots', 'final solution of the Palestinian problem', 'Israeli blitzkrieg' and the like. On the other hand, the Holocaust has also been employed as a protective shield behind which Jews can express moral indignation at the very idea of gentiles condemning the post-Auschwitz behaviour of a Jewish state. How, it is sometimes insinuated, can anyone be so insensitive (or 'antisemitic') as to charge the victims of the Holocaust with brutality? Does not Israel, born out of the ashes of Treblinka and Sobibor, have every right to defend itself by all possible means against another genocidal onslaught, this time Arab-sponsored? Thus, at both extremes, is the Holocaust invoked to add emotional, rhetorical weight to an argument the net result of which is often the distortion of moral and political reality.

The passage of time itself has had a contradictory effect: the further the horrors of Nazism recede into the past, the more the world's memory and sense of outrage fade away, while Nazism itself assumes an increasingly symbolic role in people's consciousness. More disturbingly, Adolf Hitler (and everything associated with him) continues to exert a deep and growing fascination, especially with the young, and is, as the advertising world would put it, an extremely 'marketable' commodity – more on the scale of Elvis Presley than of Winston Churchill.

At the same time, after so long a period of mourning and self-reckoning, the Holocaust experience is now so deeply etched on Jewish minds and hearts that the Jewish world is, to an extent, fixated on the event. Since the Second World War, almost every authentic Jewish response, move and reflex – whether on a political, theological or educational plane – has somehow been conditioned by a mindfulness, or remembrance, of the Holocaust. The mainstream Jewish reaction has often been characterized by an over-insistence on Jewish exclusivity: that the Holocaust was in essence a crime against the Jewish people, rather than an affront to humanity as a whole. Such a position has tended to discourage others – educationists, historians, psychologists, philosophers and theologians – from trespassing on what is perceived as 'sacred' Jewish territory.

The result of this exclusivity has unquestionably been to the pronounced detriment of serious Holocaust scholarship and education, and has served to prevent us from seeing the Holocaust as a critical means of promoting caring and responsible citizenship in a democratic framework and of encouraging harmony between different religious, national and ethnic groups. On the other hand, it must be acknowledged that the insistence on the Jewish uniqueness of the Holocaust has ensured that the event does not become lost in the banality of universalizing clichés. What is required is a balanced approach – one that sees the unique and the universal features of the Holocaust as by no means mutually exclusive.

Indeed, one of the main purposes of this book is to guard against the danger that the Holocaust, as a 'unique' event, may be isolated from other people's experiences and ghettoized within the highly charged ideological realm of 'Jewish education'. Its morals and lessons are simply too important and of too universal a concern to be incarcerated within the obsessive world of the victim, however understandable that preoccupation might be. The seeming reluctance by many Holocaust 'educators' to relate the Holocaust to other genocidal catastrophes is depressingly self-defeating. While each genocide has an independent character which demands separate investigation, it is important to go beyond the specific instance and to ask general questions about the nature and process of genocide, the multiplicity of ethical and psychological issues it raises, and what is being done to comprehend and combat it in a century during which – thus far – the estimated number of civilians done to death comes to more than 60 million.

In assessing the ironic and contradictory legacy of the Holocaust, there would seem to be another two-sided dimension. Jews, as we have seen, have fallen victim to the most paranoid and irrational conspiracy theories, from Christian times right down to our century. How curious therefore, that as a direct consequence of the Holocaust, some Jews now see much of the gentile world engaged in an anti-Jewish, or anti-Israeli, conspiracy. On the other hand, as Groucho Marx once said, 'Just 'cos I'm paranoid, don't mean I ain't got no enemies!' The Holocaust has thus helped create a guilt-edged relationship, on the one hand between the surviving Jewish world (especially Jewish communities in the United States) and the State of Israel, and on the other between many non-Jews and the Jewish people, the symbolic victims *par excellence* of human prejudice, hatred and discrimination.

The Holocaust and the State of Israel: an unbreakable connection

In the years immediately following the catastrophe, the principal objective of the organized Jewish world was to engage in whatever strategies were considered necessary to ensure the continued existence of the surviving remnant of European Jewry; to guarantee their future safety in a perilous world; and to lift the demoralized and shattered spirits of their brethren throughout the five continents. Much of this effort was to be be focused on attempts by European survivors to reach British-controlled Palestine and on the now revitalized initiative to set up a Jewish state.

Pre-1945 developments

During the years 1919–39, the rise to power in central and eastern Europe of governments which did not hesitate to include antisemitism in their political programmes had strengthened the belief of Zionist leaders that only a sovereign Jewish state could prevent a major catastrophe. It was perfectly natural, therefore, that in many quarters the Holocaust came to be viewed as the ultimate expression of that very powerlessness which, for well over half a century, Zionist thinkers and activists had warned must be brought to an end. Thus in May 1942 in New York City, the Zionist leadership, faced with incontrovertible evidence of the slaughter of their people in Europe (the full breadth of the Nazis' intentions was not yet known), had demanded the establishment of a Jewish state:

> The Conference declares that the new world order that will follow victory cannot be established on foundations of peace, justice and equality, unless the problem of Jewish homelessness is finally solved ... and that Palestine be established as a Jewish commonwealth integrated in the structure of a new democratic world.

Then and only then will the age-old problem of the Jewish people be righted.[4]

British response

During the 1920s and 1930s (as we have seen in Chapter 3), it had become painfully clear to the British authorities in Palestine that Zionist and Arab aspirations were irreconcilable. By the late 1930s, with war against Germany a decided and growing possibility, the British government decided it would be politically expedient to appease the Arabs, who might otherwise have sided with Hitler in the impending conflict (the Jews, it need hardly be stated, offered no such threat). Eventually, British vacillation over the question of Jewish immigration to Palestine, gave way to a much clearer line in 1939, when the British government issued its White Paper. This would restrict Jewish immigration to a bare minimum, at a time when Jews in Germany and Austria were desperate to escape Hitler's clutches.

1945 – conditions in Europe

After the war, General Eisenhower, the Commander of Allied Forces in Europe, had employed a general policy of repatriation of Displaced Persons, but this had proved a tragic failure in the case of east European Jewry. Consequently, the Haganah[5] leaders funnelled many Jewish refugees into the American Zone inside Germany. At such a highly charged time, the climate of opinion was such that it was not easy for the American army to maintain adequate checks on the flow of Jewish refugees. As Yehuda Bauer argues:

> From a moral and political point of view, it was impossible in 1945 to order American soldiers to use arms against the Jewish victims of Hitlerism.[6]

By late 1945, American Jewish army chaplains and welfare teams had alerted American military officials to the alarming levels of antisemitism still prevailing in eastern Europe. Washington responded by appointing Earl Harrison, a Protestant lawyer, to investigate the refugee crisis with particular reference to the Jewish predicament. His report was severely critical of the American military's treatment of Jewish Displaced Persons, spotlighting the horrendous conditions in camps and going so far as to compare American soldiers with the SS! In one truly appalling instance, Jewish internees had been incarcerated behind barbed wire in the very grounds of Landsberg Castle where Hitler, imprisoned in 1924, had written the first volume of *Mein Kampf*. There they languished in the intimidating company of former Nazi collaborators, while some of their American 'captors', oblivious of the cruel and ironic significance of their actions, actually distributed SS and regular German army uniforms as clothing to several of the Jewish inmates. Harrison suggested that the problem could be solved if 100,000 Jewish survivors were granted immediate access to Palestine.

Creation of the Jewish state

The British would eventually be forced to climb down through a combination of intense United States pressure, increasingly outraged world opinion at the treatment of Hitler's victims, domestic intolerance of the continuing loss of British life at the hands of the Jewish military underground, and the sheer strain of policing a rapidly deteriorating situation in Palestine.

Of particular importance in establishing widespread support for the Zionist cause was the spectacle of British troops clamping down on unarmed and destitute Jewish passengers aboard ships carrying their illegal immigrant cargo into Palestine. When one of the boats, the *Beauharnais* was towed into Haifa Harbour, a banner could be seen bearing this message:

> We survived Hitler. Death is no stranger to us. Nothing can keep us from our Jewish homeland. The blood be on your head if you fire on this unarmed ship.'[7]

The image of British sailors and soldiers using force against the survivors of the Holocaust and interning them behind barbed wire played right into the Zionists' hands. As Howard Morley Sachar has written:

It was precisely this message of the refugee tragedy that the Zionists were determined to convey. Its impact on world opinion and the British taxpayer turned out to be the Jews' most effective weapon.[8]

The most notorious episode concerned the ship *Exodus*, which in July 1947 had put out from Marseilles carrying 4,500 Jewish survivors. The British tried to board the ship 12 miles out of Haifa, but the Jewish passengers offered resistance and the British eventually used machine-guns, killing three and wounding over a hundred; the crew of the *Exodus* surrendered only after the ship had been rammed. The ship was first towed to Haifa, but the British authorities decided to make a special example of the passengers and sent them back to Hamburg in Germany, rather than to Cyprus as had been the customary practice. The startling insensitivity of this action was not lost on the world's onlookers. The image of Holocaust survivors being sent back to the very country which had inflicted such unspeakable barbarities upon them placed world opinion firmly on their side. For the British, this had proved a public relations disaster.

On 14 February 1947 Ernest Bevin, now seemingly resigned to the insusceptibility of the problem to a 'British' solution, chose to turn the whole Palestine question over to the United Nations. Twelve member nations sent representatives (the United Nations Special Committee on Palestine – UNSCOP) to both Europe and Palestine in an attempt to resolve the dilemma. Their considered recommendations received the required two-thirds majority approval of the UN General Assembly. On 29 November 1947, with the backing of both the United States and the Soviet Union, it passed a resolution that Palestine be partitioned into separate Arab and Jewish states, with no British presence whatsoever.[9] The Arab states were adamant that they would neither accept, nor recognize, the existence of a Jewish state in the region: the ramifications, both of the United Nations resolution and of the Arab rejection, are still with us today in the continuing Arab-Israeli conflict.

Israel: the product of the Holocaust?

We are left with a question that is often asked: did the State of

Israel come into being principally because of the murder of 6 million Jews? The answer must surely be that these two momentous, 'epoch-making' events in Jewish history are truly inseparable. Yet it would be wrong to see the State of Israel as little more than a Jewish 'answer' to Adolf Hitler. Zionism was, as we have seen, a movement that sprang up in response to nineteenth-century conditions and, by 1933, the Jews in Palestine had undoubtedly created the infrastructure for a Jewish state. On the other hand, it is also true that the level of Jewish immigration into Palestine at this time was minimal. In point of fact, in the period just prior to Hitler's accession, Zionism had become a virtually lifeless movement among the German Jewish community; they most certainly did not view emigration to Palestine as a serious alternative to living as a 'successfully' emancipated group in an integrationist European society. It was, in reality, only the rise of Nazism and the intensification of antisemitic political repression in many parts of eastern Europe that persuaded many Jews to rethink their position.

After the war, in their search for physical salvation and spiritual comfort, it was the irresistible growth of Zionism among Holocaust survivors that, in all likelihood, proved the decisive factor in the establishment of the State of Israel. For only then did it become clear that Jews wished to emigrate to Palestine in sufficiently large numbers to make a sovereign state viable. As for the United Nations partition resolution – the *sine qua non* of Jewish statehood – it is not implausible to conclude that, without the Holocaust, a compassionate and shame-filled world would have felt no need to grant political independence to the Jewish people as compensation, or as a 'guilt offering', for the extraordinary suffering they had endured. A Jewish state in Palestine was also, for many countries, a more favourable and self-interested solution than to try to accommodate the European Jews in their own countries, thus disturbing and compromising their immigration policies. On the other hand, it could be claimed that, but for the initial threat posed by Hitler, the British might never have felt so strong an urge to conciliate the Arabs during the 1930s and 1940s. These are, of course, tangled and unprovable hypotheses, but there is unquestionably some merit in George Steiner's controversial and emotive insinuation that Adolf Hitler –

unwittingly of course – was the supreme architect of the State of Israel.[10]

Israel: legacy of the Holocaust

Israel has been at 'war' since the moment of its birth on 15 May 1948. From time to time, this conflict has boiled over into what the whole world acknowledges as war – in 1948/9, in 1956, in 1967, in 1973 and in 1982 (in the Gulf War of 1991, though frequently subjected to ballistic attack, Israel was not formally a party to the conflict). Consequently, despite the smallness of its size and population, Israel has been obliged by the belligerent context in which it has found itself to become one of the most powerful military nations on earth – principally with the backing of the United States.

This transformation of the Jewish people from being a group without a land and without an army into a militaristic nation would never have come about without the constant spectre of the Holocaust. It is memory of the Holocaust that, to a great extent, informs Israel's traumatized political and military psyche. The ideology of Jewish statehood, based on a perception of, and a rejection of, the Jews' historical powerlessness – manifested most painfully and unmistakably in the Holocaust – has been replaced by an ideology of survival, rooted in the uncompromising commitment to Jewish power and nurtured by a 'never again' philosophy that was born of the Holocaust.

The enemies of Israel are identified – sometimes accurately, sometimes less so – as the 'new antisemites' (occasionally they are even referred to as 'new Nazis'). To challenge the policies of the Israeli government is one thing; but to deny the legitimacy of the State of Israel – the major ship of Jewish survival in a post-Holocaust world – is often seen, both in Israel and elsewhere, as yet another attempt to denigrate and 'denormalize' the Jewish people, to deny their right to participate on equal terms with the rest of humanity. Moreover, threats by Arab leaders to 'push the Israelis into the sea' are construed as preludes to another genocidal onslaught – a new version of the Nazi war against the Jews. It is, in short, almost impossible to separate modern Israel from her Holocaust parentage.

At first Israel may have been perceived as the culmination of a Zionist philosophy that sought to normalize the Jewish condition, thus bringing an end to Jewish helplessness, isolation and victimization. Certainly this had been the intention of her founding fathers. Increasingly, though, Israel's struggle for survival, rather than representing a revolutionary break from the burden of a Diaspora Jewish history which, at its lowest ebb, had spawned the Holocaust, has come to symbolize that very history of persecution. Far from denying the ghetto mentality of her Jewish past, Israel's continuing embroilment with her Arab neighbours, viewed through the prism of the Holocaust, is seen as a continuation of the travails of the downtrodden outsider – only this time the agony of the individual stateless Jewish pariah is re-enacted on the national and international stage.

Israeli government decision-making at the highest level has taken place somehow within a framework of Holocaust consciousness. In 1967, just prior to the Six Day War, there was a clear perception, both in Israel and elsewhere in the Jewish world, that the very survival of the Jewish nation was once again hanging in the balance. Israel, surrounded on all sides by implacable foes, felt compelled to strike first and then hold on to her conquests to ensure 'security'. Israeli Independence celebrations are closely associated with commemorations of the Holocaust. Conscripts into the Israeli army are regularly taken to the Yad Vashem Museum (the stunning national memorial to the victims of the Holocaust) to 'remember'; there they see what it is they are fighting to stave off, what they are fighting to protect.

The motivation of the Israel Defence Forces, their level of understanding of the political, moral and historical issues at the root of their own conflict, probably makes them unique in the long history of the uninformed and unquestioning obedience of the serving soldier. Such sophistication has, of course, not been without its complications (underlining the ambiguous impact of the Holocaust on Israeli society and on Jewish ethics): there are several cases of Israeli officers and enlisted men refusing to serve in the occupied territories, invoking their own Jewish history of suffering in protest at their government's policy towards the Palestinians. It is the Holocaust more than any other single ingredient that makes Israel such a vibrant, politicized and vigilant society. In short, the complexities of the Holocaust/Israel relationship are such as to bring the triple moral imperative of the Holocaust – (1) *Do not be a perpetrator*; (2) *Do not be a victim*; and (3) *Do not be a bystander* – into the sharpest possible focus.

War crimes trials

In the aftermath of the First World War, two international conferences – at Geneva and at the Hague – had laid down the rules of conduct for warfare. Distinctions were made between the treatment of civilians and military personnel, and rules were formulated relating especially to the treatment of prisoners of war.

During the Second World War, first Edvard Beneš, the exiled President of Czechoslovakia, and later representatives of other governments, had reported Nazi atrocities, particularly towards civilian populations in eastern Europe. The Nazis had been fighting an ideological, racial war, expressed from the start in their behaviour towards civilians and prisoners of war who were Slavic in origin: Russian and Polish citizens had been used as a reservoir of slave labour and the first gassing experiments at Auschwitz had been conducted on Russian prisoners. In western Europe, on the other hand, Germany's treatment of captured soldiers had generally satisfied the requirements of the Geneva Convention.

In response to appalling reports of Nazi barbarism in the east, the United Nation's War Crimes Commission (UNWCC) was formed in October 1943. Representatives from Australia, the United States, Belgium, England, Denmark, India, Holland, Yugoslavia, Greece, Luxemburg, Norway, New Zealand, China, Poland, Czechoslovakia, France and Canada began to draw up lists of wanted Nazi war criminals. Because of problems with the composition of the group, the Soviet Union was not represented.

Shortly after the war, in August 1945, the London Agreement established an International Military Tribunal to deal with Nazi war criminals. Hersh Lauterpacht, an English Jewish judge and Professor of International Law at Cambridge University, defined three indictable categories of the tribunal's Charter which laid down the terms of reference and the rules of procedure for the tribunal. The categories were as follows:

'Crimes Against Peace': – relating to the waging of an aggressive war; 'War Crimes': – those crimes which flouted the Geneva Convention's stipulations concerning the treatment of prisoners of war; and 'Crimes Against Humanity' – the wholesale murder of a civilian population.

The Nuremberg Trials

The specific issue of the Nazis' planned extermination of the Jewish people as a Crime against Humanity was first considered by the International Military Tribunal which opened in Nuremberg on 20 November 1945. Captured leaders of the Nazi regime were put on trial. The list of defendants included Hermann Göring; Rudolf Hess, formerly Hitler's Deputy; Joachim von Ribbentrop, the Nazi Minister of Foreign Affairs; Ernst Kaltenbrunner, Head of the Reich Main Security Office; Alfred Rosenberg, Hitler's leading racial ideologist; Julius Streicher, editor of the notorious antisemitic publication, *Der Stürmer*; and Hans Frank, Nazi Governor-general of occupied Poland. Hitler, Goebbels and Himmler had already evaded justice by committing suicide.

In keeping with the London Charter, indictments were jointly submitted by the four main prosecutors representing the United States, the Soviet Union, Britain and France. The proceedings continued for almost a year, ironically reaching their climax on the Jewish Day of Atonement. Twelve defendants were sentenced to death, three to life imprisonment, four were given prison sentences and three were acquitted. In delivering its judgment, the tribunal established important moral principles and legal precedents. In dismissing the claims that the accused were only following orders and that only a state could be found guilty of war crimes and crime against humanity, it underlined the moral concept of *individual* accountability for human actions, even at time of inter-state military conflict. Only by meting out punishment to individuals could the constraints of international law and convention be visibly enforced.

Subsequent trials

There were various later trials, known as Subsequent

Nuremberg Proceedings, conducted in the American Zone, but by 1949, for a variety of reasons to be discussed later, these trials were halted. Many countries which had been under Nazi occupation did continue to hold trials, mainly of Nazi collaborators. However, according to Simon Wiesenthal, a Holocaust survivor who has devoted his life since the war to tracking down Nazi war criminals, of over 100,000 known perpetrators, fewer than 10,000 have ever faced trial. The question has frequently been asked why, given the enormity of the crime, more of the murderers were not brought to justice.

One answer – unpalatable as it may seem – is that in the years immediately following the war, the prevailing political climate underwent a fairly sudden and radical change. Tensions between the anti-Nazi Allies, that had been apparent during the conflict, now came conspicuously to the surface. The Soviet Union, erstwhile wartime colleague, was rapidly emerging as the new 'enemy' of the west, as central and eastern Europe again became the focus of territorial and ideological dispute (Czechoslovakia, Hungary, Bulgaria, Poland and Romania were to fall decisively under Soviet sway – Yugoslavia somewhat less so).

Germany itself was partitioned at the end of the war, and the Western Allies were determined to strengthen the western sector as a bulwark against communism. There was scarcely a single area of the new West German society – whether in local government, the judiciary, education or the police force – that had not been deeply implicated in the Nazi regime; nevertheless, many low-profile former Nazi officials were deliberately retained in official positions to ensure the smooth running of the country. West Germany was, in effect, never fully 'deNazified', as both Churchill and Roosevelt had undertaken to achieve; anxieties about the threat from the Soviet Union, should West Germany prove bureaucratically or economically weak, ensured that many Germans were given 'protection' from prosecution, ostracism, or even occupational disabilities.[11]

The Western Allies, in particular the United States, were also committed to the belief that the mistakes of Versailles should not be repeated: Germany was never again to be demoralized and humiliated. So it has, in part, been Western fears of another possible German overreaction that has ironically helped create the favourable conditions for the postwar 'economic miracle' which has hurtled modern Germany – recently reunified – into the position of European 'superstate'.

Nazi war criminals and the Israeli courts

The State of Israel has itself held war crimes trials, the most significant – certainly on the level of education, both of its own population and of the world at large – being that in 1961 of Adolf Eichmann, the Nazi bureaucrat held responsible for organizing the murder of over 4 million Jews. Eichmann had been controversially seized by the Israeli Secret Service in Argentina, flown to Israel, tried in a very public way over a period of several months, found guilty of 'crimes against the Jewish people and humanity' and, in a judicial execution unique in the country's history, hanged in an Israeli prison. The question of the jurisdiction of Israel to hold trials relating to crimes committed before her birth and on different soil has been raised, most recently during the trial in Jerusalem of John Demjanjuk (accused of being 'Ivan the Terrible' of Treblinka).

The future?

As we enter the final decade of the twentieth century, the argument still rages as to whether ageing Nazis – 'tired and broken old men' – should be put on trial for war crimes and crimes against humanity. The arguments in favour focus on the pursuit of justice rather than on vengeance, and on the moral and 'educational' value of such trials. Opponents emphasize the 'near impossibility' of producing reliable witnesses that would ensure fair trials so long after the event. They also draw attention to the inconsistency and selectiveness, whereby Nazi 'criminals' are hunted down, while the perpetrators of other genocidal atrocities, for example Pol Pot, Saddam Hussein and their henchmen, go unpunished and, in the former's case, appear to enjoy the protection of powerful Western countries and even the United Nations.

The Nuremberg War Crimes proceedings did little more than pay lip service to the need to deal with the thousands who were guilty of monstrous crimes. Yet, for all their inadequacy, the Nuremberg Trials were exceptional in having being held at all. For *no* international tribunals have since been convened, either to examine charges against alleged Nazi war criminals or to investigate other palpable examples of genocide.

The contrast between the approach of all states to 'regular' homicide and to genocide is quite astonishing. Anyone committing an individual act of murder will do so in the sure knowledge that this deed violates the rules of that society, and that law enforcement agencies will do all in their power to prevent his escape. In the case of genocidal mass murder, however, one alarming feature has been that the crime is nearly always perpetrated with the stamp of approval, indeed at the instigation, of the government of that society. In nearly all instances, therefore, there will be neither a police investigation nor retribution; the perpetrators rarely feel guilty, nor are they apprehended.

The key issues, challenges and questions are these: Should there be a statute of limitations on the commission of genocidal crimes? Given that the victims were themselves given no second chance, can there be any moral, judicial, exemplary, or rehabilitatory justification for letting mass murderers go free merely because of the passage of time? Do later generations have the moral right to forgive or exonerate the perpetrators for their crimes? How can the international community show even-handedness in their investigation of such monstrous crimes, and thus avoid the construction of a hierarchy of suffering which condemns some genocides to virtual oblivion, while others remain at the forefront of our consciousness? While preserving the distinctiveness and unique character of each genocide, are we prepared to make 'connections' between different genocides – identify common features – which may enable us to establish early warning systems to prevent the continuing abuse, persecution and destruction of groups, and the obliteration of cultures?

Should there now be a *new* code, based on the Geneva Convention, the United Nations Genocide Convention of 1948, on other agreed rules of International Law, and – most important – on what we have learnt of the causes and nature of the Holocaust and genocide during the decades since the Second World War? Is there a case for establishing an accountable international monitoring system, which can be supported, if necessary, by United Nations force? (In 1991, the anticipated genocide against the Kurds of northern Iraq *was* averted because of the fortuitous presence of hundreds of Western journalists in the wake of the Gulf War: Western leaders and the United Nations were literally shamed into taking preventive action.) A related question concerns the possible establishment of a permanent multinational War Crimes and Genocide Tribunal which might expose, try and punish those leaders and followers found guilty of violations of the new code.

Cases of genocide after *the Holocaust*

It would be both intellectually dishonest and educationally self-defeating to wantonly *compare* the Holocaust with other cases of genocide. However, as already implied in the introductory chapter, it might be just as mistaken a course to ignore, or utterly deny, the possibility of *links* between different instances of genocide. Such links and points of similarity might include: the psychological perspective and motivation of the perpetrator; the dehumanized image of the victim; the centrality of the nation-state as the source of 'authority' for genocidal action; and the *types* of historical context which appear to serve as the necessary catalyst (though *not* the explanation) of genocide – almost always a convulsive framework such as war, revolution, imperial expansion (rooted in economic domination), and – especially in the latter half of the twentieth century – the chaos resulting from decolonization.

The Holocaust, like every historical example of genocide, was a unique event; yet its central lessons (including its moral and educational *relevance*) will arguably only be imparted and its memory usefully preserved, if its connections with other genocides (*not* straight comparisons) are considered. In other words, there will, in the future, be two ways – at the very least – of 'forgetting', of consigning the Holocaust and its message to history's scrap-heap. One would be to stress only its incomparable uniqueness, thus weakening its power to warn and inform; the other would be to place too strong an emphasis on its similarity to, and hence comparability with, 'related' cases of genocide, thus robbing it of the strength and importance born of its very distinctiveness. Only by steering a delicate middle course between these two extremes – a veritable confrontation with a Scylla and Charybdis – will long-term preventive education about the Holocaust and genocide be given a serious chance of success.

In the opinion of many, if not all, commentators, the victims of genocide in the postwar period – that is, genocides that have taken place *despite* the widely publicized precedent of the Nazi Holocaust, would include the following cases (which for reasons of space must be limited here to the barest outline details):

The Bengalis, 1971[12]

Place: Bangladesh, formerly East Pakistan.
Estimated deaths: between 1,247,000 and 3 million.
Immediate catalyst: the threatened break-up of Pakistan.
Context: decolonization in Indian subcontinent superseded by economic and political domination of one part of successor state over another.

The Hutu of Burundi, 1972[13]

Place: Burundi, formerly part of the Belgian-administered mandate of Ruanda-Urundi, East-Central Africa.
Estimated deaths: 100,000–150,000.
Immediate catalyst: Hutu rebellion against government.
Context: Process of political consolidation by minority Tutsi group over majority Hutu in the wake of decolonization.

The Ache Indians, 1968–72[14]

Place: Eastern Paraguay, South America.
Estimated deaths: 900.
Immediate catalyst: government road building project through remote eastern provinces.
Context: the 'development' and exploitation by national governments and multinational companies of South American natural resources, particularly through a policy of deforestation.

Kampucheans, 1975–9[15]

Place: Kampuchea, formerly Cambodia, South East Asia.
Estimated deaths: up to 2 million.

Immediate catalyst: takeover of power by Khmer Rouge insurgents.
Context: escalation and spread of long-term war in South East Asia. Arrested process of decolonization.

The East Timor Islanders, 1975–present[16]
Place: East Timor, formerly Portuguese colony in Indonesian archipelago, South East Asia.
Estimated deaths: between 60,000 and 200,000.
Immediate catalyst: East Timor's declaration of independence followed by Indonesian invasion.
Context: Indonesian state expansion in the wake of decolonization. Acute population pressures.

In the view of some commentators, three times as many postwar instances of genocide could be cited:

(a) the French in Algeria (then part of metropolitan France), 1945–62;
(b) the Arab governing Sudanese against black Christian southern Sudanese, 1955-present;
(c) the post-Sukarno regime versus Indonesian communists, 1965–67;
(d) the Nigerian army versus Ibos (Biafra), 1966–70;
(e) the Pinochet regime in Chile against its political opponents, 1973;
(f) the Guatemalan military against Mayan Indians, 1980–present;
(g) the Ethiopian regime against peoples of Tigray and Eritrea, 1980–present;
(h) the Iraqi government versus Kurds, 1988 and 1991;
(i) Pakistan (later Bangladesh) against Chittagong Hill Tract tribes, late 1940s–present;
(j) the Brazilian and Paraguayan governments against Ache and other Amerindians, 1960s–present;
(k) Communist China against Tibet, 1959–present;
(l) Indonesia against West Papua, 1969–present;
(m) Stalin's regime against Soviet Party and selected elements of the population, up to 1953;
(n) the Macias government of Equatorial Guinea 1968–79;

(o) the Amin government and its successors against Ugandans (especially Ugandan Asians), 1972–85;

(p) the Argentinian junta versus the political 'left', 1978–9.

Under the terms of the UN Convention of 1948:

> genocide means any of the following acts committed with intent to destroy in whole or in part, a national, ethnical, racial, or religious group, as such:
> (a) Killing members of the group;
> (b) Causing serious bodily or mental harm to members of the group;
> (c) Deliberately inflicting on the group conditions of life calculated to bring about its physical destruction in whole or in part;
> (d) Imposing measures intended to prevent births within the group;
> (e) Forcibly transferring children of the group to another group.

According to the Convention, perpetrators were to be held accountable whether they were legitimate rulers, public officials, or private individuals. They were to be tried either by a competent tribunal of the state in which the acts were perpetrated or by an international penal tribunal whose jurisdiction has been accepted by the members of the UN.

Conclusion

The twentieth century has seen remarkable advances in virtually every field of human endeavour, but it has also borne witness to some of the most barbaric events in all of human history ... and the Holocaust probably ranks as the very worst. Whether the most important lessons of the Nazi period have, even on a theoretical level, been grasped is very doubtful. Most certainly they have not been *applied*, as attested by the alarming frequency of postwar instances of genocide; by the consistent failure of the United Nations to invoke its own Genocide Convention of 1948 and to show itself ready to intervene in the 'internal' affairs of sovereign nation-states; by the seeming powerlessness and indifference of the developed world in the face of starvation and misery of millions; by the recent upsurge of European antisemitism; and by the unrelenting scourge of racial, religious and national bigotry on all continents and in nearly every society.

The amazing transition of the Jewish people, from a position of almost complete impotence (and, in Hitler's Europe, helplessness) to the possession of a mighty, sovereign state of Israel, has embroiled them in a continuing and most exacting test of their own interpretation of these newly acquired political and military responsibilities – a test in which they are the constant focus of world scrutiny and in which the highest moral standards are consistently demanded of them, not least by their fellow-Jews. As many have pointed out, some of the recent behaviour and attitudes displayed by soldiers and citizens in the State of Israel – heirs to Hitler's legacy – are evidence that the 'victims' of the Holocaust have by no means been rendered incapable of inflicting injustice – albeit of a quite different order – on others. Jews of the postwar era, it seems clear, have now taken thoroughly to heart one precept at least – a vital precept that almost shrieks at them from the bones and ashes of Auschwitz, Sobibor, Treblinka, and the other places of death: *Thou shalt never again be a victim.* Or, as Emil Fackenheim has put it: 'Jews are forbidden to hand Hitler a posthumous victory.'[17] But what of the other moral imperatives that derive from this experience?

The Second World War is now becoming a distant memory and, as consciousness of the Nazi evil recedes further and further into the past, the Holocaust has become an increasingly vague symbol, a metaphorical reference point, for man's potential for cruelty, arrogance and abuse of power. It is also a nightmarish representation of the curse of powerlessness that afflicts so many groups and individuals in our vast, depersonalized, modern societies.

The German poet Goethe wrote: 'The greatest evil that can befall man is that he should come to think ill of himself.' In a nuclear age that, in the Cold War period, gambled with weapons of 'Mutually Assured Destruction', it is difficult, perhaps, to retain a hopeful view. In the former Soviet Union, such weapons may soon be at the disposal of several independent republics, while 'developing' nations already have the potential to produce their own pernicious arsenals that may turn parts of the planet into large crematoria.

In the Nazi period, the sheer ordinariness of the

decision-makers and perpetrators stands in terrifying contrast with the quite extraordinary consequences of their decisions and actions. The destructive potential of the Cold War and post-Cold War eras is a child of the same cultural framework – rampant technology, technocracy and bureaucracy – which made possible the Holocaust. The *Nazi Holocaust* – an event with the odds stacked so heavily against its happening – became a reality. A *nuclear holocaust* – statistically a much more probable outcome – may be the next and final step in mankind's abandonment of itself. As David Biale has written:

> As a metaphor for a new politics of irrationality, the Holocaust contains a message of inescapable relevance for a nuclear world. For the first time in human history, a government sought to eradicate a whole people from the earth for reasons that had nothing to do with political realities. In a similar way, the idea of nuclear war lacks the most elementary political rationality, for it would necessarily destroy everything it meant to save: it would take genocide, invented in its most systematic form by the Nazis, to its global and ultimately suicidal conclusion.[18]

Whether an understanding of the most urgent and compelling lessons of the Holocaust – the universal need for compassion, toleration, gentleness and self-restraint – *can* and *will* be applied by a humanity apparently hell-bent on the pursuit of self, and still set – *despite* the precedent of these events – on a course of manic destruction and self-destruction, is not a claim that this book would dare enter. But in such an understanding of the Holocaust may well lie a measure of hope in our Pandora's Box of future possibilities.

> If we could learn to look instead of gawking,
> We'd see the horror in the heart of farce,
> If only we could act instead of talking,
> We wouldn't always end up on our arse.
> This was the thing that nearly had us mastered;
> Don't yet rejoice in his defeat, you men!
> Although the world stood up and stopped the bastard,
> The bitch that bore him is in heat again.
>   Bertold Brecht[19]

Notes

CHAPTER 1
The historical, educational and moral
significance of the Holocaust

1. This statement was made during a news report on British Independent Television News (ITN) in October 1989.

2. Samuel Pisar, *Of Blood and Hope* (Cassell, 1980).

3. For a more elaborate treatment of the motivation of perpetrators see Leo Kuper, *Genocide, Its Political Use in the Twentieth Century* (Penguin, 1982), and Robert Lifton and Eric Markhusen, *The Genocidal Mentality: the Nazi Holocaust and the Nuclear Threat* (Macmillan, 1991).

4. Albert Einstein is quoted in *Encyclopaedia Judaica* (Keter Publishing House, Jerusalem, 1971), Vol.6, p.537.

5. C.P. Snow, 'Either–Or', *Progressive* (February, 1964), p.24, quoted by Stanley Milgram, *Obedience to Authority* (Harper & Row, 1974), p.2.

6. Primo Levi, quoted by L.P. Billig, in *Dimensions: A Journal of Holocaust Studies* (International Center of Holocaust Studies, no. 2, 1987), p.16.

7. A questionnaire was compiled in October 1989 by the author, under the auspices of the British Holocaust Educational Project. It investigated: (a) the course framework(s) in which British teachers offered the Holocaust; (b) the age group(s) taught; (c) the time allocated to the subject in an average academic year; (d) the historical, thematic and overall educational 'contexts' within which the subject was generally approached; (e) the teachers' 'preferences' with respect to these diverse approaches; (f) what, in the teachers' view constituted the most important 'lessons' of the Holocaust; (g) the greatest difficulties experienced in teaching the subject; (h) their prioritization of needs regarding written materials for teachers and students; and (i) their willingness to attend special conferences to examine different approaches to communicating the Holocaust.

8. See Lionel Kochan, 'Life over Death' (*Jewish Chronicle*, London, 22 December 1989) where, adopting an extreme and provocative

position, the author challenges the wisdom of teaching the Holocaust at all to school and university students.

9. Source: Michael Marrus, *The Holocaust in History* (Penguin, 1989), Preface, p.xiv.

10. These words are attributed to Hitler in a speech delivered to his army chiefs shortly before the Nazi invasion of Poland on 1 September 1939; alluded to in Helen Fein, *Accounting for Genocide* (The Free Press, 1979), p.4, and cited in Margot Strom and William Parsons, *Facing History and Ourselves: Holocaust and Human Behaviour* (Intentional Educations Inc., 1982), p.319.

11. Raphael Lemkin, *Axis Rule in Occupied Europe* (Carnegie Endowment for International Peace, 1944).

12. See Yves Ternon, 'Reflections on genocide' in Gerard Chaliand (ed.), *Minority Peoples in the Age of Nation–States* (Pluto Press, 1989), p.133.

13. Much of the scholarly literature on the historiography of the Holocaust focuses on the question of uniqueness versus comparability. See especially Yehuda Bauer, 'The place of the Holocaust in contemporary history' in Jonathan Frankel, *Studies in Contemporary Jewry*, Vol.1 (Indiana University Press, 1984).

14. See especially John Pilger's investigative newspaper and television pieces, e.g. *Weekend Guardian* (London, 6–7 October 1990), pp.4–7, and *Cambodia: The Betrayal* (British ITV programme), first transmitted on 9 October 1990.

15. Nicholas de Lange, *Atlas of the Jewish World* (Phaidon, 1984), p.126.

CHAPTER 2
Survey of Jewish history: c.300 BC to c.1700

1. Jonathan Miller was appearing in *Beyond the Fringe*, a satirical review of the early 1960s (with Alan Bennett, Peter Cooke and Dudley Moore). This line comes at the end of a sketch on class prejudice.

2. Isaiah Berlin, 'Benjamin Disraeli, Karl Marx, and the search for Identity', in *Against the Current: Essays in the History of Ideas* (Oxford University Press), p.252.

3. See Nehama Leibowitz, *Studies in Shemot* [Exodus], (World Zionist Organization, 1981), Mishpatim 3, pp.379–89.

4. For a clear statement of this thesis, see Yehuda Bauer, *History of the Holocaust* (Franklin Watts, 1982), pp.3–7.

5. These kingdoms derived their names from Alexander the Great's generals, Seleucus and Lagus (the latter's son was Ptolemaeus).

6. For a fuller explanation of the concept of *Kiddush Hashem* (Sanctification of God's Name) in Jewish tradition, see *Encyclopaedia Judaica* (Jerusalem, Keter Publishing House, 1971), Vol.10, pp.977–86.

7. For the Jewish background to Jesus' life, see Geza Vermes, *Jesus the Jew* (Collins, 1973).

8. Source for map on pp.34–5: Martin Gilbert, *Jewish History Atlas* (Weidenfeld & Nicolson, 1976), Map 17.

9. See David Biale, *Power and Powerlessness in Jewish History*, *passim* (Schocken Books, 1986).

10. For a consideration of the treatment Jews received in those Islamic countries which were Arab, from the time of Muhammad to the nineteenth century, see Norman Stillman, *The Jews of Arab Lands: A History and Source Book* (Jewish Publication Society of America, 1979).

11. Source: *Encyclopaedia Judaica, op. cit.*, Vol.4, p.1120.

12. Source for map on pp.42–3: Gilbert, *op. cit.*, map 46.

13. Source: Nathan of Hanover (d.1683), *The Abyss of Despair*, translated from the Hebrew by Abraham Mesch (Bloch Publishing Company, 1950).

14. Source: Arnold Rogow (ed.), *The Jew in a Gentile World* (Macmillan, 1961), pp.101–3.

CHAPTER 3
The European Jew and the modern world

1. For an in-depth examination of the Jewish transition from medieval to modern times, see the two excellent works by Jacob Katz, *Exclusiveness and Tolerance: Studies in Jewish–Gentile Relations in Medieval and Modern Times* (Schocken Books, 1962), and *Out of the Ghetto* (Schocken Books, 1978).

2. The ambivalence of progressive thinkers of the Enlightenment towards the Jews is explored in fascinating detail in Arthur Hertzberg, *The French Enlightenment and the Jews* (Columbia University Press, 1968).

3. Source: Norman Solomon, 'Does the Shoah require a radically new Jewish theology?' in Ronnie S. Landau (ed.), *Christians, Jews and the After-Effects of the Holocaust* (forthcoming).

4. The invention of the term 'antisemitism' is commonly attributed to Wilhelm Marr, author of the seminal pamphlet, *The Victory of Judaism over Germandom: Regarded from a Non-denominational Point of View*, and founder of the League of Anti-Semites in 1879.

5. Source: Correspondence between King Ludwig II and Richard Wagner. (*Koenig Ludwig II und Richard Wagner Briefwechsel* (Karlsruhe, 1936–9, Vol.3)). This extract appears in a letter dated 22 November 1881.

6. Source: Leon Pinsker, 'Auto-Emancipation' (1882), in Arthur Hertzberg (ed.), *The Zionist Idea: An Historical Analysis and Reader* (Atheneum, 1971).

7. Quoted in Alex Bein, *Theodore Herzl: A Biography* (Jewish Publication Society of America, 1941), p.116.

8. The original was deposited by the letter's recipient, Lord Roth-schild, in the British Museum: Addl. Ms. 41178, folios 1 and 3.

For an excellent analysis of the circumstances surrounding this remarkable declaration, see Leonard Stein, *The Balfour Declaration* (Magnes Press, 1983).

9. Cited in Martin Gilbert, *Exile and Return* (Weidenfeld & Nicolson, 1978), p.120 (source: Foreign Office papers, 371/3937).

10. Source: *Illustrated London Herald* (8 February 1920), cited in Gilbert, *op. cit.*, pp.127–8.

CHAPTER 4
Nazism and Modern Germany

1. Extract from a leaflet published by the Nazi Party's Propaganda Department in Munich in 1927. Cited in Simon Taylor, *Prelude to Genocide: Nazi Ideology and the Struggle for Power* (Duckworth, 1985), p.222.

2. Ernst Bloch, *Erbschaft dieser Zeit* (Suhrkamp, Frankfurt am Main, 1962), cited in Arno Mayer, *Why Did the Heavens not Darken?* (Verso, 1990), p.92.

3. Carl Schorske, *Fin de Siècle Vienna: Politics and Culture* (Cambridge University Press, 1981).

4. The International Working Men's Association (The First International) had been founded in London by Karl Marx in 1864, to promote joint political action by the working classes of all countries (it was formally dissolved in Philadelphia in 1876). The Second International was the successor organization, founded in Paris in 1889 to celebrate the 100th anniversary of the French Revolution. The original idea of international socialist solidarity had been given a trmendous boost by the growth and success of social democratic parties in France and, particularly, Germany during the 1870s and 1880s.

5. Cited in William Carr, *A History of Germany 1815–1945*, (Edward Arnold, 1985).

6. Donald Niewyk, *The Jews in Weimar Germany* (Manchester University Press, 1980).

7. Source: Eberhard Kolb, *The Weimar Republic* (Unwin Hyman, 1988).

8. *Ibid.*

9. Martin Broszat, *Hitler and the Collapse of the Weimar Republic* (Berg, 1987).

10. Source: Adolf Hitler, *Mein Kampf*, trans. R. Manheim (Houghton Mifflin, 1943).

11. Broszat, *op. cit.*

12. Ian Kershaw, *Popular Opinion and Political Dissent in the Third Reich* (Clarendon Press, Oxford, 1983).

13. Peter Merkl, *Political Violence under the Swastika: 581 Early Nazis* (Princeton University Press, 1975).

CHAPTER 5
Nazi Germany 1933–8: Anti-Jewish policy and legislation

1. Source: Raul Hilberg, *The Destruction of the European Jews* (Harper Colophon, 1979), p.3.
2. Source: Adolf Hitler, *Mein Kampf* (Houghton Mifflin, 1943).
3. Source: *Das Programm der NSDAP* [*The Programme of the National-Socialist German Workers' Party*] (Berlin, 1933), cited in Y. Arad, Y. Gutman and A. Margaliot, *Documents on the Holocaust* (Yad Vashem, 1981), p.15.
4. Source: Joseph Goebbels, *Vom Kaiserhof zur Reichskanzlei* [*From the Emperor's Court to the Reich Chancellory*] (Munich, 1937), pp.291–2, cited in Arad, Gutman and Margaliot, *op. cit.*, p.35.
5. Source: Robert Weltsch, *Jüdische Rundschau* (editorial 4 April 1933), cited in Ludwig Lewisohn, *Rebirth* (Behrman House, 1935).
6. Heine's line is alluded to in Yisrael Gutman and Chaim Schatzker, *The Holocaust and Its Significance* (Zalman Shazar Center, Jerusalem 1984), p.40.
7. Source: Theodor Fritsch, *The Antisemitic Catechism (1883)* later renamed *Handbook on the Jewish Question*. English version appeared in Paul Massing, *Rehearsal for Destruction: A Study of Political Antisemitism in Imperial Germany* (Harper & Row, 1949).
8. Source: W. Hofer, *Der Nationalsozialismus* (Fisher, Frankfurt, 1957). English translation by C Fox appeared in *The SS* (General Studies Project – Schools Council Publication, 1972)).
9. Source: Howard Morley Sachar, *The Course of Modern Jewish History* (Delta, 1977), p.428.
10. From a speech given in Jerusalem on 25 November 1936, quoted in Meyer Weisgal and Joel Carmichael (eds), *Chaim Weizmann* (Weidenfeld & Nicolson, 1962), p.237.

CHAPTER 6
Nazi Europe 1938–41: From Kristallnacht to ghettoization in the east

1. Source: US National Archives 840.48, Division of European Affairs, Memorandum on Refugee Problems, attached to Division of American Republics, memo of 18 November 1938.
2. Arthur Morse, *While Six Million Died: A Chronicle of American Apathy* (Secker & Warburg, 1968), pp.203-4.
3. This quotation from Hitler's Königsberg address appeared in the *New York Times*, 27 March 1938.

4. Source: Helen Fein, *Accounting for Genocide* (The Free Press, 1979), p.167.

5. Quoted in Martin Gilbert, *Exile and Return* (Weidenfeld & Nicolson, 1978), p.203 (source: Cabinet Committee on Refugees: Cabinet papers, 23/94).

6. Makins is quoted to this effect in Gilbert, *op. cit.*, p.214 (source: Foreign Office papers, 371/22536).

7. Source: Fein, *op. cit.*

8. *Golda Meir, My Life* (Weidenfeld & Nicolson, 1975), p.127.

9. Source: A.J.P. Taylor, *The Origins of the Second World War* (Penguin, 1964), pp.99–100.

10. Source: Klaus Hildebrand, *The Third Reich* (Allen & Unwin, 1984), p.35.

11. The full report from which this extract is taken appears in Jeremy Noakes and Geoffrey Pridham (eds), *Nazism 1919–1945*, Vol.2: *State Society and Economy*, document 424 (Exeter University Press, 1984).

12. Source: Bernard Dov Weinryb, *Jewish Emancipation Under Attack* (American Jewish Committee, 1942).

13. Memorandum excerpted from document 58 in Yitzhak Arad, Yisrael Gutman and Abraham Margaliot (eds), *Documents on the Holocaust* (Yad Vashem, 1981).

14. *Ibid.*, document 59.

15. *Ibid.*, document 73.

16. *Ibid.*, document 88.

17. Source: Hannah Arendt, *Eichmann in Jerusalem: A Report on the Banality of Evil* (Penguin, 1983), pp.125–6).

18. Raul Hilberg, *The Destruction of the European Jews* (Harper Colophon, 1961).

19. Arendt, *op. cit.*, p.125.

20. Source: Noakes and Pridham, *op. cit.*, Vol.3: *Foreign Policy, War and Racial Extermination*, document 785 (Exeter University Press, 1988).

CHAPTER 7
The Holocaust 1941–5: From dehumanization to annihilation

1. Source: Louis Lochner (trans. and ed.), *The Goebbels Diaries (1942–1943)* (Hamish Hamilton, 1948), entry of 27 March 1942, p.103.

2. The most prominent historians in the 'Intentionalist' camp are Lucy Dawidowicz, Gerald Fleming, Eberhard Jäckel and Karl Hildebrand (see Bibliography).

3. The 'Functionalist' historians include Martin Broszat, Christopher Browning, Andreas Hilgruber and Hans Mommsen (see Bibliography).

4. Source: Jeremy Noakes and Geoffrey Pridham, *Nazism*

1919–1945, Vol.3: *Foreign Policy, War and Racial Extermination*, document 819 (Exeter University Press, 1988).

5. Source: Yad Vashem Archives 0-4/53-1

6. Source: Lucy Dawidowicz, *A Holocaust Reader* (Behrman House, 1976), pp.72–3.

7. Excerpted from Yitzhak Arad, Yisrael Gutman and Abraham Margaliot, *Documents on the Holocaust*, document 117 (Yad Vashem, Jerusalem, 1981).

8. Source: International Military Tribunal, *Trial of the Major War Criminals Before the International Military Tribunal: Official Text*, *XXXVII*, pp.670–3. (Excerpted from Dawidowicz, *op. cit.* p.96.)

9. Source: Noakes & Pridham, *op. cit.*, document 823.

10. Source: *Commandant of Auschwitz: The Autobiography of Hoess* (World Publishing, 1959).

CHAPTER 8
Perpetrators, victims and bystanders

1. From Jeremy Noakes and Geoffrey Pridham, *Nazism 1919–1945*, Vol.3: *Foreign Policy, War and Racial Extermination* (Exeter University Press, 1988) pp.1198–9.

2. See Stanley Milgram, *Obedience to Authority* (Harper & Row, 1974).

3. Gitta Sereny, *Into that Darkness: From Mercy Killing to Mass Murder* (André Deutsch, 1974), *passim*.

4. *Ibid.*, p.201.

5. For a view of the role of bureaucratic mechanisms in the destruction of human conscience, see Richard Rubenstein, *The Cunning of History* (Harper Colophon, 1975).

6. Source: Elie Cohen, *Human Behaviour in the Concentration Camp* (W. Norton, 1953).

7. Source: Noakes and Pridham, *op. cit.*, document 912.

8. Source: Yitzhak Arad, Yisrael Gutman and Abraham Margaliot, *Documents on the Holocaust* (Yad Vashem, Jerusalem, 1981), document 161.

9. *Commandant of Auschwitz: The Autobiography of Rudolf Hoess* (Weidenfeld & Nicolson, 1959).

10. Gustav Gilbert, *Nuremberg Diary* (Farrar, Straus & Giroux, 1974).

11. Bruno Bettelheim, *The Informed Heart: Autonomy in a Mass Age* (Avon Books, 1971) and *Surviving and Other Essays* (New York, 1980).

12. Isaiah Trunk, *Jewish Responses to Nazi Persecution* (Stein & Day, 1979), pp.50–1.

13. From Elie Wiesel, *Legends of Our Time* (Holt, Rinehart & Winston, 1968).

14. Source: Betty Merti, *Understanding the Holocaust* (J. Weston Walch Publishers, 1982).

15. Source: Arad, Gutman and Margaliot, *op. cit.*, document 196.

16. *Ibid.*, document 145 (written to Yitzhak Cukierman).

17. *Ibid.*, document 89.

18. Simon Sibelman's words appeared in a handout at the London-based Film Season staged by the Spiro Institute as part of the 'Remembering for the Future' conference in July 1988.

19. Source: Ian Kershaw, *Popular Opinion and Political Dissent in the Third Reich* (Clarendon Press, Oxford, 1983).

20. Martin Gilbert, *Auschwitz and the Allies* (Michael Joseph, 1982).

21. Bernard Wasserstein, *Britain and the Jews of Europe, 1939–1945* (Clarendon Press, Oxford, 1979).

22. David Wyman, *The Abandonment of the Jews: America and the Holocaust, 1941–45* (Pantheon Books, 1984).

23. *Ibid.*, p.331.

24. Quoted in *Encyclopaedia Judaica* (Keter Publishing House, Jerusalem), Vol.4, p.508.

25. Rudolf Vrba and Alan Bestic, *I Cannot Forgive* (Sidgwick & Jackson; Gibbs & Phillips, 1963).

26. Wasserstein, *op. cit.*, p.353.

27. Quoted in Menachem Shelah, 'The Catholic Church in Croatia, the Vatican and the murder of the Jews', in Ronnie S. Landau (ed.), *Christians, Jews and the After-Effects of the Holocaust* (forthcoming).

CHAPTER 9
The Jewish question: public opinion in Nazi Germany

1. Cited in David Bankier, 'German society and National Socialist antisemitism', unpublished PhD thesis, Hebrew University of Jerusalem, 1983, p.125.

2. *Ibid.*, p.126.

3. *Ibid.*, p.127.

4. See Sarah Gordon, *Hitler, Germans and the Jewish Question* (Princeton University Press, 1984).

5. Bankier, *op. cit.*, pp.157 ff.

6. *Ibid.*, p.132.

7. *Ibid.*, p.130.

8. *Ibid.*, p.132.

9. See Otto D Kulka, 'Public opinion in National Socialist Germany and the "Jewish Question"' *Zion* (40, 1975), p.228.

10. Bankier, *op. cit.*, p.134.

11. *Ibid.*, p.137.

12. For the most elaborate scholarly treatment of German indifference, see Ian Kershaw, *Popular Opinion and Political Dissent in the Third Reich* (Clarendon Press, Oxford, 1983).

13. Source: Jeremy Noakes and Geoffrey Pridham, *Nazism 1919–1945*, Vol.2 (Exeter University Press, 1984), document 424.

14. German public responses to Jews can be found in *Proceedings of the Tenth World Congress of Jewish Studies*, Division B (Jerusalem, 1990).

15. Source: Noakes and Pridham, *op. cit.*, Vol.3 (1988), document 833.

16. See also 'Memoirs of Emma Becker Cohen' (Leo Baeck Institute Archives, New York).

17. Source: Noakes and Pridham, *op. cit.*, Vol.3, document 834.

18. For a broader picture of the role of the Church, both in Germany and elsewhere in Nazi-occupied Europe, see Chapter 8.

19. Source: Noakes and Pridham, *op. cit.*, Vol.3, document 830.

20. See Kulka, *op. cit.*, p.287.

21. Source: Richard Grunberger, *A Social History of the Third Reich* (Weidenfeld & Nicolson, 1971), pp.465 and 466.

22. For the most recent scholarly investigation into the question of German 'knowledge' and responsibility , see David Bankier, *The Germans and the Final Solution* (Basil Blackwell, 1992), *passim*. See also the same author's 'The Germans and the Holocaust: what did they know?' in *Yad Vashem Studies* (20, 1990), pp.93 ff.

CHAPTER 10
The aftermath and impact of the Holocaust

1. The term 'Shoah' has been given added weight by the French film-maker Claude Lanzmann, who chose it as the one-word title of his remarkable and highly acclaimed nine-hour film.

2. Arno Mayer, *Why Did the Heavens Not Darken? The Final Solution in History* (Verso, 1990).

3. See also Robert Lifton and Eric Markusen, *The Genocidal Mentality, Nazi Holocaust and Nuclear Threat* (Macmillan, 1991).

4. Source: Paul Mendes-Flohr and Jehuda Reinharz (eds), *The Jew in the Modern World* (Oxford University Press, 1980), 'The Biltmore Program', p.471.

5. The Haganah was the mainstream underground military organization of the Jewish settlement in Palestine between 1920 and 1948. Right up to the end of the Second World War, it generally followed a policy of restraint (unlike the extremist, breakaway Irgun and Lehi groups). Thereafter, it pursued a more active policy of resistance to the British authorities. Upon the establishment of the State of Israel, it became the regular Israeli Defence Forces (IDF).

6. Source: Yehuda Bauer, *The Jewish Emergence from Powerlessness* (University of Toronto Press, 1979), p.15.

7. Cited in Howard M Sachar, *A History of Israel* (Knopf, 1976), p.270.

8. *Ibid.*, p.270.

9. As a result of this historic resolution, the State of Israel would later be born – at 4 p.m. on the afternoon of 14 May 1948, a few hours after the British had lowered the Union Jack.

10. George Steiner, *Portage to St Cristobal of A.H.* (Faber & Faber, 1981).

11. For a searing attack on the postwar Allied failure to 'deNazify' West Germany, see Tom Bower, *Blind Eye to Murder: Britain, America and the Purging of Nazi Germany – a Pledge Betrayed* (André Deutsch, 1981).

12. See Craig Baxter, *Bangladesh, New Nation in an Old Setting* (Westview Press, 1984)

13. See Minority Rights Group, *Burundi since the Genocide*, report no.20

14. See Richard Arens (ed.), *Genocide in Paraguay* (Temple University Press, 1976).

15. See François Ponchaud, *Cambodia Year Zero* (Penguin, 1977).

16. See Arnold Kohen and John Taylor, *An Act of Genocide: Indonesia's Invasion of East Timor* (Tapol, 1979).

17. Emil Fackenheim, *The Jewish Return to History* (Schocken Books, 1978). See especially Chapter 2: 'The 614th Commandment' (there are 613 basic commandments in Judaism; Fackenheim reverentially suggests that, since the Holocaust, there is now this additional one).

18. David Biale, *Power and Powerlessness in Jewish History* (Schocken Books, 1988), p.209.

19. Epilogue to Bertold Brecht, *The Resistible Rise of Arturo Ui*, trans. by George Tabori; a biting satire on Hitler's rise to power in Germany.

Bibliography

Part 1 The Background and Context

Chapter 2
Survey of Jewish history: c.300 BC to c. 1700

Agus, Irving, *The Heroic Age of Franco-German Jewry* (Yeshiva University Press, 1969).

Anderson, G.W., *The History and Religion of Israel* (Oxford University Press, 1966).

Ashtor, Eliyahu, *The Jews of Moslem Spain*, 2 vols (Jewish Publication Society of America, 1973–9).

Avi-Yonah, M., *The Jews of Palestine: A Political History from the Bar Kokhba War to the Arab Conquest* (Schocken Books, 1976).

Baer, Yitzhak, *A History of the Jews of Christian Spain*, 2 vols (Jewish Publication Society of America, 1961–6).

Baron, Salo, *A Social and Religious History of the Jews*, 16 vols (Columbia University Press, 1952–76).

Ben-Sasson, H.H. (ed.), *A History of the Jewish People* (Weidenfeld & Nicolson, 1976).

Biale, David, *Power and Powerlessness in Jewish History* (Schocken Books, 1986).

Encyclopaedia Judaica, 16 vols (Keter Publishing House, 1972).

Funkenstein, Amos, 'Passivity as the characteristic of the Diaspora Jews: myth or reality?', in *Tel Aviv University School of Historical Studies*, 1982.

Grayzel, Solomon, *A History of the Jews* (Mentor, 1986).

Jacobs, Louis, *A Jewish Theology* (Behrman House, 1973).

Josephus, *The Jewish War*, trans. G.A. Williamson (Penguin, 1970).

Kamen, Henry, *The Spanish Inquisition* (New American Library, 1965).

Katz, Jacob, *Tradition and Crisis: Jewish Society at the End of the Middle Ages* (The Free Press, 1961).

Katz, Jacob, *Exclusiveness and Tolerance: Studies in Jewish–Gentile Relations in Medieval and Modern Times* (Schocken Books, 1962).

Kedourie, Elie (ed.), *The Jewish World* (Thames & Hudson, 1979).

Lewis, Bernard, *The Jews of Islam* (Princeton University Press, 1982).

Lowenthal, Marvin, *The Jews of Germany: A Story of Sixteen Centuries* (Jewish Publication Society of America, 1938).

Polonsky, Antony (ed.), *The Jews in Old Poland* (I.B. Tauris, 1992).

Roth, Cecil, *A History of the Jews In England* (Oxford University Press, 1949).

Seltzer, Robert, *Jewish People, Jewish Thought. The Jewish Experience in History* (Macmillan, 1980).

Smallwood, Mary, 'The Jews under Roman Rule, from Pompey to Diocletian', *Studies in Judaism in Late Antiquity*, 20 (E.J. Brill, 1976).

Tcherikover, Victor, *Hellenistic Civilization and the Jews* (Jewish Publication Society of America, 1959).

Weinryb, Bernard, *The Jews of Poland: A Social and Economic History of the Jewish Community in Poland from 1100 to 1800* (Jewish Publication Society of America, 1973).

Chapter 3
The European Jew and the modern world

Arendt, Hannah, *The Origins of Totalitarianism* (Harcourt, Brace & World, 1951).

Avineri, Shlomo, *The Making of Modern Zionism. An Intellectual History of the Jewish National Movement* (Weidenfeld & Nicolson, 1981).

Baron, Salo, *A Social and Religious History of the Jews*, 16 vols (Columbia University Press, 1952–76).

Baron, Salo, *The Russian Jews Under Tsars and Soviets* (Macmillan, 1975).

Ben-Sasson, H.H. (ed.), *A History of the Jewish People* (Weidenfeld & Nicolson, 1976).

Bethel, Nicholas, *The Palestine Triangle* (Weidenfeld & Nicolson, 1979).

Brearley, Margaret, 'Hitler and Wagner: the Leader, the Master and the Jews', *Patterns of Prejudice* (1988, 22 (2), pp.3–22).

Cohn, Norman, *Warrant for Genocide: The Myth of the Jewish World-Conspiracy and the Protocols of the Elders of Zion* (Harper & Row, 1966).

Dawidowicz, Lucy, *The Golden Tradition: Jewish Life and Thought in Eastern Europe* (Holt, Rinehart & Winston, 1966).

Dubnow, Simon, *History of the Jews*, Vol. 5: *From the Congress of Vienna to the Emergence of Hitler* (Thomas Yoseloff, 1973).

Ettinger, Shmuel, *The Origins of Modern Antisemitism* (Yad Vashem, 1973).

Friesel, Evyatar, *Atlas of Modern Jewish History* (Oxford University Press, 1990).

278   The Nazi Holocaust

Gilbert, Martin, *Jewish History Atlas* (Weidenfeld & Nicolson, 1976).
Greenberg, Louis, *The Jews in Russia. The Struggle for Emancipation* (Yale University Press, 1965).
Halpern, Ben, 'Reactions to antisemitism in modern Jewish history', in Jehuda Reinharz, *Living with Antisemitism: Modern Jewish Responses* (University Press of New England, 1987).
Hertzberg, Arthur, *The French Enlightenment and the Jews* (Columbia University Press, 1968).
Katz, Jacob, *Out of the Ghetto* (Schocken Books, 1978).
Katz, Jacob, *From Prejudice to Destruction: Antisemitism 1700–1933* (Harvard University Press, 1980).
Kulka, Otto, 'Critique of Judaism in European thought: on the historical meaning of modern antisemitism', *Jerusalem Quarterly* (1989, 52, pp.126–144).
Laqueur, Walter, *A History of Zionism* (Weidenfeld & Nicolson, 1980).
Levin, Nora, *The Jews in the Soviet Union since 1917* (I.B. Tauris, 1991).
Mahler, Raphael, *A History of Modern Jewry, 1780–1815* (Macmillan, 1980).
Marrus, Michael, *The Politics of Assimilation: A Study of the French Jewish Community at the Time of the Dreyfus Affair* (Oxford University Press, 1971).
Massing, Paul, *Rehearsal for Destruction: A Study of Political Antisemitism in Imperial Germany* (Harper & Row, 1949).
Mendelssohn, Ezra, *Class Struggle in the Pale: The Formative Years of the Jewish Workers' Movement in Tsarist Russia* (Cambridge University Press, 1970).
Mendes-Flohr, Paul and Jehudah Reinharz (eds), *The Jew in the Modern World* (Oxford University Press, 1980).
Meyer, Michael, *The Origins of the Modern Jew. Jewish Identity and European Culture in Germany, 1749–1824* (Wayne State University Press, 1967).
Meyer, Michael, *Jewish Identity in the Modern World* (University of Washington Press, 1990).
Niewyk, Donald, *The Jews in Weimar Germany* (Manchester University Press, 1980).
Poliakov, Leon, *The History of Antisemitism*, 3 vols (Vanguard Press, 1965–76).
Pulzer, Peter, *The Rise of Political Antisemitism in Germany and Austria* (John Wiley, 1964).
Sachar, Howard, *The Course of Modern Jewish History* (Delta, 1977).
Schorsch, Ismar, *Jewish Reactions to German Antisemitism, 1870–1914* (Columbia University Press, 1972).
Seltzer, Robert, *Jewish People, Jewish Thought. The Jewish Experience in History* (Macmillan, 1980).
Stein, Leonard, *The Balfour Declaration* (Jewish Chronicle Publications, 1983).

Tal, Uriel, *Christians and Jews in Germany: Religion, Politics and Ideology in the Second Reich, 1870–1914* (Cornell University Press, 1975).

Verbeeck, Georgi, 'Marxism, antisemitism and the Holocaust', *German History* (1989, 7 (3), pp.319–31).

Wistrich, Robert, *Antisemitism – The Longest Hatred* (Thames/ Methuen, 1991).

Zipperstein, Steven, *The Jews of Odessa: A Cultural History* (Stanford University Press, 1985).

Chapter 4
Nazism and modern Germany

Abraham, D., *The Collapse of the Weimar Republic* (Princeton 1981).

Allen, William, *The Nazi Seizure of Power: The Experience of a Single German Town* (Franklin Watts, 1984).

Arendt, Hannah, *The Origins of Totalitarianism* (Harcourt, Brace & World, 1951).

Baranowski, Shelley, 'The sanctity of rural life: Protestantism, agrarian politics and Nazism in Pomerania during the Weimar Republic', *German History* (1991, 9 (1), pp.1–22).

Bracher, Karl, *The German Dictatorship: The Origins, Structure and Effects of National Socialism* (Praeger, 1971).

Brearley, Margaret, 'Hitler and Wagner: the Leader, the Master and the Jews', *Patterns of Prejudice* (1988, 22 (2), pp.3–22).

Breitman, Richard, *German Socialism and Weimar Democracy* (St Martin's Press, 1979).

Broszat, Martin, *Hitler and the Collapse of the Weimar Republic* (Berg, 1987).

Carr, William, *A History of Germany, 1815–1985* (Edward Arnold, 1985).

Childers, Thomas, *The Nazi Voter: The Social Foundations of Fascism in Germany, 1919–1933* (University of North Carolina Press, 1983).

Craig, Gordon, *Germany, 1866–1945* (Oxford University Press, 1980).

Diehl, J.M., *Paramilitary Politics in Weimar Germany* (Indiana University Press, 1977).

Eley, Geoff, *Reshaping the German Right. Radical Nationalism and Political Change after Bismarck* (Yale University Press, 1980).

Eley, Geoff, *From Unification to Nazism* (Allen and Unwin, 1986).

Evans, Richard, *Society and Politics in Wilhelmine Germany* (Croom Helm, 1978).

Farquharson, John, *The Plough and the Swastika: National Socialist Farm Policy, 1928–1933* (Sage Publications, 1986).

Fromm, E, *Working Class in Weimar Germany: A Psychological and Sociological Study* (Harvard University Press, 1984).

Goodrick-Clarke, Nicholas, *The Occult Roots of Nazism* (I.B. Tauris, 1992).

Halperin, William, *Germany Tried Democracy: A Political History of the Reich, 1918–1933* (W.W. Norton, 1965).

Hitler, Adolf, *Mein Kampf*, trans. R. Manheim (Houghton Mifflin, 1943).

Jäckel, Eberhard, *Hitler's World View: A Blueprint for Power* (Harvard University Press, 1972).

Jones, Larry, 'The dying middle: Weimar Germany and the fragmentation of bourgeois politics', *Central European History* (1972, 5 (1), pp.23–54)

Kershaw, Ian, *Popular Opinion and Political Dissent in the Third Reich* (Oxford University Press, 1983).

Kolb, Eberhard, *The Weimar Republic* (Unwin Hyman, 1988).

Levy, Richard, *The Downfall of the Antisemitic Political Parties in Imperial Germany* (Yale University Press, 1975).

Massing, Paul, *Rehearsal for Destruction: A Study of Political Antisemitism in Imperial Germany* (Harper & Row, 1949).

Merkl, Peter, *Political Violence under the Swastika; 581 Early Nazis* (Princeton University Press, 1975).

Michaelis, Meir, 'Fascism, totalitarianism and the Holocaust: reflections on current interpretations of National-Socialist antisemitism', *European History Quarterly* (1989, 19 (1), pp.85–103).

Mosse, George, *The Crisis of German Ideology* (Grosset & Dunlop, 1964).

Noakes, Jeremy, *The Nazi Party in Lower Saxony, 1921–1933* (Oxford University Press, 1971).

Noakes, Jeremy and Geoffrey Pridham, *Nazism 1919–1945. A Documentary Reader*, Vol.1 (Exeter University Press, 1984).

Pridham, Geoffrey, *Hitler's Rise to Power. The Nazi Movement in Bavaria, 1923–1933* (Princeton University Press, 1973).

Stern, Fritz, *The Politics of Cultural Despair: A Study of the Rise of the Germanic Ideology* (University of California Press, 1961).

Stern, Fritz, *The Failure of Illiberalism: Essays on the Political Culture of Modern Germany* (University of Chicago Press, 1976).

Taylor, Simon, *Prelude to Genocide: Nazi Ideology and the Struggle for Power* (Duckworth, 1985).

Zeman, Zbynek, *Heckling Hitler: Caricatures of the Third Reich* (I.B. Tauris, 1991).

Part 2   The Holocaust: A History

Chapters 5, 6 and 7

Arad, Yitzhak, Yisrael Gutman and Abraham Margaliot (eds), *Documents on the Holocaust: Selected Sources on the Destruction of the Jews of Germany, Austria, Poland and the Soviet Union* (Yad Vashem, 1981).

Arendt, Hannah, *The Origins of Totalitarianism* (Harcourt, Brace & World, 1951).

Arendt, Hannah, *Eichmann in Jerusalem: A Report on the Banality of Evil* (Penguin, 1983).

Bauer, Yehuda, *The Holocaust in Historical Perspective* (Sheldon Press, 1978).

Bauer, Yehuda, *The History of the Holocaust* (Franklin Watts, 1982).

Bracher, Karl, *The German Dictatorship: The Origins, Structure and Effects of National Socialism* (Praeger, 1970).

Braham, Randolph, *The Destruction of Hungarian Jewry: A Documentary Account* (World Federation of Hungarian Jews, 1963).

Breitman, Richard, 'In search of a national identity: new interpretation of the Holocaust', *Dimensions* (1987, 3 (1), pp.9–13).

Broszat, Martin, *German National Socialism, 1919–1945* (Clio Press, 1961).

Broszat, Martin, *The Hitler State* (Longman, 1981).

Browning, Christopher, *The Final Solution and the German Foreign Office* (Holmes & Meier, 1978).

Browning, Christopher, *Fateful Months: Essays on the Emergence of Final Solution* (Holmes & Meier, 1985).

Browning, Christopher, 'Nazi ghettoization policy in Poland: 1939–1941', *Central European History* (1987, 19 (4), pp.343–68).

Bullock, Alan, *Hitler: A Study in Tyranny* (Penguin, 1962).

Chartock, Roselle and Jack Spencer (eds), *The Holocaust Years: Society on Trial. A Collection of Readings* (Bantam Books, 1979).

Cohen, Asher, 'Pétain, Horthy, Antonescu and the Jews, 1942–1944: towards a comparative view', *Yad Vashem Studies* (1987, 18, pp.275–91).

Czech, Danuta (ed.), *Auschwitz Chronicle, 1939–1945* (I.B. Tauris, 1991).

Czerniakow, Adam, *The Warsaw Diary of Adam Czerniakow* (Stein & Day, 1979).

Dallin, Alexander, *German Rule in Russia, 1941–1945: A Study of Occupation Policy* (Macmillan, 1957).

Davies, Norman, *God's Playground: A History of Poland*. 2 vols, (Oxford University Press, 1981).

Dawidowicz, Lucy, *The War Against the Jews* (Penguin, 1975).

Dawidowicz, Lucy, *A Holocaust Reader* (Beacon Press, 1976).
Dobroszycki, Lucjan, *The Chronicle of the Lodz Ghetto, 1941–44*, (Yale University Press, 1984).
Donat, Alexander, *The Holocaust Kingdom* (Holt, Rinehart & Winston, 1965).
Fackenheim, Emil, 'Holocaust and Weltanschaung: philosophical reflections on why they did it', *Holocaust and Genocide Studies* (1988, 3 (2), pp.197–208).
Fein, Helen, *Accounting for Genocide: National Responses and Jewish Victimization during the Holocaust* (The Free Press, 1979).
Fleming, Gerald, *Hitler and the Final Solution* (Oxford University Press, 1982).
Friedlander, Albert (ed.), *Out of the Whirlwind: A Reader of Holocaust Literature* (Schocken Books, 1976).
Friedlander, Saul, 'From antisemitism to extermination: an historiographical study of Nazi policies towards the Jews', *Yad Vashem Studies*, Vol.16, (1984).
Gilbert, Martin, *Atlas of the Holocaust* (Michael Joseph, 1982).
Gilbert, Martin, *Auschwitz and the Allies* (Michael Joseph, 1982).
Gilbert, Martin, *The Holocaust: The Jewish Tragedy* (Collins, 1986).
Gross, Leonard, *The Last Jews of Berlin* (Bantam Books, 1983).
Gross, Jan, 'Polish–Jewish relations during the war: an interpretation', *Dissent* (1987, 34 (1), pp.73–81).
Hilberg, Raul, *The Destruction of the European Jews* (Quadrangle Books, 1961).
Hilberg, Raul, *Documents of Destruction – Germany and Jewry, 1933–1945* (W.H. Allen, 1972).
Hildebrand, Karl, *The Third Reich* (Allen & Unwin, 1984).
Hilgruber, Andreas, 'War in the east and the extermination of the Jews', *Yad Vashem Studies* (1987, 18, pp.103–32).
Hitler, Adolf, *Mein Kampf* (Houghton Mifflin, 1971).
Hoehne, Heinz, *The Order of the Death's Head: The Story of Hitler's SS* (Coward McCann, 1970).
Horwitz, Gordon, *In the Shadow of Death: Living Outside the Gates of Mauthausen* (I.B. Tauris, 1991).
Jäckel, Eberhard, *Hitler's World View: A Blueprint for Power* (Harvard University Press, 1981).
Jäckel, Eberhard, *Hitler in History* (Brandeis University Press, 1984).
Kaplan, Chaim, *The Warsaw Ghetto Diary of Chaim A Kaplan* (Collier Books, 1973).
Kershaw, Ian, *The Nazi Dictatorship: Problems and Perspectives of Interpretation* (Edward Arnold, 1985).
Kieler Wieslaw, *Anus Mundi* (Time Books, 1980).
Kosinski, Jerzy, *The Painted Bird* (Houghton Mifflin, 1976).
Kubar, Zofia, 'With a flower in her hair', *Partisan Review* (1988, 55 (1), pp.97–112).

Lanzmann, Claude, *Shoah* (Pantheon Books, 1985).
Le Chene, Evelyn, *Mauthausen: The History of a Death Camp* (Methuen, 1971).
Levi, Primo, *The Drowned and the Saved* (Summit Books, 1987).
Levi, Primo, *If This Is A Man / The Truce* (Penguin, 1979).
Levin, Nora, *The Holocaust: The Destruction of European Jewry, 1933–1945* (Schocken Books, 1973).
Maccoby, Haim, *The Sacred Executioner* (Thames & Hudson, 1982).
Marrus, Michael, *The Unwanted: European Refugees in the Twentieth Century* (Oxford University Press, 1985).
Marrus, Michael, *The Holocaust in History* (Penguin, 1987).
Marrus, Michael (ed.), *The Nazi Holocaust (Selected Articles)*, Vol.3:, *The Final Solution* (Meckler, 1989).
Marrus, Michael, 'History of the Holocaust: a survey of recent literature', *Journal of Modern History* (1987, 59 (1), pp.114–60).
Marrus, Michael, 'Recent trends in the history of the Holocaust', *Holocaust and Genocide Studies* (1988, 3 (3), pp.257–65).
Marrus, Michael, 'The strange story of Herschel Grynszpan', *American Scholar* (1988, 57 (1), pp.69–79).
Mayer, Arno, *Why Did the Heavens Not Darken? The 'Final Solution' In History* (Verso, 1990).
Mommsen, Hans, 'The realization of the unthinkable: The "Final Solution of the Jewish Question" in the Third Reich', Gerhard Hirschfeld (ed.), *The Policies of Genocide: Jews and Soviet Prisoners of War in Nazi Germany* (Allen & Unwin, 1986).
Mord, Rollbahn, 'The early activities of Einsatzgruppe C', *Holocaust and Genocide Studies* (1987, 2 (2), pp.221–41).
Noakes, Jeremy and G. Pridham (eds), *Nazism 1919–1945 – A Documentary Reader*, Vol.2: *State, Economy and Society*, and Vol.3: *Foreign Policy, War and Racial Extermination* (Exeter University Press, 1984 (Vol.2) & 1988 (Vol.3)).
Pincus, Oskar, *The House of Ashes* (I.B. Tauris, 1991).
Pisar, Samuel, *Of Blood and Hope* (Cassel, 1980).
Pulzer, Peter, 'German historians debate the Holocaust', *Patterns of Prejudice* (1987, 21 (3), pp.3–14).
Read, Anthony and David Fisher, *Kristallnacht: Unleashing the Holocaust* (Papermac, 1991).
Reitlinger, Gerald, *The Final Solution: The Attempt to Exterminate The Jews of Europe* (A.S. Barnes, 1961).
Ringelbaum, Emmanuel, *Notes from the Warsaw Ghetto* (McGraw Hill, 1958).
Rottenstreich, Nathan, 'The Holocaust as a unique historical event', *Patterns of Prejudice* (1988, 22 (1), pp.14–20).
Schleunes, Karl, *The Twisted Road to Auschwitz: Nazi Policy towards German Jews, 1933–1939* (University of Illinois Press, 1970).
Schleunes, Karl, 'The first and last night of "Broken Glass"', *Dimensions* (1988, 4 (2), pp.5–10).

Schwartz-Bart, André, *The Last of the Just* (Penguin, 1983).
Shirer, William, *The Rise and Fall of the Third Reich* (Fawcett, 1960).
Steinberg, Jonathan, *All or Nothing: the Axis and the Holocaust, 1941–1945* (Routledge, 1990).
Taylor, A.J.P., *The Origins of the Second World War* (Penguin, 1964).
Trunk, Isaiah, *Judenrat: The Jewish Councils in Eastern Europe Under Nazi Occupation* (Macmillan, 1972).
Volavkova, Hana (ed.), *I Never Saw Another Butterfly: Children's Drawings and Poems from Terezin Concentration Camp* (Schocken Books, 1978).
Wiesel, Elie, *Night* (Penguin, 1958).
Wistrich, Robert, *Who's Who in Nazi Germany* (Weidenfeld & Nicolson, 1982).
Yahil, Leni, *The Rescue of Danish Jewry* (Jewish Publication Society of America, 1969).
Zariz, Ruth, 'Officially approved emigration from Germany after 1941: a case study', *Yad Vashem Studies* (1987, 18, pp.275–91).

Part 3   Themes, Issues and Protagonists

Chapter 8
Perpetrators, victims and bystanders

Allport, Gordon, *The Nature of Prejudice* (Addison-Wesley, 1954).
Arendt, Hannah, *Eichmann in Jerusalem: A Report on the Banality of Evil* (Penguin, 1983).
Bettelheim, Bruno, *Surviving and Other Essays* (Knopf, 1979).
Bettelheim, Bruno, *The Informed Heart* (Penguin, 1986).
Bezwinska, Jadwiga and Danuta Czech (eds), *Kl Auschwitz Seen by the SS* (Publications of Panstwowe Museum w Oswiecimiu, 1978).
Buscher, Frank and Michael Phayer, 'German Catholic bishops and the Holocaust', *German Studies Review* (1988, 11 (3), pp.463–85).
Cohn-Sherbok, Dan, *Holocaust Theology* (Lamp Press, 1989).
Donat, Alexander, *The Holocaust Kingdom* (Holt, Rinehart & Winston, 1965).
Eckardt, Roy and Alice Eckardt, *Long Night's Journey into Day* (Wayne State University Press, 1982).
Fenelon, Fania, *Playing For Time* (Atheneum, 1977).
Friedlander, Saul (ed.), *Pius XII and the Third Reich* (Chatto & Windus, 1966).
Gilbert, Martin, *Auschwitz and the Allies* (Michael Joseph, 1982).
Greenberg, Irving and Alvin Rosenfeld, *Confronting the Holocaust: The Impact of Elie Wiesel* (Indiana University Press, 1978).
Gutman, Yisrael, *Fighters Among the Ruins: the Story of Jewish Heroism in World War II* (B'nai B'rith Books, 1988).
Hoess, Rudolf, *Commandant of Auschwitz* (World Publishers, 1959).

Hoffmann, Peter 'Roncalli in the Second World War: peace initiatives, the Greek famine and the persecution of the Jews', *Journal of Ecclesiastical Studies* (1989, 40 (1), pp.74–99).

Lanzmann, Claude, *Shoah* (Pantheon Books, 1962).

Laqueur, Walter, *The Terrible Secret: Suppression of the Truth about Hitler's 'Final Solution'* (Penguin, 1980).

Lifton, Robert, *The Nazi Doctors: Medical Killing and the Psychology of Genocide* (Basic Books, 1986).

Lipstadt, Deborah, 'Finessing the truth: the press and the Holocaust', *Dimensions* (1982, 4 (3), pp.10–14).

Marrus, Michael, *The Unwanted: European Refugees in the Twentieth Century* (Oxford University Press, 1985).

Marrus, Michael, *The Holocaust in History* (Penguin, 1987).

Marrus, Michael, *The Nazi Holocaust (Selected Articles)*, Vol.5: *Public Opinion and Relations to the Jews in Nazi Europe*; Vol.6: *The Victims of the Holocaust*; Vol.7: *Jewish Resistance to the Nazis*; Vol.8: *Bystanders to the Holocaust* (Meckler, 1989).

Marrus, Michael, 'Jewish leaders and the Holocaust', in *French Historical Studies* (1987, 15 (2), pp.316–31).

Milgram, Stanley, *Obedience to Authority* (Harper & Row, 1974).

Robinson, Jacob, *And the Crooked Shall Be Made Straight* (Macmillan, 1968).

Rubenstein, Richard, *The Cunning of History* (Harper Colophon, 1975).

Sereny, Gitta, *Into That Darkness: From Mercy Killing to Mass Murder* (André Deutsch, 1974).

Shelah, Menachem, 'The Catholic Church in Croatia, the Vatican and the murder of the Croatian Jews'. In Ronnie Landau (ed.), *Christians, Jews and the After-Effects of the Holocaust* (Pergamon Press, forthcoming).

Speer, Albert, *Inside the Third Reich: Memoirs* (Macmillan, 1970).

Sternberg, Lucien, *Not As a Lamb* (Saxon House, 1970).

Stern Strom, Margot and William Parsons, *Facing History and Ourselves. Holocaust and Human Behaviour* (Intentional Educations Inc., 1982).

Trunk, Isaiah, *Judenrat: The Jewish Councils in Eastern Europe Under Nazi Occupation* (Macmillan, 1972).

Trunk, Isaiah, *Jewish Responses to Nazi Persecution* (Stein & Day, 1979).

Wasserstein, Bernard, *Britain and the Jews of Europe, 1939–1945* (Institute of Jewish Affairs, 1979).

Wyman, David, *The Abandonment of the Jews: America and the Holocaust, 1941–45* (Pantheon Books, 1984).

Chapter 9
The Jewish question: public opinion in Nazi Germany

Bankier, David, *The Germans and the Final Solution* (Basil Blackwell, 1992).

Bankier, David, 'The Germans and the Holocaust: What did they know?', *Yad Vashem Studies* (1990, 20).

Broszat, Martin, 'The Third Reich and the German People'. In Hedley Bull (ed.), *The Challenge of the Third Reich* (Oxford University Press, 1986).

Buttner, Ursula, 'The persecution of Christian-Jewish families in the Third Reich', *Leo Baeck Institute Year Book* (1989, 34, pp.267–89).

Davies, A.J., *Antisemitism and the Christian Mind* (Herder & Herder, 1969).

Dipper, Christopher, 'The German Resistance and the Jews', *Yad Vashem Studies* (1984, 16).

Gordon, Sarah, *Hitler, Germans and the Jewish Question* (Princeton University Press, 1984).

Grunberger, Richard, *A Social History of the Third Reich* (Weidenfeld & Nicolson, 1971).

Kater, Michael, 'Everyday antisemitism in prewar Nazi Germany: the popular bases', *Yad Vashem Studies*, (1984, 16).

Kershaw, Ian, *Popular Opinion and Political Dissent in the Third Reich* (Oxford University Press, 1983).

Kershaw, Ian, 'The persecution of the Jews and German popular opinion in the Third Reich', *Yearbook of the Leo Baeck Institute* (1981, 26).

Kershaw, Ian, 'German popular opinion during the "Final Solution": information, comprehension, reactions'. In A. Cohen, J. Gelber and C. Wardi (eds), *Comprehending the Holocaust* (Peter Lang, 1989).

Kulka, Otto, 'Public opinion in National Socialist Germany and the Jewish Question', *Zion* (1975, 40).

Laqueur, Walter, *The Terrible Secret. Suppression of the Truth about Hitler's 'Final Solution'* (Penguin, 1980).

Littell, Franklin, *The Crucifixion of the Jews* (Harper & Row, 1975).

Marrus, Michael, *The Unwanted: European Refugees in the Twentieth Century* (Oxford University Press, 1985).

Marrus, Michael, *The Holocaust in History* (Penguin, 1987).

Muller, Ingo, *Hitler's Justice: The Courts of the Third Reich* (I.B. Tauris, 1991).

Merkl, Peter, *Political Violence under the Swastika: 581 Early Nazis* (Princeton University Press, 1975).

Noakes, Jeremy and G. Pridham, *Nazism, 1919–1945: A Documentary Reader*, Vols 2 and 3 (Exeter University Press, 1984 & 1988).

Rothfels, Hans, *The German Opposition to Hitler* (Oswald Wolff, 1961).

Stokes, Lawrence, 'The German people and the destruction of the European Jews', *Central European History* (1973, 6).

Chapter 10
The aftermath and impact of the Holocaust

Bauer, Yehuda, *The Jewish Emergence from Powerlessness* (University of Toronto Press, 1979).
Bauer, Yehuda, *History of the Holocaust* (Franklin Watts, 1982).
Bauer, Yehuda, *Out of the Ashes* (Pergamon Press, 1989).
Bauman, Zygmunt, *Modernity and the Holocaust* (Polity Press, 1989).
Bauman, Zygmunt, 'Sociology after the Holocaust', *British Journal of Sociology* (1988, 39 (4), pp.469–97).
Begin, Menachem, *The Revolt: Story of the Irgun* (Henry Schumann, 1951).
Bethel, Nicholas, *The Palestine Triangle* (André Deutsch, 1979).
Bettelheim, Bruno, 'The Holocaust in the undermind of the West', *Dimensions* (1988, 4 (1), pp.5–8).
Bower, Tom, *Blind Eye To Murder: Britain, America and the Purging of Nazi Germany – A Pledge Betrayed* (André Deutsch, 1981).
Biale, David, *Power and Powerlessness in Jewish History* (Schocken Books, 1988).
Conquest, Robert, *Harvest of Sorrow, Soviet Collectivization and the Terror-Famine* (Hutchinson, 1986).
Chaliand, Gerard (ed.), *Minority Peoples in the Age of Nation-States* (Pluto Press, 1989).
Elliot, Gil, *Twentieth Century Book of the Dead* (Penguin, 1972).
Evans, Richard, *In Hitler's Shadow: West German Historians and the Attempt to Escape from the Nazi Past* (I.B. Tauris, 1991).
Fackenheim, Emil, *The Jewish Return into History* (Schocken Books, 1978).
Fein, Helen, 'The Holocaust – what it means and what it doesn't', *Present Tense* (1987, 15 (1), pp.24–9).
Fein, Helen, 'Political functions of genocide comparisons'. In *Remembering for the Future*, Vol.3 (Pergamon Press, 1988).
Gilbert, Martin, *Exile and Return – The Emergence of Jewish Statehood* (Weidenfeld & Nicolson, 1978).
Gutman, Yisrael and Chaim Schatzker, *The Holocaust and Its Significance* (Zalman Shazar Center, Jerusalem, 1983).
Hass, Aaron, *In the Shadow of the Holocaust: The Second Generation* (I.B. Tauris, 1991).
Hertzberg, Arthur, *The Zionist Idea: an Historical Analysis and Reader* (Atheneum Publishers, 1972).
Horowitz, Irving, *Taking Lives, Genocide and State Power* (Transaction Books, 1980).
Hughes, Robert, *The Fatal Shore* (Pan, 1987).

Insdorf, Annette, *Indelible Shadows: Film and the Holocaust* (Cambridge University Press, 1989).

Irwin-Zarecka, Iwona, 'National attitudes to Jews: Catholics and Jews in Poland today', *Holocaust and Genocide Studies* (1989, 4 (1), pp.27–40).

Katz, Steven 'Quantity and interpretation – issues in the comparative historical analysis of the Holocaust', *Holocaust and Genocide Studies* (1989, 4 (2), pp.127–48).

Kiernan, Ben, *How Pol Pot Came to Power* (Verso, 1985).

Kohen, Arnold and John Taylor, *An Act of Genocide: Indonesia's Invasion of East Timor* (Tapol, 1979).

Kuper, Leo, *Genocide, Its Political Use in the Twentieth Century* (Penguin, 1982).

Landau, Ronnie (ed.), *Christians, Jews and the After-Effects of the Holocaust* (Pergamon Press, forthcoming).

Laqueur, Walter, *The History of Zionism* (Weidenfeld & Nicolson, 1980).

Lifton, Robert and Eric Markhusen, *The Genocidal Mentality: the Nazi Holocaust and the Nuclear Threat* (Macmillan, 1991).

Melson, Robert, 'Revolutionary genocide: on the causes of the Armenian genocide of 1915 and the Holocaust', in *Remembering for the Future*, Vol.2 (Pergamon Press, 1988).

Mendes-Flohr, Paul and Jehuda Reinharz, *The Jew in the Modern World* (Oxford University Press, 1980).

Morse, Arthur, *While Six Million Died: A Chronicle of American Apathy* (Secker & Warburg, 1968).

Muller, Jerry, 'German historians at war', *Commentary* (1989, 87 (5), pp.33–41).

Pisar, Samuel, *Of Blood and Hope* (Cassell, 1980).

Rabinbach, Anson 'The Jewish Question in the German Question', *New German Critique* (1988, 44, pp.159–62).

Robinson, Jacob, *And the Crooked Shall Be Made Straight* (Macmillan, 1968).

Sachar, Howard Morley, *A History of Israel* (Knopf, 1976).

Sigal, John and Morton Weinfeld, *Trauma and Rebirth: Inter-generational Effects of the Holocaust* (Praeger, 1989).

Solomon, Norman, 'Does the Shoah require a radically new Jewish theology?'. In Ronnie Landau (ed.), *Christians, Jews and the After-Effects of the Holocaust* (Pergamon Press, forthcoming).

APPENDIX A

Euphemisms of Death

At first glance, the following document may seem innocuous enough, a rather tedious technical memorandum written by a welder to his 'line manager' – of no interest or concern to the superficial reader, one of millions of such bureaucratic records. On closer inspection, however, and when the reader is informed of the context, it becomes transformed into arguably one of the most alarming documents of the twentieth century.

Few pieces of paper convey more effectively the astonishing detachedness and amoral devotion to duty on the part of thousands of bureaucrats and minor functionaries. Despite their lowly status, their role would prove indispensable to the carrying out of the 'Final Solution', all sense of moral perspective hidden behind the jargon and obedience to 'higher authority'.

Translation of euphemisms: the writer here expresses his opinion that the trucks used for poisoning Jewish prisoners with carbon monoxide gas could be converted into more efficient killing machines by reducing the space into which the condemned were to be crammed.

The van's load is usually nine per square yard. In Saurer vehicles, which are very spacious, maximum use of space is impossible, not because of any possible overload, but because loading to full capacity would affect the vehicle's stability. So reduction of the load space seems necessary. It must absolutely be reduced by a yard, instead of trying to solve the problem, as hitherto, by reducing the number of pieces loaded. Besides, this extends the operating time, as the empty void must also be filled with carbon monoxide. On the other hand, if the load space is reduced, and the vehicle is packed solid, the operating time can be considerably shortened. The manufacturers told us during a discussion that reducing the size of the van's rear would throw it badly off balance. The front axle, they claim, would be overloaded. In fact, the balance is automatically restored, because the merchandise aboard displays during the operation a natural tendency to rush to the rear doors, and is mainly found lying there at the end of the operation. So the front axle is not overloaded.

The lighting must be better protected than now. The lamps must be enclosed in a steel grid to prevent their being damaged. Lights could be eliminated, since they apparently are never used. However, it has been observed that when the doors are shut, the load always presses hard against them [against the doors] as soon as darkness sets in. This is because the load naturally rushes towards the light when darkness sets in, which makes closing the doors difficult. Also, because of the alarming nature of darkness, screaming always occurs when the doors are closed. It would therefore be useful to light the lamps before and during the first moments of the operation.

For easy cleaning of the vehicle, there must be a sealed drain in the middle of the floor. The drainage hole's cover, eight to twelve inches in diameter, would be equipped with a slanting trap, so that fluid liquids can drain off during the operation. During cleaning, the drain can sometimes be used to evacuate large pieces of dirt.

The aforementioned technical changes are to be made to vehicles in service only when they come in for repairs. As for the ten vehicles ordered from Saurer, they must be equipped with all innovations and changes shown by use and experience to be necessary.*

* Source: Memorandum written on 5 June 1942 by Willy Just, a welder in the RSHA transport department. Cited in Claude Lanzmann, *Shoah – An Oral History of the Holocaust* (Pantheon Books, 1985), pp.1035.

Yossel Rakover's Appeal to God (an excerpt) by Zvi Kolitz

In the ruins of the Ghetto of Warsaw, among heaps of charred rubbish, there was found, packed tightly into a small jar, the following testament, written during the ghetto's last hours by a Jew named Yossel Rakover.

Warsaw, April 28, 1943

I, Yossel, son of David Rakover of Tarnopol, a Chasid of the rabbi of Ger and a descendant of the great and pious families of Rakover and Meisel, inscribe these lines as the houses of the Warsaw Ghetto go up in flames. The house I am in is one of the last unburnt houses remaining. For several hours an unusually heavy artillery barrage has been crashing down on us, and the walls are disintegrating under the fire. It will not be long before the house I am in is transformed, like almost every other house of the ghetto, into a grave for its defenders. ...

In a forest where I once hid, I encountered a dog one night, sick and hungry, his tail between his legs. Both of us immediately felt the kinship of our situation. He cuddled up to me, buried his head in my lap, and licked my hands. I do not know if I ever cried so much as that night. I threw my arms around his neck, crying like a baby. If I say that I envied the animals at that moment, it would not be remarkable. But what I felt was more than envy. It was shame. I felt ashamed before the dog to be a man. That is how matters stand. That is the spiritual level to which we have sunk. Life is a tragedy, death a saviour; man a calamity, the beast an ideal; the day a horror, the night – relief.

When my wife, my children and I – six in all – hid in the forest, it was the night and the night alone that concealed us in its bosom. The day turned us over to our persecutors and murderers. I remember with the most painful clarity the day when the Germans raked with a hale of fire the thousands of refugees on the highway from Grodno to Warsaw. As the sun rose, the airplanes zoomed over us and the whole day long they murdered us. In this massacre, with our seven-month old child in her arms my wife perished. Two of my five remaining children also disappeared that day without a trace. Their names were David and Yehuda; one was four years old, the other six.

At sunset the handful of survivors continued their journey in the direction of Warsaw, and I, with my three remaining children, started out to comb the fields and woods at the site of the massacre in search of the children. The entire night we called for them, but only echoes replied. I never saw my two children again, and, later, in a dream, I was told that they were in God's hands.

My other three children died in the space of a single year in the Warsaw Ghetto. Rachel, my daughter of ten, heard that it was possible to find scraps of bread in the public dump outside the ghetto walls. The ghetto was starving at the time, and the people who died of starvation lay in the streets like heaps of rags. The people of the ghetto were prepared to face any death but the death of hunger. Against no death did they struggle so fiercely as against death by starvation.

My daughter, Rachel, told me nothing of her plan to steal out of the ghetto, which was punishable by death. She and a girl friend of the same age started out on the perilous journey. She left home under cover of darkness, and at sunrise she and her friend were caught outside the ghetto walls. Nazi ghetto guards, together with dozens of their Polish underlings, at once started in pursuit of those two Jewish children who dared to venture out to hunt for a piece of bread in a garbage can. People witnessing the chase could not believe their eyes. It was unusual even in the ghetto. It looked like a pursuit of dangerous criminals ... my child, running with her last ounce of strength, fell exhausted to the ground and the Nazis put a bullet through her head. The other child saved herself, but, driven out of her mind, died two weeks later.

The fifth child, Yacob, a boy of thirteen, died on his Bar Mitzvah day of tuberculosis. The last child, my fifteen-year-old daughter, Chaya, perished during a Kinderaktion – a children's operation – that began at sunrise late Rosh Hashanah [Jewish New Year] and ended at sundown. That day, before sunset, hundreds of Jewish families lost their children.

Now my time has come. And like Job, I can say to myself, nor am I the only one who can say it, that I return to the soil naked, as naked as the day of my birth.

I am forty-three years old, and when I look back on the past I can assert confidently, as confident as a man can of himself, that I have lived a respectable, upstanding life, my heart full of love for God. I was once blessed with success, but never boasted of it. My possessions were extensive. My house was open to the needy. I served God enthusiastically, and my single request to Him was that He should allow me to worship Him with all my heart, and all my soul, and all my strength.

I cannot say that my relationship to God has remained unchanged after everything I have lived through. But I can say with absolute certainty that my belief in Him has not changed by a hair's breadth. Previously, when I was happy and well off, my relation to God was as to one who granted me a favour for nothing, and I was eternally obliged to Him for it. Now my relations to Him are as to one who owes me something, too, who owes me very much in fact, and since I feel it so, I believe I have the right to demand it of Him. But I do not say like Job that God should point out my sin with His finger so that I may know why I deserve this; for greater and saintlier men than I are now firmly convinced that it is not a question of punishing sinners: something entirely different is taking place in the world. ... It is, namely, a time when God has veiled His countenance from the world, sacrificing mankind to its wild instincts. This, however, does not mean that the pious members of my people should justify the edict, saying that God and His judgments are correct. For to say that we deserve the blows we have received is to malign ourselves, to desecrate the Holy Name of God's children. And those who desecrate our name desecrate the Name of the Lord; God is maligned by our self-deprecation.

In a situation like this I naturally expect no miracles, nor do I ask Him, my Lord, to show me mercy. May he treat me with the same indifference with which He treated millions of His people. I am no exception, and I expect no special treatment. I will no longer attempt to save myself, nor flee any more. I will facilitate the work of the fire by moistening my clothing with gasoline. I have three bottles of gasoline left after having emptied several scores over the heads of the murderers. It was one of the finest moments of my life when I did this, and I was shaken with laughter by it. I never dreamed that the death of people, even of enemies – even such enemies – could cause me such great pleasure....

I have three more bottles of gasoline. They are as precious to me as wine to a drunkard. After pouring one over my clothes, I will place the paper on which I write these lines in the empty bottle and hide it among the bricks filling the window of this room. If anyone ever finds it and reads it, he will perhaps, understand the emotions of a Jew, one of millions, who died forsaken by the God in Whom he believed unshakeably. I will let the two other bottles explode on the heads of the murderers when my last moment comes.

There were twelve of us using this room at the outbreak of the rebellion. For nine days we battled against the enemy. All eleven of my comrades had fallen, dying silently in battle, including the small boy of about five – who came here only God knows how and who now lies dead near me, with his face wearing the kind of smile that appears on children's faces when dreaming peacefully – even this child died with the same epic calm as his older comrades. ... Unless my face is eaten by the flames, a similar smile may rest on it after my death. Meanwhile, I still live, and before my death I wish to speak to my Lord as a living man, a simple, living person who had the great but tragic honour of being a Jew.

I am proud that I am a Jew not in spite of the world's treatment of us, but precisely because of this treatment. I should be ashamed to belong to the people who spawned and raised the criminals who are responsible for the deeds that have been perpetrated against us or to any people who tolerated these deeds.

I am proud to be a Jew because it is an art to be a Jew. It is no art to be an Englishman, an American or a Frenchman. It may be easier, more comfortable to be one of them, but not more honourable. Yes, it is an honour, a terrible honour to be a Jew!

I believe that to be a Jew means to be a fighter, an everlasting swimmer against the turbulent human current. The Jew is a hero, a martyr, a saint. You, our evil enemies, declare that we are bad. I believe that we are better and finer than you, but even if we were worse, I should like to see how you would look in our place!

I am happy to belong to the unhappiest of all peoples of the world, whose precepts represent the loftiest and most beautiful of all morality and laws. These immortal precepts which we possess have now been even more sanctified and immortalized by the fact that they have been so debased and insulted by the enemies of the Lord.

I believe that to be a Jew is an inborn trait. One is born a Jew exactly as one is born an artist. It is impossible to be released from being a Jew. That is our godly attribute that has made us a chosen people. Those who do not understand this will never understand the higher meaning of our martyrdom. If ever I doubted that God once designated us as the chosen people, I would believe now that our tribulations have made us the chosen one.

I believe in You, God of Israel, even though You have done everything to stop me from believing in You. I believe in Your laws even if I cannot excuse Your actions. My relationship to

You is not the relationship of a slave to his master but rather that of a pupil to his teacher. I bow my head before Your greatness, but I will not kiss the lash with which You strike me.

You say, I know, that we have sinned, O Lord. It must surely be true! And therefore we are punished? I can understand that too! But I should like You to tell me whether *there is any sin in the world deserving of such a punishment as the punishment we have received?*

You assert that You will yet repay our enemies? I am convinced of it! Repay them without mercy? I have no doubt about that either! I should like You to tell me, however, – *is there any punishment in the world capable of compensating for crimes that have been committed against us?*

You say, I know, that it is no longer a question of sin and punishment, but rather a situation in which Your countenance is veiled, in which humanity is abandoned to its evil instincts. But I should like to ask You, O Lord – and this question burns in me like a consuming fire – *what more, O, what more must transpire before You unveil Your countenance again to the world?*

I want to say to You that now, more than in any previous period in our eternal path of agony, we, we the tortured, the humiliated, the buried alive and burned alive, we the insulted, the mocked, the lonely, the forsaken by God and man – we have the right to know *what are the limits of Your forbearance?*

I should like to say something more: do not put the rope under too much strain, lest, alas, it snaps! The test to which You have put us is so severe, so unbearably severe, that You should – You must – forgive those members of Your people who, in their misery, have turned from You.

Forgive those who have turned from You in their misery, but also those who have turned from You in their happiness. You have transformed our life into such a frightful, perpetual ordeal that the cowards among us have been forced to flee from it; and what is happiness but a place of refuge for cowards? Do not chastise them for it. One does not strike cowards, but has mercy on them. Have mercy on *them*, rather than *us*, O Lord.

Forgive those who have desecrated Your name, who have gone over to the service of other gods, who have become indifferent to You. You have castigated them so severely that they no longer believe that You are their Father, that they have any Father at all.

I tell You this because I do believe in You, because I believe in You more strongly than ever, because now I know that You are my Lord because after all You are not, You cannot possibly be after all the God of those whose deeds are the most horrible expression of ungodliness!

If You are not *my* Lord, then whose Lord are You? The Lord of the murderers?

If those that hate me and murder me are so benighted, so evil, what then am I if not he who reflects something of Your light, of Your goodness?

I cannot extol You for the deeds that You tolerate. I bless You and extol You, however, for the very fact of Your existence, for Your awesome mightiness!

The murderers themselves have already passed sentence on themselves and will never escape it, but may You carry out a doubly severe sentence on those who are condoning the murder.

Those who condemn murder orally, but rejoice at in their hearts. ... Those who meditate in their foul hearts: it is fitting, after all to say that he is evil, the tyrant, but he carries out a bit of work for us for which we will always be grateful to him!

It is written in Your Torah that a thief should be punished more severely than a brigand, in spite of the fact that the thief does not attack his victim physically and merely attempts to take his possessions stealthily.

The reason for this is that a robber by attacking his victim in broad daylight shows no more fear of man than of God. The thief, on the other hand, fears man, but not God. His punishment, therefore, is greater.

I should be satisfied if You dealt with the murderers as with brigands, for their attitude towards You and towards us is the same.

But those who are silent in the face of murder, those who have no fears of You but fear what people might say ... those who express their sympathy with the drowning man but refuse to rescue him though they can swim – punish them, O Lord, punish them, I implore, with a doubly severe sentence!

Death can wait no longer. From the floors above me, the firing becomes weaker by the minute. The last defenders of this stronghold are now falling, and with them falls and perishes the great, beautiful, and God-fearing Jewish part of Warsaw. The sun is about to set, and I thank God that I will never see it again. Fire lights my small window, and the bit of sky that I can see is flooded with red like a waterfall of blood. In about an hour at the most I will be with the rest of my family and with the millions of other stricken members of my people in that better world where there are no more questions.

I die peacefully, but not complacently; persecuted, but not enslaved; embittered, but not cynical; a believer, but not a supplicant; a lover of God, but no blind amen-sayer of His.

I have followed Him even when He rejected me. I have followed His commandments even when He castigated me for it; I have loved Him and I love Him even when He hurls me to the earth, tortures me to death, makes me an object of shame and ridicule.

My rabbi would frequently tell the story of a Jew who fled from the Spanish Inquisition with his wife and child, striking out in a small boat over the stormy sea until he reached a rocky island where a flash of lightning killed his wife; A storm rose and hurled his son into the sea. Then, as lonely as a stone, naked, barefoot, lashed by the storm and terrified by the thunder and the lightning, hands turned up to God, the Jew, setting out on his journey through the wastes of the island, turned to his maker with the following words:

God of Israel, I have fled to this place in order to worship You without molestation, to obey Your commandments and sanctify Your name. You, however, have done everything to make me stop believing in You. Now lest it seem to You that You will succeed by these tribulations to drive me from the right path, I notify You, my God and the God of my fathers, *that it will not avail You in the least!* You may insult me, You may castigate me, You may take from me all that I cherish and hold dear in the world, You may torture me to death – I shall believe in *You*, I shall love You no matter what You do to test me.

And these are my last words to You, my wrathful God: nothing will avail You in the least. You have done everything to make me renounce You, to make me lose my faith in You, but I die exactly as I have lived, a *believer!*

Eternally praised be the God of the dead, the God of vengeance, of truth and of law, Who will soon show His face to the world again and shake its foundations with His almighty voice.

Hear, O Israel, the Lord our God the Lord is One.

Into your hands, O Lord, I consign my soul.

Note: Though this 'document' is, in fact, a work of literary reconstruction, there was a Chasidic family called Rakover who perished during the Holocaust. And one of them, Yossel, died in the flames of the Warsaw ghetto. Here the author, Zvi Kolitz recreates the last thoughts of this pious Jew.
Source: Albert Friedlander (ed.), Out of the Whirlwind: A Reader of Holocaust Literature (New York: Schocken, 1976).

The Jewish Question: Excerpts from Hitler's Writings

A Letter on the Jewish Question

Antisemitism as a political movement should not and cannot be determined by emotional factors, but rather by a realization of the facts. And these are:

First, Jewry is clearly a racial and not a religious group. ... All that which is for men a source of higher life – be it religion, society or democracy – is for the Jew merely a means to an end, namely the satisfaction of his lust for power and money.

His actions will lead to a racial tuberculosis of peoples.

Hence it follows: antisemitism based on purely emotional grounds will find its ultimate expression in the form of pogroms (which are capricious and thus not truly effective). Rational antisemitism, however, must pursue a systematic, *legal* campaign against the Jews, by revocation of the special privileges they enjoy in contrast to the other foreigners living among us. But the final objective must the complete removal of the Jews [*die Entfernung der Juden überhaupt*].

[Source: Adolf Hitler to Adolf Gemlich, 16 September 1919, translated by Paul Mendes-Flohr.]

Extracts from *Mein Kampf*

Today it is difficult, if not impossible to say, for me to say when the word 'Jew' first gave me ground for special thoughts. At home I do not remember having heard the word during my father's lifetime. I believe that the old gentleman would have regarded any special emphasis on this term as cultural backwardness. In the course of his life he had arrived at more or less cosmopolitan views which, despite his pronounced national sentiments, not only remained intact, but also affected me to some extent.

Likewise at school I found no occasion which could have led me to change this inherited picture. ...

Not until my fourteenth or fifteenth year did I begin to come across the word 'Jew', with any frequency, partly in connection with political discussions. This filled me with a mild distaste, and I could not rid myself of an unpleasant feeling that always came over me whenever religious quarrels occurred in my presence.

At that time I did not think anything else of the question.

There were few Jews in Linz. In the course of the centuries their outward appearance had become Europeanized and had taken on a human look; in fact, I even took them for Germans. The absurdity of this idea did not dawn on me because I saw no distinguishing feature but the strange religion. The fact that they had, as I believed, been persecuted on this account sometimes almost turned my distaste at unfavourable remarks about them into horror. ... Then I came to Vienna. [Gradually], I encountered the Jewish question. ...

My views with regard to antisemitism thus succumbed to the passage of time, and this was my greatest transformation of all.

It cost me the greatest inner soul struggles and only after months of battle between my reason and my sentiments did my reason begin to emerge victorious. Two years later, my sentiment had followed my reason, and from then on became its most loyal guardian and sentinel.

At the time of this bitter struggle between spiritual education and cold reason, the visual instruction of the Vienna streets had performed invaluable services. There came a time when I no longer, as in the first days, wandered blindly through the mighty city; now with open eyes I saw not only the buildings but also the people.

Once, as I was strolling through the Inner City, I suddenly encountered an apparition in a black caftan and black hair locks. Is this a Jew? was my first thought.

For, to be sure, they had not looked like this in Linz. I observed the man furtively and cautiously, but the longer I stared at this foreign face, scrutinizing feature for feature, the more my first question assumed a new form: Is this a German?

As always in such cases, I now began to try to relieve my doubts by books. ...

I could no longer very well doubt that the objects of my study were not Germans of a special religion, but a people in themselves; for since I had begun to concern myself with this question and to take cognizance of the Jews, Vienna appeared to

me in a different light than before. Wherever I went, I began to
see Jews, and the more I saw, the more sharply they became
distinguished from the rest of humanity. ...

The cleanliness of this people, moral and otherwise, I must say,
is a point in itself. By their very exterior you could tell that these
were no lovers of water, and, to your distress, you often knew it
with your eyes closed. Later I often grew sick to my stomach from
the smell of these caftan-wearers. Added to this, there was their
unclean dress and generally unheroic appearance.

All this could scarcely be called very attractive; but it became
positively repulsive when, in addition to their physical unclean-
liness, you discovered the moral stains on this 'chosen people'.

In a short time I was made more thoughtful than ever by my
slowly rising insight into the type of activity carried on by the
Jews in certain fields.

Was there any form of filth or profligacy, particularly in
cultural life, without at least one Jew involved in it?

If you cut even cautiously into such an abscess, you found, like
a maggot in a rotting body, often dazzled by the sudden light – a
kike [Yid]!

What had to be reckoned heavily against the Jews in my eyes
was when I became acquainted with their activity in the press,
art, literature and the theatre. All the unctuous reassurances
helped little or nothing. It sufficed to look at a billboard, to study
the names of the men behind the horrible trash they advertised,
to make you hard for a long time to come. This was pestilence,
spiritual pestilence, worse than the Black Death of olden times,
and the people was being infected with it! ...

And now I began to examine my beloved 'world press' from this
point of view.

And the deeper I probed, the more the object of my former
admiration shrivelled. The style became more and more unbearable; I could not help rejecting the content as inwardly shallow
and banal; the objectivity of exposition now seemed to me more
akin to lies than honest truth; and the writers were – Jews.

The relation of the Jews to prostitution and, even more, to the
white-slave traffic, could be studied in Vienna as perhaps in no
other city of Western Europe, with the possible exception of the
southern French ports. If you walked at night through the streets
and alleys of Leopoldstadt, at every step you witnessed proceedings which remained concealed from the majority of the German
people until the War gave the soldiers on the eastern front
occasion to see similar things, or, better expressed, forced them to
see them.

When for the first time I recognized the Jew as the cold-
hearted, shameless and calculating director of this revolting vice

traffic in the scum of the big city, a cold shudder ran down my back.

But then a flame flared up within me. I no longer avoided discussion of the Jewish question; no, now I sought it. And when I learned to look for the Jew in all branches of cultural and artistic life and its various manifestations, I suddenly encountered him in a place where I would least have expected to find him.

When I recognized the Jew as the leader of the Social Democracy, the scales dropped from my eyes. A long soul struggle had reached its conclusion ...

Only now did I become thoroughly acquainted with the seducer of our people. ...

The Jewish doctrine of Marxism rejects the aristocratic principle of Nature and replaces the eternal privilege of power and strength by the mass of numbers and their dead weight. Thus it denies the value of personality in man, contests the significance of nationality and race, and thereby withdraws from humanity the premiss of its existence and its culture. As a foundation of the universe, this doctrine would bring about the end of any order intellectually conceivable to man. And as, in this greatest of all recognizable organisms, the result of an application of such a law could only be chaos, on earth it could only be destruction for the inhabitants of this planet.

If, with the help of his Marxist creed, the Jew is victorious over the other peoples of the world, his crown will be the funeral wreath of humanity and this planet will, as it did thousands of years ago, move through the ether devoid of men.

Eternal Nature inexorably avenges the infringement of her commands.

Hence today I believe that I am acting in accordance with the will of the Almighty Creator: *by defending myself against the Jew, I am fighting for the work of the Lord.*

To what an extent the whole existence of this people is based on a continuous lie is shown incomparably by the *Protocols of the Elders of Zion,* so infinitely hated by the Jews. They are based on a forgery, the *Frankfurter Zeitung* moans and screams once every week: the best proof that they are authentic. ... For once this book has become the common property of a people, the Jewish menace may be considered as broken.

His [i.e. the Jew's] unfailing instinct in such things scents the original soul in everyone, and his hostility is assured to anyone who is not spirit of his spirit. Since the Jew is not the attacked but the attacker, not only anyone who attacks passes as his enemy, but also anyone who resists him. But the means with which he seeks to break such reckless but upright souls is not honest warfare, but lies and slander.

Here he stops at nothing, and in his vileness he becomes so gigantic that no one need be surprised if among our people the personification of the devil as the symbol of all evil assumes the living shape of the Jew.

The ignorance of the broad masses about the inner nature of the Jew, the lack of instinct and narrow-mindedness of our upper classes, make the people an easy victim for this campaign of lies.

While from innate cowardice the upper classes turn away from a man whom the Jew attacks with lies and slander, the broad masses from stupidity or simplicity believe everything. The state authorities either cloak themselves in silence or, what usually happens, in order to put an end to the Jewish press campaign, they persecute the unjustly attacked, which, in the eyes of such an official ass, passes as the preservation of state authority and the safeguarding of law and order. Slowly fear and the Marxist weapon of Jewry descend like a nightmare on the mind and soul of decent people.

They begin to tremble before the terrible enemy and thus have become his final victim.

The Jew's domination in the state seems so assured that now not only can he call himself a Jew again, but he ruthlessly admits his ultimate national and political designs. A section of his race openly owns itself to be a foreign people, yet even they lie. For while the Zionists try to make the rest of the world believe that the national consciousness of the Jew finds its satisfaction in the creation of a Palestinian state, the Jews again slyly dupe the dumb *Goyim*. It doesn't even enter their heads to build up a Jewish state in Palestine for the purpose of living there; all they want is a central organization for their international world swindle, endowed with its own sovereign rights and removed from the intervention of other states; a haven for convicted criminals and a university for budding crooks.

It is a sign of their rising confidence and sense of security that at a time when one section is still playing the German. Frenchman or Englishman, the other with open effrontery comes out as the Jewish race.

How close they see approaching victory can be seen by the hideous aspect which their relations with the members of other peoples takes on.

With satanic joy in his face, the black-haired Jewish youth lurks in wait for the unsuspecting girl whom he defiles with his blood, thus stealing her from her people. With every means he tries to destroy the racial foundations of the people he has set out to subjugate. Just as he himself systematically ruins women and girls, he does not shrink back from pulling down the blood barriers for others, even on a large scale. It was and it is Jews who bring the negroes into the Rhineland, always with the same secret thought and clear aim of ruining the hated white race by the necessarily resulting bastardization, throwing it down from its cultural and political height, and himself rising to be its master.

For a racially pure people which is conscious of its blood can never be enslaved by the Jew. In this world he will forever be master over bastards and bastards alone.

And so he tries systematically to lower the racial level by a continuous poisoning of individuals.

And in politics he begins to replace the idea of democracy by the dictatorship of the proletariat.

In the organized mass of Marxism he has found the weapon which lets him dispense with democracy and in its stead allows him to subjugate and govern the peoples with a dictatorial and brutal fist.

He works systematically for revolutionization in a two-fold sense: economic and political.

Around peoples who offer too violent a resistance to attack from within he weaves a net of enemies, thanks to his international influence, incites them to war, and finally, if necessary, plants a flag of revolution on the very battlefields.

In economics he undermines the states until the social enterprises which have become unprofitable are taken from the state and subjected to his financial control.

In the political field he refuses the state the means for its self-preservation, destroys the foundations of all national self-maintenance and defense, destroys faith in the leadership, scoffs at its history and past, and drags everything that is truly great into the gutter.

Culturally, he contaminates art, literature, the theatre, makes a mockery of natural feeling, overthrows all concepts of beauty and sublimity, of the noble and the good, and instead drags men down into the sphere of his own base nature.

Religion is ridiculed, ethics and morality represented as outmoded, until the last props of a nation in its struggle for existence in this world have fallen.

Now begins the great last revolution. In gaining political power the Jew casts off the few cloaks that he still wears. The democratic people's Jew becomes the blood-Jew and tyrant over peoples. In a few years he tries to exterminate the national intelligentsia and by robbing the peoples of their natural intellectual leadership makes them ripe for the slave's lot of permanent subjugation.

The most frightful example of this kind is offered by Russia, where he killed or starved about thirty million people with positively fanatical savagery, in part amid inhuman tortures, in order to give a gang of Jewish journalists and stock exchange bandits domination over a great people.

The end is not only the end of the freedom of the peoples oppressed by the Jew, but also the end of this parasite upon the nations. After the death of his victim, the vampire sooner or later dies too.

Excerpts: Adolf Hitler, *Mein Kampf* [My Struggle], (Munich, 1925), (Houghton Mifflin, 1943. Translated by Ralph Manheim). Quoted in P. Mendes-Flohr and J. Reinharz, *The Jew in the Modern World* (Oxford University Press, 1980) and in Y. Arad, Y. Gutman and A. Margaliot, *Documents on the Holocaust* (Yad Vashem, 1981).

Extracts from Hitler's Secret Book (c.1928)

Just as every people ... possesses a powerful urge for self-preservation as its driving force, likewise is it exactly so with Jewry, too. Only here, in accord with their basically different dispositions, the struggle for existence of Aryan peoples and Jewry is also different in its forms. The foundation of the Aryan struggle for life is the soil, which he cultivates and which provides the general basis for an economy satisfying primarily its own needs within its own orbit through the productive forces of its own people.

Because of the lack of productive capacities of its own the Jewish people cannot carry out the construction of a state, viewed in a territorial sense, but as a support of its own existence it needs the work and creative activities of other nations. Thus the existence of the Jew himself becomes a parasitical one within the lives of other peoples. Hence the ultimate goal of the Jewish struggle for existence is the enslavement of productively active peoples. In order to achieve this goal, which in reality has represented Jewry's struggle for existence at all times, the Jew makes use of all weapons that are in keeping with the whole complex of his character.

Therefore in domestic politics within the individual nations he fights first for equal rights and later for super-rights. The characteristics of cunning, intelligence, astuteness, knavery, dissimulation, etc., rooted in the character of his folkdom, serve him as weapons thereto. They are as much stratagems in his war of survival as those of other peoples in combat.

In foreign policy he tries to bring other nations into a state of unrest, to divert them from their true interests, and to plunge them into reciprocal wars and in this way gradually rise to mastery over them with the help of the power of money and propaganda.

His ultimate goal is the denationalization, the promiscuous bastardization of other peoples, the lowering of the racial level of the highest peoples as well as the domination of this racial mish-mash through the extirpation of the folkish intelligentsia and its replacement by the members of his own people.

The end of the Jewish world struggle therefore will always be a bloody Bolshevization. In truth this means the destruction of all the intellectual upper classes linked to their peoples so that he can rise to become master of a mankind become leaderless....
The economic conquest of Europe by the Jews was pretty much completed around the turn of the century, and now he began to safeguard it politically. That means, the first attempts to extirpate the national intelligentsia were undertaken in the form of revolutions.

He utilized the tensions between European nations, which are in great part to be ascribed to their general need for territory with the consequences which arise therefrom, for his own advantage by systematically inciting them to the World War.

The aim is the destruction of inherently antisemitic Russia as well as the destruction of the German Reich which in the administration and the army still offers resistance to the Jew. The further aim is the overthrow of those dynasties which had not yet been made subject to a democracy dependent upon and led by Jews. ... The bitterest struggle for the victory of Jewry at the present time is being waged in Germany. Here it is the National Socialist movement which alone has taken upon itself the struggle against this execrable crime against mankind.

From *Hitlers Zweites Buch* (Stuttgart, 1928). (English translation: *Hitler's Secret Book* (New York, 1961)).

The Programme of the National-Socialist German Workers' Party

The Programme of the German Workers' Party is a programme for our time. The leadership rejects the establishment of new aims after those set out in the programme have been achieved, for the sole purpose of making it possible for the Party to continue to exist as the result of the artificially stimulated dissatisfaction of the masses.

1. We demand the uniting of all Germans within one Greater Germany, on the basis of the right to self-determination of nations.
2. We demand equal rights for the German people with respect to other nations, and the annulment of the peace treaty of Versailles and St. Germain.
3. We demand land and soil to feed our People and settle our excess population.
4. Only Nationals can be Citizens of the State. Only persons of German blood can be Nationals, regardless of religious affiliation. No Jew can therefore be a German National.
5. Any person who is not a Citizen will be able to live in Germany only as a guest and must be subject to legislation for Aliens.
6. Only a Citizen is entitled to decide the leadership and laws of the State. We therefore demand that only Citizens may hold public office, regardless of whether it is a national, state or local office.

We oppose the corrupting parliamentary custom of making party considerations, and not character and ability, the criterion for appointments to official positions.

7. We demand that the State make it its duty to provide

opportunities of employment first of all for its own Citizens. If it is not possible to maintain the entire population of the State, then foreign nationals (non-citizens) are to be expelled from the Reich.

8.　Any further immigration of non-Germans is to be prevented. We demand that all non-Germans who entered Germany after August 2 1914, be forced to leave the Reich without delay.

9.　All German citizens must have equal rights and duties.

10.　It must be the first duty of every Citizen to carry out intellectual or physical work. Individual activity must not be harmful to the public interest and must be pursued within the framework of the community and for the general good.

　　We therefore demand:

11.　The abolition of all income obtained without labour or effort.

　　Breaking the Servitude of Interest.

12.　In view of the tremendous sacrifices in property and blood demanded of the Nation by every war, personal gain from the war must be termed a crime against the Nation. We therefore demand the total confiscation of all war profits.

13.　We demand the nationalization of all enterprises (already) converted into corporations (trusts).

14.　We demand profit-sharing in large enterprises.

15.　We demand the large-scale development of old-age pension schemes.

16.　We demand the creation and maintenance of a sound middle class; the immediate communalization of the large department stores, which are to be leased at low rates to small tradesmen. We demand the most careful consideration for the owners of small businesses in orders placed by national, state or community authorities.

17.　We demand land reform in accordance with our national needs and a law for expropriation without compensation of land for public purposes. Abolition of ground rent and prevention of all speculation in land.

18.　We demand ruthless battle against those who harm the common good by their activities. Persons committing base crimes against the People, usurers, profiteers, etc., are to be punished by death without regard to religion or race.

19.　We demand the replacement of Roman Law, which serves a materialistic World Order, by German Law.

20.　In order to make higher education – and thereby entry into leading positions – available to every able and industrious German, the State must provide a thorough restructuring of our entire public educational system. The courses of study at all educational institutions are to be adjusted to meet the requirements of practical life. Understanding of the concept of the State must be achieved through the schools (teaching of civics) at the earliest age at which it can be grasped. We demand the education at the public expense of specially gifted children of poor parents, without regard to the latters' position or occupation.

21. The State must raise the level of national health by means of mother-and-child care, the banning of juvenile labour, achievement of physical fitness through legislation for compulsory gymnastics and sports, and maximum support for all organizations providing physical training for young people.

22. We demand the abolition of hireling troops and the creation of a national army.

23. We demand laws to fight against *deliberate* political lies and their dissemination by the press. In order to make it possible to create a German press, we demand:

(a) all editors and editorial employees of newspapers appearing in the German language must be German by race;

(b) non-German newspapers require express permission from the State for their publication. They may not be printed in the German language;

(c) any financial participation in a German newspaper or influence on such a paper is to be forbidden by law to non-Germans and the penalty for any breach of this law will be the closing of the newspaper in question, as well as the immediate expulsion from the Reich of the non-Germans involved.

Newspapers which violate the public interest are to be banned. We demand laws against trends in art and literature which have a destructive effect on our national life, and the suppression of performances that offend against the above requirements.

24. We demand freedom for all religious denominations, provided they do not endanger the existence of the State or offend the concepts of decency and morality of the Germanic race. The Party as such stands for positive Christianity, without associating itself with any particular denomination. It fights against the Jewish-materialistic spirit *within* and *around* us, and is convinced that a permanent revival of our Nation can be achieved only from *within*, on the basis of:

Public Interest Before Private Interest

25. To carry out all the above we demand: the creation of a strong central authority in the Reich. Unquestioned authority by the political central Parliament over the entire Reich and

over its organizations in general. The establishment of trade and professional organizations to enforce the Reich basic laws in the individual states.

The Party leadership promises to take an uncompromising stand, at the cost of their own lives if need be, on the enforcement of the above points.

Munich, February 24, 1920.

Source: *Das Programm der NSDAP* (Berlin, 1933). Translation appears in Y. Arad, Y. Gutman, and A. Margaliot, *Documents on the Holocaust* (Yad Vashem, 1981).

APPENDIX E

The Nuremberg Laws

Excerpts from the two Nuremberg Laws and the
Implementing Decree

Reich Citizenship Laws
15 September, 1935

Paragraph 2

1) A Reich citizen is a subject of the State who is of German or related blood, who proves by his conduct that he is willing and fit faithfully to serve the German people and Reich.
2) Reich citizenship is acquired through the granting of a Reich Citizenship Certificate.
3) The Reich citizen is the sole bearer of full political rights in accordance with the Law.

Law for the Protection of German Blood and Honour
15 September, 1935

Moved by the understanding that purity of the German Blood is the essential condition for the continued existence of the German people, and inspired by the inflexible determination to ensure the existence of the German nation for all time, the Reichstag has unanimously adopted the following Law, which is promulgated herewith:

Paragraph 1
1) Marriages between Jews and subjects of the State of German or related blood are forbidden. Marriages nevertheless concluded are invalid, even if concluded abroad to circumvent this law.

2) Annulment proceedings can be initiated only by the State Prosecutor.

Paragraph 2
Extra-marital sexual relations between Jews and subjects of the State of German or related blood are forbidden.

Paragraph 3
Jews may not employ in their households female subjects of the State of German or related blood who are under 45 years of age.

Paragraph 4
1) Jews are forbidden to fly the Reich or National flag or to display the Reich colours.
2) They are, on the other hand, permitted to display the Jewish colours. The exercise of this right is protected by the State.

Paragraph 5
1) Any person who violates the prohibition under Paragraph 1 will be punished by a prison sentence with hard labour.
2) A male who violates the prohibition under Paragraph 2 will be punished with a prison sentence with or without hard labour.
3) Any person violating the provisions under Paragraphs 3 or 4 will be punished with a prison sentence of up to one year and a fine, or with one or the other of these penalties.

First Decree to the Reich Citizenship Law
14 November, 1935

Paragraph 4
1) A Jew cannot be a Reich citizen. He has no voting rights in political matters; he cannot occupy a public office.
2) Jewish officials will retire as of 31 December, 1935. ...

Paragraph 5
1) A Jew is a person descended from at least three Jewish grandparents who are full Jews by race.
2) A subject of the State of mixed descent [Mischling] who is descended from two full Jewish grandparents is also considered a Jew if: (a) he belonged to the Jewish religious community at the time this law was issued or joined the community later; (b) he was married to a Jew at the time the law was issued, or if he married a Jew subsequently; (c) he is the offspring of a marriage with a Jew, which was contracted after the Law for the Protection of German Blood and

Honour went into effect; or (d) he is the offspring of extra-marital intercourse with a Jew and will be born out of wedlock after 31 July, 1936.

Source: *Reichsgesetzblatt, I* (1935, p.1333). English translation by Priscilla Fishman in Y. Gutman and C. Schatzker, *The Holocaust and its Significance* (Zalman Shazar Center, 1984), except for paragraph 5 (2) which appears in Bernard Dov Weinryb, *Jewish Emancipation Under Attack* (American Jewish Publication Committee, 1942) reproduced in Paul Mendes-Flohr and Jehuda Reinharz, *The Jew in the Modern World* (Oxford University Press, 1980).

German Foreign Ministry Memorandum on 'The Jewish Question', 25 January 1939*

Subject: The Jewish Question as a Factor in Foreign Policy in 1938.

1. Germany's Jewish policy as condition and consequence of foreign policy decisions in 1938.
2. The aim of German Jewish policy: emigration.
3. Means, ways and destinations of Jewish emigration.
4. The Jewish emigre as the best propaganda for Germany's Jewish policy.

It is probably no coincidence that the fateful year of 1938 brought not only the realization of the concept of a Greater Germany, but at the same time has brought the Jewish Question close to solution. For the Jewish policy was both pre-condition and consequence of the events of 1938. More than the power politics and hostility of the former enemy in the World War it was the penetration of Jewish influence and the corrupting Jewish mentality in politics, economy and culture which paralysed the strength and the will of the German people to rise once more. ...

But the need for a radical solution of the Jewish question also resulted from the developments in foreign affairs which added 200,000 persons of the Jewish faith in Austria to the 500,000 living in the old Reich. The influence of the Jews in the Austrian economy made it necessary to take immediate steps to eliminate the Jews from the German economy. ...

The campaign launched in reprisal for the assassination of Secretary of Legation vom Rath has speeded up this process so greatly that Jewish retail trade – so far with the exception of

313

foreign-owned stores – has vanished completely from our streets. The liquidation of Jewish wholesale and manufacturing enterprises, and of houses and real estate owned by Jews, is gradually progressing so far that within a limited period of time the existence of Jewish property will in Germany be a thing of the past. ...

The ultimate aim of Germany's policy is the emigration of all Jews living in German territory. ... The Jew has been eliminated from politics and culture, but until 1938 his powerful economic position in Germany and his tenacious determination to hold out until the return of 'better times' remained unbroken. ...

But the Jew had underestimated the consistency and strength of the National-Socialist idea.

The ... question, to which countries the organized emigration of the Jews should be directed, could (not) be solved by the Evian Conference; each of the countries taking part expressed its agreement in principle to help solve the refugee problem, but declared that it was unable to accept large masses of Jewish emigres into its territory. While in the years 1933–4 more than 100,000 Jews from Germany made their way abroad, legally or illegally, and were able to gain a foothold in a new host nation, either with the aid of relatives living abroad, or the pity of humanitarian circles, by now almost all countries in the world have sealed their borders hermetically against the burdensome Jewish intruders. ...

Even the migration of only about 100,000 Jews has been sufficient to waken the interest in, if not the understanding of, the Jewish danger in many countries, and it can be foreseen that the Jewish question will develop into an international political problem when large numbers of Jews from Germany, Poland, Hungary and Rumania are set in motion by the increasing pressure of their host nations. Even for Germany the Jewish question will not be solved when the last Jew has left German soil. ...

Palestine, which has already been designated by a popular catchword as the target of emigration, cannot be considered as such because its absorptive capacity for a mass influx of Jews is insufficient. Under pressure of Arab resistance the British Mandatory government has limited Jewish immigration into Palestine to a minimum.

At first the emigration of German Jews to Palestine received extensive support from Germany through the conclusion of an agreement with Jewish representatives in Palestine. ...

But Germany is obliged to discern the danger in the creation of a Jewish State, which even in a miniature form could provide world Jewry with a basis for action similar to that of the Vatican

State for political Catholicism, and could absorb only a fraction of the Jews. The realization that Jewry will always be the implacable enemy of the Third Reich forces us to the decision to prevent any strengthening of the Jewish position. A Jewish State would give world Jewry increased power in international law and relations. ...

Germany has an important interest in seeing the splintering of Jewry maintained. Those who argue that this will cause the creation of sources of boycott and anti-German centres all over the world disregard a development already evident, that the influx of Jews arouses the resistance of the native population in all parts of the world and thus provides the best propaganda for Germany's policy towards the Jews.

In North America, in South America, in France, in Holland, Scandinavia and Greece – wherever the stream of Jewish migrants has poured in, a clear increase in antisemitism has already been recorded. It must be the aim of German foreign policy to strengthen this wave of antisemitism. ...

The poorer the Jewish immigrant is and the greater the burden he constitutes for the country into which he has immigrated, the stronger the reaction will be in the host country, and the more desirable the effect in support of German propaganda. The aim of this German policy is a future international solution of the Jewish question, dictated not by false pity for a 'Jewish religious minority that has been driven out' but by the mature realization by all nations of the nature of the danger that Jewry spells for the national character of the nations.

* Excerpted from document 58 in Yitzhak Arad, Yisrael Gutman and Abraham Margaliot (eds), *Documents on the Holocaust* (Yad Vashem, 1981).

Numbers of Jews Murdered in Europe: An Estimate*

Country	Jewish population September 1939	Number of Jews murdered	Percentage of Jews murdered
1 Poland	3,300,000	2,800,000	85.0
2 USSR (occupied territories)	2,100,000	1,500,000	71.4
3 Romania	850,000	425,000	50.0
4 Hungary	404,000	200,000	49.5
5 Czechoslovakia	315,000	260,000	82.5
6 France	300,000	90,000	30.0
7 Germany	210,000	170,000	81.0
8 Lithuania	150,000	135,000	90.0
9 Holland	150,000	90,000	60.0
10 Latvia	95,000	85,000	89.5
11 Belgium	90,000	40,000	44.4
12 Greece	75,000	60,000	80.0
13 Yugoslavia	75,000	55,000	73.3
14 Austria	60,000	40,000	66.6
15 Italy	57,000	15,000	26.3
16 Bulgaria	50,000	7,000	14.0
17 Others	20,000	6,000	30.0
Total	8,301,000	5,978,000	72.0

* Source: Leon Poliakov and Josef Wulf (eds), *Das Dritte Reich und die Juden: Dokumente und Aufsätze* (Arani-Verlag, GmbH, Berlin, 1955), cited in Paul Mendes-Flohr and Jehuda Reinharz, *The Jew in the Modern World* (Oxford University Press, 1980).

Chronology of the Holocaust, 1933–45

1933

30 January. Hitler appointed Chancellor. In the following weeks and months the Nazis assume total control of German state, abolishing its federalist structure, dismantling democratic government and outlawing political parties and trade unions.

20 March. Dachau concentration camp set up on Himmler's orders. First inmates include communists, socialists, homosexuals and Jews.

1 April. Nazi boycott of Jewish businesses and professions accompanied by a wave of terror.

7 April. The Restoration of the Professional Civil Service Act dismisses Jews and those considered politically undesirable from the Civil Service.

22 April. Jews disqualified from working in hospitals.

25 April. Law against the Overcrowding of German Schools begins the elimination of Jewish teachers and pupils from German schools system.

10 May. Public book-burning in Berlin organized by Goebbels targets 'Jewish' books and others considered 'degenerate' by the Nazis.

August. *Ha'avara* (transfer) agreement between German Ministry of Economics and Zionist Organization facilitates large-scale emigration of Jews from Germany to Palestine.

29 September. Hereditary farm law bans Jews from ownership of land. On the same day a further law bans Jews from all aspects of German cultural and sporting life.

1934

1 May. Nazi propaganda weekly, *Der Stürmer*, revives ritual murder accusation against Jews.

30 June. Murder of Röhm and other SA leaders in 'The Night of the Long Knives'.

2 August. Death of President Hindenburg. Hitler declares himself 'Führer'.

1935

15 September. Hitler uses the occasion of the Nazi rally in Nuremberg to issue the Nuremberg Laws: (1) the Reich Citizenship Law which removes Jewish equality before the law; and (2) The Law for the Protection of German Blood and Honour which prohibits marriage or sexual relations between Jews and non-Jews.

1 November. Supplement to the Reich Citizenship Law disqualifies Jews from German citizenship. Thirteen days later a further supplement defines categories of *Mischling* or 'part Jews'.

1936

March. Spate of anti-Jewish pogroms in Poland, abetted by an inflammatory speech by Polish Cardinal Hlond against Jewish 'usury, fraud and white slavery'.

August. Anti-Jewish discriminatory measures eased during Olympic Games which are held in Berlin but reapplied and extended after its conclusion to cover all areas of economic and social activity.

1937

19 July. Buchenwald concentration camp established.

1938

12 March. Nazi troops enter Vienna, effecting Austrian Anschluss with Germany. Rash of antisemitic incidents follow. German anti-Jewish laws swiftly applied to new province. Austrian Jews flee in their thousands.

26 April. Personal property of German Jews over 5,000 marks in value to be officially registered – first of a series of regulations aimed at registering all Jewish-owned domestic and foreign property, as a prelude to confiscation by the state.

4 May. Hungarian government introduces *numerus clausus* restricting Jewish entry into liberal professions, administration, commerce and industry.

14 June. All Jewish firms in Germany to be registered with the Ministry of Economics.

6–15 July. International conference held at Evian in France discusses and fails to find solution to Jewish refugee problem precipitated by the Anschluss.

25 July. Licences of Jewish doctors cancelled.

August. Eichmann opens a Vienna office for Jewish emigration.

17 August. Jewish women have to add 'Sarah' and Jewish men 'Israel' to their first names for official purposes.

September–October. Munich crisis culminates in Anglo-French decision to cede Czech Sudetenland to the Germans. Nazi occupation the following month leads to mass flight of Jews from region.

27 September. Licences of Jewish lawyers cancelled.

5 October. Following confiscation of Jewish passports, new passports to Jews now issued with suffix 'J'.

28 October. 17,000 Polish-born Jews living in Germany expelled.

7 November. Herschl Grynszpan assassinates German official in Paris in response to the expulsion of his parents.

9–10 November. *Kristallnacht*, the Nazi response to the assassination. Night-long campaign of violence and physical destruction against synagogues and shops leaves 91 dead. Jews held responsible by Nazis. Approx. 25,000 sent to concentration camps. 1,000 million marks required of Jews in 'reparations'.

12 November. Göring convenes conference of Nazi officials to plan the complete 'Aryanization' of Jewish businesses in Germany.

16 November. Decree forbids Jewish children to attend German schools. From now on they may only attend Jewish schools.

1939

24 January. Heydrich assigned by Göring to remove all Jews from Reich through emigration. The Reichsvertretung, the Jewish representative organization in Nazi Germany, reformed as the

Reichsvereiningung (State Association) under Nazi supervision for this purpose.

30 January. Hitler delivers Reichstag speech in which he threatens that, if international Jewry plunge the world into war, the Jews of Europe will be annihilated.

21 February. Decree requires Jews to surrender all gold and silver in their possession.

15 March. German troops enter Prague, absorbing formerly Czech provinces of Bohemia and Moravia into Greater Germany. Leads to mass flight of Czech Jews. Eichmann sets up a Jewish emigration office in Prague. Slovakia becomes independent ally of Nazi Germany.

21 March. German troops occupy Lithuanian-administered Memel. Jewish population flees.

30 April. Revocation of tenancy protection for Jews paves way for their relocation in 'communal Jewish houses'.

May. British government White Paper sets a limit for entry of 75,000 Jewish refugees into Palestine over following five years.

22 August. Hitler's speech to generals urges liquidation of Poles in forthcoming war in order to gain *Lebensraum* for Germany.

23 August. Non-aggression pact between Nazi Germany and the Soviet Union, which includes secret conditions for the division of eastern Europe, prepares the way for the Nazi attack on Poland.

1 September. Nazi invasion of Poland accompanied by accelerating violence against both Poles and Jews. *Einsatzgruppen* begin executions of Poles. German Jews placed under curfew and have radio sets confiscated.

3 September. Britain and France declare war on Germany.

21 September. Beginning of dissolution of traditional Polish Jewish communities. Parallel movement towards enforced resettlement of Jews in ghettos. Order for expulsion of all Jews and gypsies from areas of Poland annexed to Greater Germany.

28 September. Total defeat of Poland leads to partition between Nazi Germany and the Soviet Union under terms of Non-Aggression Pact.

October. Euthanasia programme begins leading to the deaths of over 70,000 mentally and physically disabled people by August 1941.

23 November. All Jews in Nazi-occupied Poland ordered to wear Star of David.

28 November. Jewish Councils (*Judenräte*) ordered into existence in German-occupied Poland.

12 December. Labour camps set up throughout German-occupied Poland. All Jewish males between 14 and 60 required for forced labour.

1940

9 April. German blitzkrieg in the west begins.

1 May. The Lodz Ghetto, containing 160,000 Jews and with Chaim Rumkowski at its head, is sealed off from outside world.

22 June. France defeated. Pétain sues for peace leading to creation of collaborative Vichy government in the south.

July. German Foreign Office proposes that European Jews be deported to French Madagascar.

October. Deportations into Warsaw Ghetto begin. Wall is built to isolate Jews from rest of city. By early 1941 there are 400,000 confined here in rapidly deteriorating conditions.

3 October. Vichy government debars Jews from public offices and most areas of French economic life and a day later authorizes internment of foreign Jews. Similar anti-Jewish legislation enacted by Antonescu regime in Romania.

1941

January. Major anti-Jewish pogrom by Romanian fascist Iron Guard in Bucharest.

February. Deportations of several hundred Dutch Jews to Buchenwald and Sachsenhausen concentration camps in reprisal for the self-defence killing of a Dutch Nazi. Two-day general strike in Amsterdam in support of Jews is crushed.

1 March. Himmler sets in motion plans for expansion of Auschwitz complex.

6 April. German invasion of Yugoslavia and Greece triggers pogroms against Jews and Serbs, carried out by pro-Nazi militia in Croatia.

May. Beginning of internment of foreign-born Jews in Paris.

4 June. German army directive to troops about to invade the Soviet Union to eliminate all resistance. Jews are included in this category. Commissar Order, two days later, spells out that all Soviet officials are to be liquidated.

22 June. Operation Barbarossa, the invasion of the Soviet Union by Nazi Germany and her Hungarian, Romanian and Finnish allies.

Precipitates local massacres of Jews in Baltic states and the western Ukraine. Four commandos of *Einsatzgruppen* begin mass slaughter of Jews, Gypsies and soviet officials.

22 July. Vichy government commences expropriation of French Jewish businesses.

31 July. Heydrich receives orders from Göring, on Hitler's instructions, to begin preparations for the 'intended Final Solution of the Jewish Question'.

August. Romanians begin expelling Jews from Bessarabia and Bukovina, which they had reoccupied during Operation Barbarossa, into Transnistria across the River Dneister. Thousands perish on death marches.

23 August. Hitler officially calls off euthanasia programme after Bishop von Galen's denunciatory sermon on the subject.

26 August. Bloody massacre of Hungarian Jewish refugees by SS units and Ukrainian militia at Kamenets Podolsk in the Ukraine. Mass executions throughout Nazi-occupied Soviet regions intensify.

September. Zyclon B gas tested for the first time at Auschwitz on Soviet prisoners of war. Construction of killing centre at Birkenau (adjacent to existing Auschwitz complex) begins.

6 September. Vilna Jews ghettoized.

29–30 September. Bloodbath in Babi Yar gorge, near the Ukrainian capital of Kiev. Jews and gypsies butchered by SS units and Ukrainian militia.

14 October. Mass deportations of Jews from Greater Germany to the east begins. Thousands are shot on arrival.

23 October. Nazi emigration policy towards Jews officially ends. No more Jews allowed to leave the Reich or Nazi sphere of influence. Concurrently Romanian troops perpetrate horrendous massacre of Jews in Black Sea port of Odessa.

24 November. New 'model' ghetto created at Theresienstadt for thousands of central European Jews.

30 November. Executions of Riga Jews in the Rumbuli forest.

December. *Generalplan Ost* (General Plan for the East), drawn up under Himmler's directions, proposes deportation of 31 million non-Germans in conquered East to make *Lebensraum* for German colonists.

5 December. Soviet counteroffensive in front of Moscow signals failure of Operation Barbarossa.

8 December. Gas killings of Jews and Gypsies in mobile vans begin in Chelmno, western Poland.

11 December. Following Japanese bombing of Pearl Harbor, Germany declares war on the United States.

1942

January. Jewish resistance and partisan groups organized in Vilna and Kovno.

20 January. The Wannsee Conference in Berlin. Nazi officials agree plans for the coordination of the 'Final Solution'.

24 February. The ship, the *Struma*, carrying Jewish refugees from Romania, having been refused permission to sail to British-controlled Palestine is sunk in the Black Sea. All bar one passenger are drowned.

16 March. Operations Reinhard, the liquidation of Polish Jewry, begins. First transports to Belzec, Sobibor, Majdanek and Treblinka death camps.

24 March. First deportations of Jews to Auschwitz from Slovakia. Followed four days later by first Jewish refugees from France.

2 June. BBC broadcast extracts from a report smuggled out of Poland by the Jewish socialist Bund. It tells of extermination of 700,000 Jews at Chelmno and elsewhere.

9 June. Mobile gas van killings begin in Riga, Latvia.

10 June. Czech village of Lidice liquidated in revenge for the assassination of SS chief Heydrich. Additional round-ups of Czechs in Prague and Jews in Berlin.

14 July. Mass deportation of Dutch Jews to Auschwitz begins, followed shortly afterwards by Jews from Belgium and Luxemburg.

22 July. Deportation of Warsaw Jews to Treblinka death camp begins.

28 July. Underground Jewish Combat Organization formed in Warsaw Ghetto.

8 August. Gerhard Riegner, the World Jewish Congress representative in Geneva, sends telegram to British and American governments with information about the Final Solution.

15 October. Horrendous slaughter of Jews by SS in Brest-Litovsk, Soviet Russia.

25 October. Deportation of Norwegian Jews to Auschwitz begins, despite resistance and escape routes provided by many Norwegians.

2 November. Start of major round-up of all Jews in Bialystok region of Poland. 170,000 killed in one week.

4 November. Tide of war turns with British victory at El Alamein, followed on 19 November by Russian counter-offensive at Stalingrad.

27 November. Mass expulsion of Poles from Zamosc region of Poland to provide *Lebensraum* for Germans.

16 November. Deportations of German gypsies to Auschwitz begin.

17 November. Inter-Allied declaration denounces murder of European Jewry and states that those responsible will be punished.

1943

January. Jewish transport to Treblinka attacks guards on arrival.

8 March. Deportations of Greek Jews to Treblinka (and later Auschwitz) begins.

14 March. Cracow Ghetto liquidated.

17 March. Bulgarian parliament vetoes proposed deportation of Bulgarian Jews to the death camps.

5 April. Massacres of Lithuanian Jews in Ponary woods begin.

19 April. Warsaw Ghetto Uprising begins, as SS finalizes plans for its complete liquidation. At the same time, Bermuda Conference of American and British officials fails to implement plans for rescue of European Jewry or provide assistance for European refugees.

12 May. In despair at his failure to gain Allied military assistance for the uprising, Bundist leader Shmuel Zygelboym commits suicide in London. Liquidation of the Warsaw ghetto is completed.

June. Himmler's Unit 1005 slave-labour battalions begin work exhuming corpses from death camps and execution sites in order to obliterate evidence of the Holocaust.

21 June. Lwow ghetto liquidated.

1 July. Final order of Reich Citizenship Act removes all legal protection from the Jews of Germany.

2 August. Attempted mass revolt and break-out from Treblinka crushed.

16 August. Bialystok ghetto liquidated. Attempted Jewish revolt is put down.

September–October. Danes sabotage Nazi deportation plans for

Danish Jews, most of whom are ferried to safety in neutral Sweden.

23 September. Vilna ghetto liquidated.

14 October. Partial break-out of Jews and Soviet prisoners of war from Sobibor.

16 October. Deportation of Italian Jews to Auschwitz begins following Nazi occupation of northern Italy.

1944

22 January. United States President Roosevelt sets up War Refugees Board to assist relief and rescue efforts.

19 March. Nazis occupy Hungary following fears that the Hungarian regime is about to sue for peace with the Allies. Eichmann arrives to supervise anti-Jewish measures.

May. Proposals from Jewish leaders to Allies that they bomb railway lines leading to Auschwitz.

15 May. Deportation of Hungarian Jews to Auschwitz begins and quickly accelerates as Red Army breaks into eastern Hungary.

6 June. Allies open 'Second Front' with Normandy landings.

8 June. International pressure from Sweden, the Red Cross, the Vatican, and the Allies leads to Hungarian government halting deportations. Eichmann concurrently involved in negotiations with Jewish leaders, offering to exchange lives of Hungarian Jews for war materials.

20 July. Bomb plot to assassinate Hitler fails.

23 July. Red Army advance liberates Majdanek concentration camp in Poland coinciding with large-scale German evacuations of death camp inmates to Dachau, Bergen-Belsen and Stutthof.

6 August. 70,000 remaining Jews in Lodz, including the *Judenrat* leader Chaim Rumkowski, are deported to Auschwitz (except for several hundred Jews who are mysteriously left behind).

7 October. Inmates blow up one of the four Auschwitz crematoria in abortive and suicidal revolt.

15 October. The Arrow Cross, the Hungarian fascist party, stages successful coup in Budapest in the Nazi interest.

2 November. Swedish diplomat, Raoul Wallenberg, intervenes to save 4,000 Budapest Jews as SS and Arrow Cross begin six-day orgy of mass murder.

28 November. Last gassings in Auschwitz. Himmler (already in direct contact with the War Refugees Board), orders gas chambers to be destroyed.

1945

January. Death marches of Jewish and non-Jewish slave labour from east towards Germany at their height.

28 January. Auschwitz–Birkenau complex liberated by Red Army.

March–April. Himmler in series of secret negotiations with Swedish Red Cross and with Jewish World Congress to stop the continuing concentration camp killings.

11 April. Buchenwald liberated by American troops.

15 April. British troops liberate Bergen-Belsen. Reality of Nazi atrocities send shock waves throughout the world. Simultaneously, SS death march evacuations from camps still under Nazi control continue.

25 April. Soviet and American forces meet on the Elbe. Red Army engages German army remnants in Berlin.

28 April. Dachau liberated.

30 April. Hitler commits suicide in his Berlin bunker, after dictating a last political testament in which he blames international Jewry for Germany's downfall.

2 May. Berlin captured by Red Army.

1–5 May. Continuing death marches in diminishing Nazi enclave.

8 May. Nazi Germany surrenders unconditionally to Allies. War in Europe ends but many liberated camp survivors continue to die from malnutrition, sickness and exhaustion.

Glossary of Basic Terms

Anschluss
Literally 'annexation' or 'joining together'. In this case Austria's annexation by Hitler's Germany on 12 March 1938.

Blitzkrieg
German term, literally meaning 'lightning war', used to describe the intensity and speed of German military onslaught against their enemies' territory.

Bund
Jewish socialist movement founded in tsarist Russia in 1897. Committed to secular non-territorial nationalism, Jewish cultural and linguistic (Yiddish) autonomy, and strongly antagonistic to Zionism.

Concentration camp
A camp for the detention of perceived enemies of the Nazis. Originally set up after Hitler's seizure of power in 1933, the concentration camp regime involved forced labour and systematic use of terror. Massively extended to territories and people coming under Nazi occupation during the war, usually with a high percentage of Jewish prisoners.

Death camp
As distinct from both labour and concentration camps, a centre whose sole purpose was to annihilate its inmates. The main Nazi death camps were sited on Polish soil – Auschwitz-Birkenau, Belzec, Chelmno, Majdanek, Sobibor and Treblinka.

Death marches
The evacuation and forced marches of camp inmates during the latter stages of the war, when the Nazis felt threatened by the proximity of Allied troops. Tens of thousands of victims died while on these marches.

Der Stürmer
Nazi propaganda weekly, luridly antisemitic, founded in 1923 and edited by Julius Streicher.

Deportation
Process whereby Nazis removed people from their normal place of residence, often via a deportation centre, to a labour, concentration, or death camp.

Displaced Persons
Those millions of Europeans – Jews and non-Jews – who, by the war's end, had been forced out of their homes, both by Nazi decrees and by the overall effects of the war.

Einsatzgruppen
Special mobile units organized by the Reich Security Main Office for the elimination of the Nazis' enemies in countries occupied by them. Primarily responsible for the large-scale massacres of Russian Jews, communists and intellectuals during Operation Barbarossa, 1941, and for the slaughter of Poles throughout the war years.

Final Solution
The term used by the Nazis for their plans for comprehensive annihilation of European Jewry.

General Government
Administrative area in central and southern Poland created by the Nazis following the country's partition between Germany and the Soviet Union. Became the centre of the death camp system.

Genocide
A term created by the international jurist Raphael Lemkin in 1943 to denote a conscious attempt at the physical destruction of a defined group of people.

Gestapo
The German state secret police. Directly under the control of Himmler from 1936.

Ghetto
The quarters of European towns in which Jews were compulsorily required to reside in the Middle Ages. Resurrected by the Nazis following their takeover of Poland.

Haganah
The underground military organization of the Jewish community in Palestine under the British Mandate.

Hitler Youth
Organization originally founded in 1926 to inculcate racial, social and militaristic values into young Germans. After 1936, membership for 10 to 18 year olds was obligatory.

Judenrat
German term meaning 'Jewish Council'. used to describe the Jewish representative body established by the Nazis in various ghettos and communities. The purpose behind their establishment was to provide the Nazis with vital administrative and supervisory assistance and to implement Nazi decrees.

Labour camp
A camp contributing to Germany's wartime production through the use of slave labour, mostly involving prisoners of war, Jews and foreign nationals.

Lebensraum
Literally 'living space'. The acquisition of additional *Lebensraum* to be colonized by German people in the east was central to Hitler's racial vision of the future and therefore a key to his foreign policy and military preparations.

Operation Barbarossa
The name of the Nazis' military campaign to destroy the Soviet state, starting on 22 June 1941.

Reichstag
German parliament, largely ornamental during the Nazi era.

RSHA (German, *Reichssicherheitshauptampt* – Reich Security Main Office)
The security apparatus of the Nazi state formed from an amalgamation of the Gestapo and Kripo (criminal police) state police forces with the SD (Nazi Party intelligence service) in 1939.

SA (German, *Sturmabteilung*)
Literally Stormtroopers, also known as 'Brownshirts'. Shock troops of Nazi Party founded in 1921. Eclipsed by the SS after the 'Night of the Long Knives' of 30 June 1934 when the SA leadership was murdered.

SD (German, *Sicherheitsdienst*)
The security and intelligence wing of the SS founded, under Heydrich, in 1932. The core of the Reich Security Main Office (RSHA) founded in 1939.

SS (German, *Shutzstaffeln*)
Literally 'protection squads', also known as 'Blackshirts'. The paramilitary body created in 1925 to protect the Nazi Party and its leader, Hitler. After the Nazi seizure of absolute power, Himmler turned it into the most powerful organization within the state. All functions of the concentration and death camp system were controlled by it.

Vichy France
Puppet regime set up in southern France after Nazi conquest. Northern France continued to be ruled directly by Nazi Germany.

Weimar Republic The democratic republican regime which was established in Germany after the First World War. Lasted until Hitler's destruction of democratic government shortly after his accession to power.

Wehrmacht
German regular armed forces.

White Paper, 1939
British policy statement of May 1939, rigidly adhered to throughout the war years, restricting the number of Jewish immigrants to Palestine to a total of 75,000 over the subsequent five-year period (i.e. an annual average of 15,000 per year).

Zionism
Jewish nationalist movement which sought a response to antisemitism in the founding of a Jewish national home. The outcome would be the creation of the State of Israel in 1948.

Principal Characters

Mordechai Anielewicz
Young Zionist activist who, as head of the Jewish Combat Organization, led (and died in) the Warsaw Ghetto Uprising of April–May 1943.

Leo Baeck
Leading German Jewish rabbi, scholar and spokesman, who became president of the newly formed Reichsvertretung der deutschen Juden (National Organization of German Jewry) after the Nazi takeover in 1933. Continued in this role until deported to Theresienstadt.

David Ben-Gurion
Zionist leader of the Jewish community in Palestine. Given its slender resources, he was opposed to rescue efforts which might detract from his primary goal of building a Jewish national home in Palestine. In 1961, as Israeli Prime Minister, he used the Eichmann trial as a way of bringing world attention to the facts of the Holocaust.

Walther Darré
Nazi head of the Race Office, Agriculture Minister and advocate of the special German relationship between 'blood and soil'. Argued that only pure 'Aryans' could own land and in a series of laws eliminated Jews from all aspects of German agricultural production and trade.

Simon Dubnow
Leading Jewish historian, whose last words to his fellow-Jews before his deportation in December 1941 from his home in Riga, Latvia, are said to have been 'Write and record'.

Adolf Eichmann
Career bureaucrat in the SS, who became a specialist in 'Jewish affairs'. He oversaw first the expulsions of Jews from Greater Germany and later the transport and other administrative arrangements necessary for the implementation of the Final Solution. Sprung by Israeli agents from Argentina where he had gone into

hiding after the war, Eichmann was tried and sentenced to death by an Israeli court in 1961.

Hans Frank
Head of the General Government (Nazi-occupied central and southern Poland) – the heartland of the ghetto and death camp system. Exploited its 2.5 million Jewish population for slave labour, while at the same time ensuring their removal through starvation, expulsion and extermination.

Wilhelm Frick
Nazi Minister of the Interior until 1943. Responsible for Nazi racial and anti-Jewish legislation, including the 1935 Nuremberg Laws and 1938 'Aryanization' of Jewish businesses.

Bishop Clemens von Galen
Catholic Bishop of Münster who publicly criticized the Nazi 'euthanasia' killings in a sermon in August 1941, leading to its official (though not in practice complete) termination. Later imprisoned by the Nazis.

Joseph Goebbels
Nazi Minister of Propaganda, organizing in this capacity repeated anti-Jewish campaigns. Responsible for the *Kristallnacht* pogrom in November 1938 and later the deportation of Jews from Berlin. Committed suicide in Hitler's bunker on 30 April 1945.

Hermann Göring
Close Nazi associate of Hitler who acquired wide powers over Germany's economy and its war preparations. Responsible for the expropriation of German Jewish assets in the 1930s and the extension of this policy to the whole of Nazi-occupied Europe during the war. Committed suicide at Nuremberg in 1946.

Herschl Grynszpan
Seventeen-year-old Jew who assassinated a German official in the Paris embassy in November 1938, in retaliation for the maltreatment and deportation of his parents from Germany to the Polish border. His action precipitated the *Kristallnacht* pogrom.

Rudolf Hess
Hitler's official deputy. Flew to Scotland in a personal attempt to make peace with the British in 1941. Tried for war crimes at Nuremberg and sentenced to life imprisonment.

Reinhard Heydrich
Himmler's right hand man in the SS and head of the SD, the organization's own security police. Co-responsible with Himmler for

the creation of the Nazi police state and concentration camp system. Creator and organizational chief of the *Einsatzgruppen* with executive responsibility for the implementation of the Final Solution. Convened Wannsee Conference in January 1942 for this purpose. From October 1941, he was Reich Protector of the Czech provinces of Bohemia and Moravia which had been incorporated into the Nazi state. Assassinated by Czech agents in cooperation with the British in May 1942.

Heinrich Himmler

Head of the SS and Nazi police apparatus, with overall responsibility for eliminating all enemies of Hitler's new order. Also after 1943 Minister of the Interior. Chief architect of the concentration camp system and prime mover and organizer of the Final Solution. Captured by the British in May 1945 and committed suicide.

Paul von Hindenburg

Head of the imperial German army in the First World War, and last President of the Weimar Republic. His death in 1934 paved the way for the complete consolidation of Nazi power.

Adolf Hitler

Austrian-born leader of the Nazi party, self-styled Führer of the German people and obsessive Jew-hater. A charismatic demagogue whose mixture of opportunism and planning plunged Europe into the Second World War. His decision to invade the Soviet Union, in June 1941, precipitated the implementation of the Final Solution. The total defeat of Nazism by the Allies, culminating in the Red Army's breakthrough to Berlin, led to his suicide in his Chancellery bunker on 30 April, 1945.

Rudolf Hoess

Zealous concentration camp functionary who became commandant of Auschwitz and Birkenau, working closely with the I.G. Farben company in the construction of gas chambers and in the use of Zyclon B gas for the extermination of soviet prisoners of war and later Jews. Hanged by the Polish authorities in 1947.

Chaim Kaplan

Polish Jewish educator and writer, whose Warsaw Ghetto diary minutely chronicled its fate until his own deportation to Treblinka in September 1942.

Pastor Martin Niemöller

German Lutheran priest who publicly criticized the Nazi persecution of the Jews. His outspokenness led to his incarceration in the Sachsenhausen and later Dachau concentration camps.

Marshal Philippe Pétain
Considered saviour of France after its army had collapsed in the First World War. He was acclaimed saviour for a second time in 1940 when, following the French army's defeat, he negotiated a peace treaty with Hitler. The Vichy regime which he led from the south of the country cooperated with the Nazis in the deportation to the death camps of French Jews and Jewish refugees from other parts of Europe.

Pope Pius XII
Head of the Catholic Church during the Nazi years. Pursued an equivocal and controversial policy towards Nazism, condemning it in the 1937 encyclical *Mit brennender Sorge* ('With Burning Worry'), but failing to speak out publicly against its persecution of the Jews.

Field Marshal Walter von Reichenau
Professional German soldier notorious for his role in wedding the Wehrmacht to the Nazi regime. As chief of the Sixth Army during Operation Barbarossa, he issued an infamous order in October 1941 calling on the Wehrmacht 'to discharge its historical mission of once and for all delivering the German people from the Asiatic-Jewish peril'.

Joachim von Ribbentrop
Hitler's Foreign Minister after 1938. Chief architect of the Nazi Non-Aggression Pact with Stalinist Russia, August 1939. Hanged at Nuremberg in 1946.

Ernst Röhm
Head of the SA Stormtroopers and a potential challenger to Hitler's leadership of the Nazi Party. Murdered in the 'Night of the Long Knives', 1934.

Alfred Rosenberg
Baltic German obsessed by the idea that the Russian revolution was a facet of the 'international Jewish conspiracy'. The Nazi's key exponent on racial theory. As wartime Reich Minister for the Occupied Eastern Territories, Rosenberg concocted schemes for a subjugated Russia, free of Jews and colonized by Germans.

Chaim Rumkowski
Controversial and 'despotic' leader of the Jewish Council in the Polish ghetto of Lodz. He believed that, by demonstrating their economic indispensability to the Nazis, the Jews of Lodz might be spared. He perished in Auschwitz, killed by his fellow-Jews who felt he had betrayed them.

Bernhard Rust
Nazi ex-schoolmaster appointed Reich Minister of Science, Education and Culture in 1934. Subordinated school system to the interests of Nazism, which included the 'dejudaization' of its teachers and pupils.

Franz Stangl
Austrian-born policeman involved in the euthanasia programme and later Commandant of Sobibor and Treblinka death camps. Extradited from Brazil in 1967, he was later sentenced by a German court to life imprisonment, dying soon afterwards.

Julius Streicher
Nazi publisher of the violently antisemitic weekly, *Der Stürmer*, and heavily involved in the boycott and other anti-Jewish campaigns in Hitler's Germany.

Raoul Wallenberg
Swedish diplomat in Budapest who, in late 1944, personally intervened, under the cover of diplomatic immunity, to save thousands of Hungarian Jews destined for the gas chambers. Disappeared after the Red Army's entry into the city in January 1945.

Chaim Weizmann
Zionist leader based in London who attempted, in the summer of 1944, to persuade the British government to bomb the railway lines leading to Auschwitz. Later became first President of the State of Israel.

Robert Weltsch
German Zionist, whose editorial in the *Jüdische Rundschau* 'Wear the Yellow Badge with Pride' became a famous riposte to the Nazi anti-Jewish boycott of 1 April 1933.

Christian Wirth
German police bureaucrat, whose efficient 'euthanasia' killings of the mentally and physically disabled in Germany paved the way for his later promotion within the death camp system, with responsibility for Belzec, Treblinka and Sobibor.

Index

350 *Index*

ARGARINE JEWELL MEMORIAL LIBRARY
BAKER COLLEGE OF MUSKEGON
MUSKEGON, MICHIGAN 49442